So Others Will Remember

So Others Will Remember

HOLOCAUST HISTORY AND SURVIVOR TESTIMONY

EDITED BY

Ronald Headland

Véhicule Press

Véhicule Press acknowledges the support of The Canada Council
for the Arts for its publishing program.
Ray Shankman's poem "To My Virtuous Jewish Woman" was
published in *For Love of the Wind*, Medicine Label Press, 1991.
Endre Farkas' poems, "Witnesses Report" and "Heirloom"
were published in *Surviving Words*, The Muses' Company, 1994.

Cover design: J.W. Stewart
Typeset in Perpetua by Simon Garamond
Printing: AGMV-Marquis Inc.

CANADIAN CATALOGUING IN PUBLICATION DATA
Main entry under title:
So others will remember : holocaust history and survivor testimony

ISBN 1-55065-120-X

1. Holocaust, Jewish (1939-1945). 2. Holocaust, Jewish
(1939-1945) – Personal narratives.
I. Headland, Ronald, 1946-

D804.3.S6 1999   940.53'18   C99-900333-X

Published by Véhicule Press
www.vehiculepress.com

Distributed by General Distribution Services

Printed in Canada on alkaline paper

Contents

HISTORY

POETRY

MEMORY

Preface

NEIL CAPLAN

THE LIFE OF PETER KLEINMANN, a retired St-Laurent businessman, has followed a pattern familiar to many Holocaust survivors. After arriving in Canada in 1949, he worked hard to rebuild his life and deliberately avoided discussing his harrowing adolescent years with anybody. Buried deep in his past were experiences of the ghettoization of Jews in the Carpathian town of Munkács (Mukacevo), round-ups and deportations to Auschwitz and elsewhere, the loss of many members of his family, the death march from the slave-labour camp at Gross-Rosen to Flossenbürg, and the liberation of the latter concentration camp by the American Army in April 1945.

But after forty years of self-imposed silence, Peter Kleinmann decided to go public about his personal Holocaust nightmare. When approached by a neighbour who was enrolled in a Humanities course which I taught at Montreal's Vanier College (CEGEP), he accepted an invitation to speak to the students in this class. Peter is still fond of recalling how his shirt was drenched with perspiration after, pacing back and forth, he told his story and answered questions for the first time that day in March 1988 before two groups of mesmerized students. In finally finding the strength and the words to speak in public about his experiences, he was expressing a need to reach out particularly to non-Jewish teenagers, many of whom were surprisingly unaware of the basic history of Nazism and the Second World War. An even more disturbing incentive for him and others to speak out during the mid- and late 1980s was the growing respectability of historical revisionism, which denied the fact that the Nazis systematically murdered millions of European Jews.

9

By 1993, Peter Kleinmann had participated twice in the March of the Living, an internationally-organized tour of senior high-school students to the death camps of Poland and to Israel, and had spoken to thousands of students not only in the Montreal region, but also in schools in Ontario and upper New York state. In the fall of 1993, Peter hosted a few lunch meetings with college teachers in a restaurant at the corner of de l'Eglise and St-Germain streets in the Montreal suburb of Saint-Laurent. There we brainstormed over ideas for a sustained programme that would go beyond periodic visits of Holocaust survivors to CEGEP and high schools. With the energetic involvement of the Hillel Student Society, the Montreal Holocaust Memorial Centre, and in cooperation with student services departments of each college and various student clubs and associations on campus, we launched what we hoped would become an annual Symposium.

The Esther and Peter Kleinmann Annual CEGEP Holocaust Symposium (now called The Kleinmann Family Foundation Annual CEGEP Holocaust Symposium) brought into dozens of classrooms and lecture-halls a variety of scholarly lectures, artistic representations and survivor testimonies. The Symposium proved to be a very successful, innovative educational experience, reaching thousands of students in the context of ongoing classes offered in the Humanities, History, English, Anthropology, Sociology and other academic departments. The aim of the Symposium was to educate CEGEP students about the Holocaust and to sensitize them to the moral responsibility all people have toward one another. This emphasis on universal themes has been, I believe, the main key to its success.

The volume before you is but a sampling of the more than fifty lectures and presentations given at Montreal-area colleges—Vanier, Dawson, Marianopolis and John Abbott—during the first three years of the Kleinmann Holocaust Symposium. Most of the published papers are expanded and updated versions of the topics covered during the original Symposium sessions.

The main purpose of this volume is to share the talents, testimonies, insights and research fruits of the Symposium's local and international presenters with an even larger public. This collection is one more proof of Montreal's remarkable activity as a centre for Holocaust education, as already evidenced by the work of the Montreal Institute for Genocide Studies and the Azrieli Holocaust Collection, both at Concordia University; McGill University's Living Testimonies Holocaust Video Documentation Archive; and the Montreal Holocaust Memorial Centre's permanent exhibition ("Splendor and Destruction: Jewish Life that Was"), its collection of survivors' testimonies and its outreach to school-age children.

The volume does not pretend to reflect or offer any orthodoxies in Holocaust scholarship or Holocaust education. The collection deals with a variety of subjects and perspectives, offered by a variety of researchers and survivors. Given the enormously complex nature of the Holocaust and our efforts to understand it, this book tackles only some of the many possible approaches. The selection—offering history, poetry and testimony—attempts to deal with topics which are less often found in existing literature, and to highlight and salute the work of many of the Canadian and Montreal participants.

Introduction

IN HIS BOOK ON ADOLF HITLER, the German writer Joachim Fest made the observation that Hitler taught the world some things it will never forget. Paramount in the Hitler legacy is the realization that it is possible to murder millions of helpless people in cold blood, in relative secrecy over a period of years, across an entire continent. How and why this cataclysm came about, and how centuries of moral and legal structures within German and European society were insufficient to prevent it, have remained central questions of our time. During the half century since this event took place an enormous amount of knowledge has been gained about what happened. We have learned much. Yet nagging doubts persist. In spite of what we know, the question lingers as to whether or not the world has really learned the horrible lessons of the past. In light of recent events throughout the world, one may well ask: Has the world forgotten the things that Hitler taught it?

The Holocaust—the planned, systematic annihilation of the Jews of Europe by the Nazis and their collaborators—has, during the last twenty years or so, been a subject very much in the public eye. In memoirs, scholarly publications, as well as the popular media, more and more attention has been focused on it. This increased emphasis has led some people, Jews and non-Jews, to question whether dwelling on this subject is, in fact, a good thing. (I refer here, of course, not to Holocaust deniers, but to those who suggest that, among other arguments, too much emphasis on the Holocaust causes Jews and non-Jews to view Jews solely as victims, while ignoring the many positive contributions the Jews have given to the world.)

Undoubtedly these are valid concerns, put forward by thoughtful people. Yet this question of over-emphasis brings to mind a newspaper article that I read several years ago which dealt with the sorry state of American education. It described a survey in which American teenagers were asked basic questions about history. One sixteen-year old girl was asked what the Holocaust was. She wasn't sure, but she said she thought it was some sort of Jewish holiday! Here, certainly, was at least *one* person who had not been saturated by information about this subject.

One suspects that the ignorance as evidenced by this teenager's response is not untypical. This book is published in the belief that there *is* an urgent and ongoing need for young people and others to be made aware of the catastrophe that engulfed the Jews of Europe. Furthermore, it is hoped that awareness of this tragedy can help sensitize people to the larger issue of racial injustice in its many forms and provide awareness of the necessity of affirming individual and collective moral responsibility in ensuring human freedoms for all groups within society, issues very much a part of today's world. The Holocaust casts a wide shadow; it falls within the ambit of many areas of human thought. Therefore, this book approaches its subject from a wide range of perspectives.

This book begins with a historical section dealing, roughly chronologically, with aspects of Holocaust history. Following this are several poems inspired by the Holocaust. Personal testimonies of five survivors complete the picture, as they look back on their lives and reach out to the present generation. The book, thus, is mainly a combination of history and memory, or perhaps, more precisely, of historical analysis and painful recollection. In this way the book reflects two of the major perspectives, that of the historian and the survivor, that have informed fifty years of Holocaust discourse.

The historian, in approaching the Holocaust, does so from a standpoint very different from that of the survivor. Unlike the survivor, the historian must detach himself from the enormous horror of the subject. In spite of the harrowing, emotional nature of the material, he must employ the tools of his trade objectively and dispassionately. However difficult this may be, and however mindful the historian may be of the uniqueness of this tragedy, he must approach the subject as he would any other historical event. Yet the dilemma of the historian is how to arrive at an explanation, if not an understanding, of this perplexing subject, one which is often viewed as being ultimately incomprehensible, even by many men and women who have spent their lives studying it. How does one give meaning to a calamity so varied and contradictory in its essential causes and structure—an event powered by perpetrators who at once combined fanatic ideology and racial anti-Semitism with bureaucratic momentum, who combined personal ambition and careerism with unquestioned devotion to a *Führer*, who combined selfless idealism with crass material gain? How does one place all these things into an interpretive mold?

Josef Schmidt makes clear in his essay that Nazi anti-Semitism did not appear overnight, nor did it exist in a vacuum. Schmidt examines the presence of anti-Semitic language within German society decades prior to Hitler's assumption of power. He underlines how easily entrenched, anti-Semitic slogans could be transformed into the "condensed expression of a political program," how metaphorical allusions to annihilation could later form the grounding for genocide. Moving on to the early years of the Third Reich, in his paper the late Klaus Herrmann distinguishes the different reactions of the various sectors of German Jewry to the unfolding anti-Jewish actions within Germany. The first to bear the brunt of Nazi persecution, the German Jews ultimately failed in their efforts to be treated as proud and loyal Germans. Tragically for the Jews, and despite the substantial contributions of Jews to German science, culture and the economy, the German leadership made little or no distinction between the various factions of Jews within their midst. For the German leaders, all those deemed to be Jews by the Nazi racial laws were considered unworthy of being citizens and were to be removed from the fabric of German society.

Several years and a world war were required for the passage from anti-Semitism to outright mass murder. The German invasion of Poland in September 1939, which marked the beginning of the Second World War, led to a radicalisation of German goals with respect to the Jews. Polish Jews were forced into ghettos and underwent terrible persecution at the hands of their German captors. Not until the attack on the Soviet Union in June 1941, however, did the systematic mass murder of the

Jews begin. It was the mobile German Security Police units, known as *Einsatzgruppen*, who began the mass shooting of the Jews, communist officials, Gypsies, and others in the occupied Soviet territories. Not only did the *Einsatzgruppen* carry out their horrific task but they also wrote top-secret reports describing in precise statistical detail what they were doing. These reports (one complete set survived the war) provide us not only with a mind-boggling day-by-day account of mass killing, but also offer valuable insight into the mind of the perpetrators and the process of mass killing itself.

Both Avraham Sela and Neil Caplan take us further afield and approach the Holocaust in relation to the complex world of Middle East politics. Sela studies the connections between Arab nationalists and Nazi Germany, noting the appeal German nationalism and militarism had for Arab nationalists in their quest for independence from Anglo-French influence. In particular he examines the ongoing attempt of the Mufti of Palestine, al-Haj Amin al-Hussaini, to forge ties with an at times reluctant German leadership. It was the Mufti's active collaboration with the Germans that contributed to the unfavourable positions of many allied countries towards the Palestinian Arab cause after the war. Neil Caplan summarizes the broad history of Arab-Israeli relations, presenting a succinct and balanced overview of all sides of the issues involved. He stresses the importance of the Holocaust to the political climate surrounding the emergence of an independent Israel. The abandonment of the Jews by the world during the war made it apparent to Jews that they could never again depend entirely on others. They would have to protect themselves by their own means. For many Jews the creation of the state of Israel in 1948 was seen as the most fitting monument to the murdered Jews of Europe. Caplan further explores the psychic wound left by the Holocaust, pointing out the profound effect it has had on the makeup of Israeli life and politics and its continuing presence as an undercurrent in the rhetoric surrounding the Arab-Israeli conflict.

Anti-Semitism, and its manifestation in hate literature, as both Stanley Asher and Irwin Cotler remind us, have not been confined exclusively to the past or to Europe. The papers of both scholars bring the subject of anti-Semitism to our own doorsteps here in Canada. We are made aware that the wellsprings of hatred run deep and are very much a part of our own society. Asher traces the anti-Semitism in Quebec during the 1930s, with particular reference to Adrien Arcand. Arcand was a journalist whose several weekly publications, replete with the vilest of anti-Semitic cartoons, graced the news-stands of Montreal. Arcand's cause has been taken up in recent years by Ernst Zundel, one of an international network of people who deny that the Holocaust ever took place. Those who deny the Holocaust claim it is their right to do so in an open society where freedom of speech is protected. The problem in combatting neo-Nazi Holocaust denial and hate propaganda—something which at the very least is clearly harmful to a specific segment of society, on the one hand, and the maintaining of the individual's right to free speech, on the other— has been an evolving issue addressed by the courts of Canada. Irwin Cotler identifies the issues involved in this debate. Noting the difficulties of legislating on this issue, Cotler discusses in depth the specific reasoning behind the Supreme Court of Canada's rulings. If, in a free and democratic society, one is committed to fight against the wilful promotion of hatred, Cotler's paper indicates that the jurisprudential precepts of Canadian courts likely offer a sound and balanced framework for doing so.

The Nazi murder of millions of Jews has elicited artistic responses from many writers. It is this literary aspect that Yossi Lévy deals with. Following a brief review of the history of the Sephardi Jews Lévy outlines their oppression by the Nazis during the war. He then offers examples of Holocaust-related poetry written from a Sephardi viewpoint. Lévy demonstrates how both traditional religious and secular interpretations have been used by Sephardi poets to confront the Holocaust. Included as well in his analysis is the major writer/survivor Primo Levi. Among other things, the author takes note of Levi's belief that even though the experience of the concentration camp was an extreme one, it is still something from which one may gather fundamental truths about human nature.

With Robert Frederick Jones we move into the realm of music with a comparison of two musical compositions by two of the greatest composers of the twentieth century: Arnold Schoenberg's *A Survivor from Warsaw* and Dmitri Shostakovich's *Babi Yar Symphony*. Jones' study is not only an examination of these two major works and their place within their respective composer's oeuvre, but is also a telling look at the relationship between a work of art and the particular environment in which it was created. In the case of Schoenberg, it was a matter of his personal response, late in his career, to the Holocaust and the changing sense of his own Jewishness. With Shostakovich (and the poet Yevgeny Yevtushenko, who wrote the text for this symphony), it was a question of making a statement against anti-Semitism as it currently existed in the Soviet Union, by evoking the memory of the 1941 mass murder of the Jews at Babi Yar, near Kiev.

Forming the middle section of this book are poems by two poets and a student, Carrie Bacher, whose poem, "Thoughts as We Walked," was written in response to a recent trip with thousands of other students to death camps in Poland. As the students walk, hand in hand, complex feelings of the moment contrast with thoughts of those for whom, years before, this same path was a journey of despair and death. Both Endre Farkas and Ray Shankman tell of the indifference of bystanders to the annihilation of their Jewish neighbours. Farkas identifies directly with the murdered Jews, with their unspeakable suffering, and with those precious moments, stolen between the endless routine of horror and death, when their humanity could not be silenced. Ray Shankman speaks of love fulfilled in a world blessed by survival and comfort. Can the spirit of those who perished evoke in us the right words "so others will remember?"

It is from Holocaust survivors that one receives the most immediate and gripping sense of what happened to the Jews. Survivors are, of course, for the most part, ordinary people. They are generally not writers, trained to express fine nuances of thought. Survivors in Canada speak to audiences in a language which is not their mother tongue. Given the terrible stories they have to tell and the profundity of their experiences, survivors more often than not achieve a remarkable degree of eloquence and insight. Furthermore, while survivors share with all Jews one fundamental characteristic—they were all slated to be murdered—every survivor's story is unique.

Many survivors have faced a number of problems in their attempts to come to grips with their past. First and foremost is the pain of dredging up the memory of what they have endured and lost. In addition, they feel the necessity for the world to know and remember. They bear witness to what happened, they try to speak for those who cannot. Yet many survivors realize that it is impossible to truly convey their experiences to those who did not themselves live through these events. In spite of their efforts, many feel that there is a gap in understanding that may never be bridged.

Two of the survivors in this volume, Peter Kleinmann and Avrum Feigenbaum, articulate another dilemma common to survivors. This is the fact that while they survived, while they were formally liberated from Nazi oppression, they have never really been truly liberated from their past. Both Feigenbaum and Kleinmann ask in what sense can one speak of liberation when the memory of the appalling suffering and the murder of loved ones still permeates their daily thoughts? As Feigenbaum, who spent most of the war in the Lodz ghetto before being sent to Auschwitz and then to Gorlitz camp, puts it, "I am not a young man. I feel almost at the edge of my grave. If I have not yet felt the happiness of liberation, do not feel it now, I, and others like me, will never feel it." The oppressive presence of the past is perhaps expressed most directly by Stefan Lesniak, who concludes his lecture simply with the following: "For years after the war, I was haunted by terrible nightmares, the illusion of the sweetish smell of burning human flesh in my nostrils, depressed feelings, and I had difficulties in remaking my life."

For many Jews who survived, therefore, there is often a contradiction between coping with their memories of the past and a desire to tell their story to others. They recognize that something of what they were before the Holocaust has been severed, that there is for them a lack of true "liberation," of closure, and that they themselves can never fully comprehend even their own experience, let alone convey this adequately to others. Although the problem is a difficult one, compounded by the fact that many survivors see themselves as different from other people because of the uniqueness of what they underwent, the urge to teach people about the Holocaust is a strong one. It is an urge shared by all the survivors in this book. However arduous the task of spanning the gap of understanding may be, and however imperfect the results of such an attempt, survivors feel the gap must be somehow bridged.

Unlike the other survivors in this book who were sent to various labour and concentration camps during the war, Ann Kazimirski miraculously survived mainly by hiding in attics and basements. On one such occasion, in December 1943, Ann and her husband became separated from her mother. Watching in helpless anguish from her hiding place, Ann saw her mother and four other people lined up against a wall and shot. Liberated finally by the Russian army, Ann and her husband came to Canada after the war. They built a new life and raised a family in Sainte Agathe, north of Montreal. The past continued to haunt Ann even in her new home, in the person of Danka, a victim of inhuman medical experiments in Auschwitz, who was also living in that small town in the Laurentian mountains. Both Ann's daughter, Heidi Berger, and her grandson, Jason Berger, speak of what it is like to be part of a survivor's family. For Heidi, childhood memories include the dreadful nightmares of her parents, her father's desperate attempts at overprotection, the reluctance of her mother to talk about the war. Above all, and in spite of what her parents had been through, it was a childhood filled with love. But anti-Semitism in the form of racial slurs and segregation was also a reality. For Jason, the shock of encountering neo-Nazi hate literature in Montreal has reinforced his sense of the urgency to combat all forms of racism.

In recent years the most well-known work to deal with the Holocaust has been the film *Schindler's List*. Both Stefan Lesniak and Willie Sterner worked for Oskar Schindler, the German businessman who saved over a thousand Jews. Repeatedly throughout the war years in the various work camps where he was interned, Willie Sterner was able to put his trade as a house painter to good use, doing diverse jobs for the Germans. In the spring of 1943 Sterner found himself working for Schindler, and along with the other Jews working there, Sterner benefited from Schindler's kindness. Separated from the other workers in August 1944, Sterner wound up in Mauthausen concentration camp and, later, other camps, where again his painting skills served him well. Like Sterner, Stefan Lesniak lost both his parents and other members of his family, and like Sterner, he too wound up working for Schindler. In Lesniak's case, both he and his brother Roman were included on Schindler's list of names of those protected Jews who escaped death by being able to continue working for Schindler in his ammunition factory in Czechoslovakia. It was there that Lesniak was liberated by Russian soldiers on 8 May 1945.

The analyses, poems, and testimonies found in this book are but a small part of a vast worldwide body of work related to the Holocaust. As with all historical phenomena, it is inevitable that the passage of time, more recent events, increased knowledge, and new questions, will colour our perception of the past. These changes are to be expected. Our view of the Holocaust will no doubt be affected by this process. One such change will soon be upon us, when the voices of survivors will be heard no more. When this happens we will have turned a corner, for then all that will be left will be the written and recorded documents of the past.

How we proceed with our knowledge of the past depends, therefore, on factors that we both can and cannot control. My belief is, that to a great degree, we can and must shape what we do with this legacy. If we are not to repeat the injustices of the past, the past must not be forgotten. The destruction of the Jews is not the only example of genocide, even in the twentieth century. It is, however, the *extreme* act of genocide and, for a variety of reasons, it is also the one that we know the most about. It is therefore the one that can continue to teach us the most and help us shape our future for the betterment of mankind. To date, the teaching of the Holocaust has been based principally on two different dimensions: its *specific nature*—it was something done to Jews by Germans; and its *universal implications*—it can be done again, by anyone to anyone else. While, as this volume attests, the uniqueness of the Holocaust can hardly be ignored, its universal aspect is already assuming increasing importance as we move further and further in time from the original source and as new perpetrators and victims emerge throughout the world.

The lessons of the Holocaust are many. Let me conclude by touching on one such lesson. Though quite straightforward, it is no less illustrative of the Holocaust's educative power for being so. We began our collection with a study of anti-Semitic jargon in the press and in public debate within Germany. In a real sense, this burgeoning verbal anti-Semitism marked the first step on a long and twisted road to mass murder. To these already-existing anti-Jewish tendencies was added during the 1930s the legalized removal of the rights of Jews as citizens. It did not necessarily follow that annihilation was an ineluctable consequence of these earlier anti-Jewish measures. *But it was. The result was industrialized mass murder. It did happen that way.* Who could have known in 1933 when Hitler came to power that the expanding assaults on the Jews would end in the calculated murder of millions? The answer is: no one could have known. Of course, some Jews said they knew and left Germany in time. But they were simply fortunate. No one could have predicted the eventual outcome with certainty. Even the German leaders themselves did not know where they were going with the Jews until the fateful year of 1941.

The lesson here is that the *long-term* consequences of allowing any form of racial discrimination within society and permitting it to flourish unchecked cannot always be immediately apparent. But the destructive legacy left by Hitler shows us how, given the right circumstances, such consequences can be devastating. And surely it does this with a directness and clarity unmatched by anything else in modern history.

Editor's Note

PREPARING THIS BOOK has involved a number of unusual editorial problems. One difficulty stemmed from the inherent difference between the spoken and written word. What works orally in front of an audience does not automatically work on the printed page. Most of the survivors spoke spontaneously, usually without the aid of extensive written notes. Fortunately, most of the talks were filmed. By using a combination of transcriptions of videotapes, survivors' notes and additional written materials, and a measure of editorial maneuvering of my own, I have come up with somewhat altered, but reasonably faithful, versions of the original presentations. In the transposition to printed form I have endeavored to retain some of the immediacy of the spoken word. In the case of the historical papers, my task was easier. Here, the authors revised, expanded, and, in some cases, updated, earlier drafts of their lectures.

I must express my appreciation for the friendly co-operation of all those who contributed to this book. In particular, I wish to extend special thanks to my friend and colleague, Neil Caplan. If it was Peter Kleinmann who provided the inspiration and generous funding that made the Symposia possible, it was Neil as co-ordinator who furnished the organizational glue that enabled the whole project to be realized. As well, Neil offered continuous and invaluable advice to me in my role as editor of this book. For this, and for his hard work in making the Symposia a success, I am especially grateful.

It simply remains to be said it is my fervent hope that someday books like this one will no longer have to be written.

History

The Contribution of Late 19th-Century German Anti-Semitism to the Holocaust

Josef Schmidt

THE INFAMOUS *Commentary on German Racial Laws* (1936), co-authored by Hans Globke, who after the war was made secretary of state (1953-1963) by Catholic chancellor Konrad Adenauer, summarizes in Nazi jargon the hideous premise behind the ultimate extermination of the Jews with inimitable hypocritical cynicism:

> ...the National Socialist state guarantees Jewry the free exercise of religion (*freie Religionsausübung*) of cultural life, and education. Economic activity is also permitted to Jews without hindrance (*ungestört*) within the framework of existing laws. However, from now on Jewry will never again (*für alle Zukunft*) be able to mix with the German people, and any participation in, and formation of, the political, economic, and cultural sphere of the Reich will be impossible (*unmöglich gemacht*) for them...Jews have to resign themselves to the fact that their influence on the formation of German life (*deutsches Leben*) is over, once and for all (*ein für allemal vorbei*).[1]

This short excerpt is representative of the multiple and complex role that language played in the Holocaust. The blueprint quoted above for the ultimate marginalization of Jews in the Third Reich also clearly and conclusively demonstrates the verbal duplicity that was so typical of this endeavour. The three predominant functions of this kind of discourse of death are a pseudo-legalistic objectivity designed to provide the proposed measures with a quasi-legal normalcy for the measures; the use of absolute and all-exclusive adverbs that deliberately strikes terror into those who are affected by these all-exclusive measures; and the employment of pseudo-philosophical argumentation which reflects the attempt, in the tradition of social Darwinism, to keep the nation free from incompatible elements that threaten to destroy it.

Such a total and unconditional exclusion had its historical genesis and was not an irrational short-term phenomenon originating in political expediency. During the second half of the nineteenth century, the public discourse in Germany prepared the ground for making the unspeakable thinkable: that a scapegoat group of people, onto whom a host of fears in the face of modernity had been projected, be removed from the nation. The brutalization process of World War I had not yet happened. Official mass murder had not yet been envisaged. But the anti-Semitic vocabulary did propose a progressive marginalization of the Jews, ranging from the curtailing of civil rights and liberties to the forced expulsion from German soil. In this respect, much in the Nuremberg racial laws sanctioned what had been said at least three generations before.

This essay, in a modest way, tries to shed light onto this part of the unresolved past in the way that Alexander and Margaret Mitscherlich demanded in their pioneering study *Die Unfähigkeit zu Trauern* (*The Inability to Mourn*, 1967). The task, they wrote, was, instead of blindly letting time take its course to do the real mourning:

> To work it through, if only with an eye for detail, starting with the particulars that smack not yet of inhumanity but which, through their innumerable propagation created the general climate, for example, for the project and the fanatical (*verbissen*) execution of "the final solution."[2]

For the foundation of the German Reich in 1871 coincided with a renewed outburst of anti-Semitic views in relation to "the Jewish question/problem."[3] Historians generally recognized that the two new dimensions entering the anti-Semitic discourse at that time originated in the domains of social innovation and the emergence of national-racial theories. Jews in Germany and elsewhere came to symbolize the disquieting modernization of society, and were consequently feared and despised by societal groups that felt threatened and disadvantaged by new economic conditions; and Darwin's revolutionizing theory of evolution was translated into a popular tribal discourse that made blood and race the basic conditions of a nationalistic social contract. The new literacy created a powerful populist language that disseminated such notions through daily newspapers, brochures, pamphlets, magazines, and so on.

I shall illustrate this new dimension with three concrete examples using a rhetorical perspective that takes into account the text's pragmatic context, situating specific anti-Semitic articulations according to a broad understanding of the history of mentalities. Since my premise seems to coincide with the basic assumptions put forward by Daniel Jonah Goldhagen in his much-discussed *Hitler's Willing Executioners: Ordinary Germans and the Holocaust*, I would like to briefly state why this is not so.[4] Like Goldhagen, I believe, on the one hand, that the "eliminationist mind-set" was in existence long before "the final solution" was set in motion, and that the instrumental anti-Semitic stereotypes were fostered in an ever-expanding radicalism; on the other hand, I reject his basic thesis of a monocausal explanation (signalled in the title of the book) of the Holocaust.[5] Different social groups, while sharing many common hostile prejudices, had very specific and different agendas in their nefarious and reprehensible activities.

In the following observations I shall make use of new and original text materials[6] that belong to a larger project about the role Catholics played in the development of modern German anti-Semitism. It is important, in my view, to investigate the emergence of this hostile attitude that was guilty of the contribution and omission that allowed a totalitarian state to carry out the most extreme form of marginalization: industrialized mass murder.[7] My contention, briefly, is that the Nazis, in the Holocaust, carried out what had been articulated, literally, long before the movement took absolute totalitarian power. Furthermore, I think that a rhetorical study is needed to provide a modern reader with a differentiated analysis of Nazi euphemisms.

As an introductory remark, let me quote two key terms of the

Holocaust vocabulary and briefly touch on their socio-linguistic connotations. The underlying notion is, of course, that the "appellative" use of invective does contain the potential of inciting actual murder. One of the words for deportation/liquidation used was the word "*Entfernung*." A modern dictionary, *Cassell's*, lists the following three basic meanings: distance...deviation/departure...removal. For the native German speaker, however, there exist several other contexts. At the most banal level, the word can be used for the removal of a stain. But in a global sense, it can mean the absolute disappearance of something. Matters get more complex when one turns to the Nazis' predilection for compounds, the stringing together of two or more words. "*Judenrein*" literally means 'purified of Jews'; the common English translation, in horrible irony, is "free of Jews." The term applied to mass executions of Jews carried out in occupied territories. Its etymology, however, dates back to the days of the emergence of social Darwinism when one of the deadliest slurs was coined: the Jew as a social parasite; "*rein*" in that context referred to racial purity, the functional use implied what one was supposed to do with parasites: remove or exterminate them!

The most direct and brutal example of an open-ended anti-Semitic condemnation is the slogan coined by the eminent historian Heinrich von Treitschke: *Die Juden sind unser Unglück!* (The Jews are our misfortune.) It was a conclusion in an essay entitled "Our Prospects/ *Unsere Aussichten*" that appeared in the *Preussische Jahrbücher* (November 1879), a very respected publication. The essay was written in the context of a renewed debate about "the Jewish problem," and von Treitschke introduced this appeal with the following explanatory remarks:

> ...the present loud agitation may appear on the one hand as a brutal and vituperative reaction of the Germanic nation's emotions (*des germanischen Volksgefühls*), but on the other it is a natural reaction against a foreign element that has been taking up too much room in our society...Up to the highest academic circles, and even among men who would reject any idea of ecclesiatical intolerance or national arrogance, there is but one outcry: the Jews are our misfortune![8]

What the Prussian professor rightly articulates is of rhetorical significance: that at this crucial stage of the emergence of the modern German state it had become acceptable in the dominant culture to overtly engage in an anti-Semitic discourse that openly advocated an "eliminationist" policy towards Jews. Universities and churches had joined the lower-class hate culture created for "the Jewish problem." Once again one has to keep in mind the limited meaning of the English translation of the term "*Unglück*." The German term is used to annotate everything from "bad luck, mischance, accident, calamity, catastrophe, tragedy, and disaster," words that certainly apply to the Holocaust! Two generations later this horrific falsification of social realities, reducing a complex situation to a negative simplification, proved its potency with deadly power. This slogan not only became the motto on every title page of the most notorious Nazi publication, Julius Streicher's *Der Stürmer*, where the message of suppression, exclusion and elimination was preached with crude and direct brutality. It also became one of the most quoted slogans on banners at Nazi mass rallies.[9] The transformation and elevation of a primitive message to the level of serious social discourse had been completed by its becoming a condensed expression of a political program.

A second text does not seem, at first sight, to be much out of the ordinary. At the height of the "*Kulturkampf*," where the (predominantly Protestant) Prussian central government tried to muzzle the Catholic minorities (about a third of the population of the Reich), the following text appeared in the confessionally oriented daily newspaper *Germania* (Berlin, No. l74, 1875-8-4):

> Without Jews there wouldn't have been any "*Kulturkampf*," a fiasco at the stock market would have done away with the defamation campaign. But the Jews not only satisfy here their need for revenge (*Rachsucht*) but with their defamation campaign against Catholics they obfuscate their shady manoeuvers at the stockmarket...For the Jews the "*Kulturkampf*" has the highly political purpose to deliver what their money could only facilitate in an indirect way: to be able, on the shoulders of Protestant

fanaticism and the hate of the liberal party, to rise to a quasi-co-governing position (*mitregierender Stellung*).

In a nutshell, one can see the frustration regarding the situation of a minority turning into the venting of this anger in the form of an anti-Semitic outburst; it also reflects the fear of modern social realities (the stockmarket), whose origins are attributed to a readily available scapegoat. The causes of a complex conflict are reduced to a monocausal measure. This process can be documented innumerable times; the dailies of that time were full of similarly crude attacks when discussing "the Jewish problem." It had very little to do with the actual political reality. But in a horrendous twist of historical irony, Adolf Hitler used a similar technique in *Mein Kampf* when trying to pose as a defender of Christianity against the Jews. Under the sub-heading "Confessional Discord" (*konfessionelle Zwietracht*) it is stated that the modern animosity between the Protestant and Catholic faiths had been instigated by Jews in order to divert attention from their problems, and that the Jew, "the archenemy (*Todfeind*) of Aryan mankind and the whole of Christianity was laughing himself silly because of that."[10] Nazi jargon in the mid-nineteen twenties used prejudice and random historical claims to create an inflammatory vocabulary that targeted the "archenemies" for eventual elimination. The journalistic slur had become part of a political program.

A third example should illustrate one more dimension of what was part of the anti-Semitic discourse in the nineteenth century that became an integral part of Nazi propaganda: the projection of global threats in an apocalyptic manner. Preaching about judgement through the biblical imagery of violent punishment was a potent way to utter threats. The following text appeared on 11 January, 1881, in one of the most vocal Catholic dailies, the *Augsburger Postzeitung*:

There is in actual fact no sector in the social network whose structure has not been damaged or completely destroyed through the defection from a Christian spirit, a defection provoked or demanded by the Jewish mentality (*Judengeist*)...
Enormous are the ruins and the destruction caused by an anti-

Christian egotism whose dynamic force is almost always Jewish; it can be observed in commerce and trade, in an exclusive emphasis of the power of the capital that seeks aquisition without, or at least with effortless production. Through the making of laws the legal means have been provided to continue this process of destruction of sucking things dry to the point of total ruin (*durch Aussaugung bis zur gänzlichen Verwüstung fortzusetzen*)...
Revise the laws in a Christian spirit and you will have burnt and destroyed these nests of robbery more thoroughly than if you had done it—may the Lord prevent it—by sword and fire.[11]

One has to remind oneself that this was not some anonymous hate brochure. It was part of a feature article in one of the most prominent newspapers that was read far beyond its immediate Bavarian territory. The most significant feature of this passage is the combination of an appeal to violence in the name of religion; and again there is this element of absolute and total enmity. There is also another key feature: resentment.[12] The wish to gain revenge in the form of regaining control through the political process is overtaken in the last paragraph by the violent outburst in the last paragraph. The threat of ultimate and total elimination is couched in open metaphors.

When looking for the origins and dominant voices of the discourse of anti-Semitism in the nineteenth century, one of the obvious objective correlatives is to note how similar phenomena in other national European cultures articulated the problem. In a fascinating study, Marc Angenot has investigated the French context. *"Un Juif Trahira." Le thème de l'espionnage militaire dans la propagande antisémitique 1886-1894,*[13] an analysis of the context of the Dreyfus affair, has independently arrived at a similar conclusion that I have encountered when dealing with Catholic anti-Semitism in Germany during the nineteenth century. The antimodernistic *Syllabus errorum prohibitorum* (1864) of Pope Pius IX, a global condemnation of modern social life, was packaged into eighty key conditions. They absolutely refuted everything according to the century-old slogan that there was no salvation whatsoever outside the church; and this list contains a litany that reverberates with the list of terms used for the enemies of modern society in the anti-Semitic catechism. Significantly, it was one of the first instances where the church hierarchy did not restrict this message to church authorities but disseminated it in the various vernaculars to a broad public. In our context the important aspect is the absolute refusal to have anything to do with the social groups that were perceived to be the archenemies of Catholic Christianity. The apodictic condemnation of anything and anybody not adhering to traditional Christian values is absolute. And in France, this was carried directly into the anti-Semitic policies of the *Action Française* and the Vichy regime.[14]

In conclusion, I would suggest that the vocabulary that was instrumental in bringing about the Holocaust had been in the making for a long time. It was appropriated, repeated and applied by an ever-widening number of mainstream social groups, and finally transformed from a revanchist all-purpose litany of accusations into a deadly political program. When analysing the historical process, one of the most depressing features that comes to light is the contribution of religious fanaticism to the dynamics of "the final solution," a contribution all the more depressing and distressing since the churches have not yet adequately acknowledged this fact.

The Initial Reactions of German Jews to Adolf Hitler's Accession to Power

Klaus J. Herrmann

THE FOLLOWING EXCERPT is from a speech given by Rabbi Dr. Elie Munk in his synagogue in the city of Ansbach in Bavaria which was subsequently published in 1933 :

It has got to be justifiably recognized that the establishment of National Socialism has in ideal respects specifically extracted the most dangerous poisonous fangs of Marxism, retaining that which can be characterized as acceptable to us, from the position of Judaism. In this context it has got to be prefaced that racialism is a sideshow, which bears not the slightest relationship to the essence of Nationalism, as a glance into the nationalism of other lands convincingly proves. As long as anti-Semitism remains, there is for us, of course, no possibility of a joint spiritual community. Without anti-Semitism, however, National Socialism would find its most loyal adherents among the Orthodox Jews.

The National Revolution preponderantly eliminated aforementioned ideological confrontations. It has mounted a battle both against the loosening of morals and consciousness of what is right, as well as against the emancipation of the female sex. It has replaced the democratic majority principle by the principle of Führerdom. It has said Halt to the progress of collectivistic economic order. All of these measures are completely in place within the ambits of our religious demands. Above all, it (the National Revolution) has exterminated the most dangerous scourge of the present, namely the Atheist movement.

Suppression of this Bolshevist danger we accept the more gratefully, as it had begun to act subversively also within Jewish circles, with the Jewish leaders proving themselves nearly powerless insofar as it was concerned.

A calmer epoch will arrive in which much of the New that now proceeds will be welcomed by us. The previously threatening danger that the progressively growing proletarization of German Jewry would self-compulsorily lead to complete assimilation appears now to be moderated. It will be possible, even on the lowest social rung, to remain morally pure and godly, like our brethren in the East. The detour via Jew-hatred which the present takes will, as so frequently in history, carry humanity a step forward. Israel has got to suffer so that its ideals, like the newly born, will elevate themselves illuminatingly over a rejuvenated world![1]

Elie Munk, one of the principal spokesmen for German Orthodox Judaism, was born in Paris on 15 September 1900, the son of Orthodox-religious German-Jewish parents who returned to Germany at the outbreak of World War I in August 1914. His 1925 doctoral degree from the University of Marburg projected Elie Munk into the avant-garde of Germany's Orthodox Judaism as represented by the Union of Law-True Jewish Communities of Germany, known as the "Halberstadt Union", after its central office location. This *Bund gesetzestreuer jüdischer Gemeinden Deutschlands* comprised all of those Orthodox communities whose membership refused to be represented by the *Deutsch-Israelitischer Gemeindebund* (German-Israelitic Communal Union) founded in 1921, a year after the Orthodox *Bund* was established. Under the leadership of Elie Munk and his rabbinical and lay colleagues, the *Bund* (not to be confused, of course, with the Labour *Bund* of eastern Europe) immediately approached Adolf Hitler in 1933 to offer its unconditional cooperation and support. The *Bund* proclaimed that Orthodox Jewry was consistently in the vanguard of the struggle against Communism and all other types of godless ideologies, the emancipation of women, pacifism, and moral corruption via the media. As well, Orthodox Jewry opposed the assimilation of the Jewish *"Volk"* into the German *Volk* and particularly so by way of "race" mixtures via intermarriages with gentiles.

The absolute limit of these endeavours to ingratiate themselves with Adolf Hitler personally and with his National-Socialist Movement as such was illustrated by a story making the rounds among Germany's Jews in 1933. Rabbi Munk had led a delegation of Orthodox rabbis to the *Gauleiter* (Nazi provincial governor) of Bavaria in 1933, trying in vain to obtain an interview with him. Rabbi Munk's plea to the *Gauleiter* was to be an attempt to sway him into accepting Orthodox Jews as members of the Nazi party and its various formations, provided that these Orthodox Jews would not be compelled to violate the Sabbath or Holy Day and dietary laws incumbent on them![2]

In any event, Rabbi Munk, one of the foremost scholars of Judaism, having extensively published in the area of Jewish liturgy, left Ansbach in 1937, moving to Paris where he assumed the pulpit of its Secessionist-Orthodox synagogue on Rue Cadet. He subsequently was able to emigrate to New York City where he died in 1981.

Adolf Hitler's appointment as Reich-Chancellor on 30 January 1933 occurred not in consequence of any nationwide elections, but in conformity with powers granted the Reich-President under the Weimar Constitution. Subject to these powers, the then Reich-President Paul von Hindenburg was entitled to appoint a "presidial cabinet". Since he was not obliged to assure himself of the support of the *Reichstag's* parliamentary assent, the eighty-six-year-old von Hindenburg listened to the misbegotten advice of his counsellors and that of his son, Major Oskar von Hindenburg. The Reich-President believed that the "Bohemian private," as he called Adolf Hitler,[3] would be completely encircled by a cabinet of trustworthies from the ranks of the German-National Peoples' Party. This *Deutschnationale Volkspartei* was a reactionist, monarchist, anti-democratic political party led by Privy Counsellor Alfred Hugenberg, a newspaper and publishing house tycoon.

> We welcome the new year 1933, in which the number 3 twice returns as a fortuitous symbol, confident that it will be the year of progress for Germany, for the world, and therefore as well for German Jewry.[4]

Truly, if ever a prediction turned out to be totally misguided and disoriented, it has got to be this 1932 New Year's Eve statement of Germany's most influential Jewish organization, the *Central-Verein deutscher Staatsbürger jüdischen Glaubens* (Central Union of German Citizens of the Jewish Faith), then close to forty years in existence. The *Central-Verein* and its associated organizations comprised well over half of all (religiously identified and thereby church-tax paying) Jews. The *Central-Verein* might be regarded as analogous to a national union of the Anti-Defamation League and the American Jewish Committee in the United States. Consistent insofar as its adherence to the values of a democratic society was concerned, the *Central-Verein*, however, opposed Zionism and the Zionist message about a Jewish "*Volk*." Thus the *Central-Verein* considered itself as representing the majority of German Jews who regarded themselves as members of the German People and therefore not of the Jewish "People", except insofar as the term "Jewish People" was used in a religion-oriented sense. To be sure, the *Central-Verein* had but small support among the German gentiles because to them even those Jews who or whose ancestors converted to Christianity continued to be regarded as members of a distinctively-defined "*Volk*", even "race". Religion had long ceased to be the defining factor in the minds both of the "anti-Semites" (German-Folkists) and the "pro-Semites" in Germany, a perception which strengthened the emergence and development of the Zionist movement.[5]

Heaven knows why the leadership of the *Central-Verein* was as presumptuous as to completely misread the signs of the times. As late as 1928, Adolf Hitler's National-Socialist German Workers' Party (of which commentators opined that it was neither national nor socialist nor German nor for the workers nor a party) was regarded as little more than a relatively unimportant splinter party. Only 810,000 or 2.5 percent of all voters then cast their ballots for it, but a couple of years thereafter, on 14 September 1930, that number increased exponentially to no less than 6,388,000 votes, or 18.2 percent of the electorate. While the aged Reich-President acted in conformity with the Weimar constitution in appointing Adolf Hitler as Reich-Chancellor on that tragic 30 January 1933, he acted in contravention to the very spirit of the Weimar constitution. In effect, he thereby eliminated or bluntly deceived all constitutionally responsible institutions or persons.[6]

Yet there was one final democratic election after Hitler's appointment as Reich-Chancellor, an election that was to sound the death knell to democratic government in Germany until the establishment of the Federal Republic of Germany in May 1949. Scheduled for 5 March 1933, the election proceeded under the cloud of the *Reichstag* fire of 27 February 1933, which led immediately to the outlawing of the Communist Party of Germany, whose leadership was falsely charged with having set the fire. The Communists in turn accused the National-Socialists, but this claim was as untrue as the other, although widely believed until 1962, when Fritz Tobias of Hannover published his definitive work on the fire's actual origins and perpetrator.[7] In any event, the *Reichstag* fire furnished the Nazis with an entirely unexpected advantage and provided electoral grist for their mills. Notwithstanding all of these advantages, the Nazi party, while securing an unprecedented 17,277,000 votes, or 43.9 percent of all votes cast, failed to obtain a parliamentary majority. Tragically, the Nazis were able to draw on the 3,137,000 votes cast for the German-National Peoples Party (*Deutschnationale Volkspartei*) of Alfred Hugenberg and his followers. This party had allied itself with the Nazis in a so-called "Combat Front Black/White/Red" (*Kampffront Schwarz-Weiss-Rot*, these were the imperial German colours as of 1871, which were replaced by the democratic Black-Red-Gold flag after Germany's defeat in November 1918 and the establishment of the republic), thereby lifting Hitler and his parliamentary retinue above the 50 percent mark. These 8 percent of Hugenberg's party enabled Hitler to realize his ambitions for the destruction of parliamentary government via an "Enabling Law" (*Ermächtigungsgesetz*). By its vote for this law the *Reichstag* committed suicide, with all political parties dissolved in short order, leaving Adolf Hitler's National Socialist party as the only authorized political party of Germany. Reich-President von Hindenburg died in August 1934, but even until then, he was unable or not disposed to intervene into any number of outrages and murders committed by a victorious Nazi movement.

We are here concerned exclusively with the reactions of Germany's

Jews to Hitler's subjugation of the German nation and people to his absolute dictates. Neither he nor his cohorts ever made a secret of their unalterable hatred of Jews by religion or by biological descent. This significant differentiation failed to impress Hitler and his adherents. In order to expedite an immediate elimination of Jews from governmental, military, civil service, professorial and teaching positions, from the stock market and the media, a new term of reference was to be employed, namely "non-Aryan"; one which suited the Nazis' goal of depriving also those of some identifiable Jewish descent of their livelihood and station in German life. By the middle of September 1935, via the so-called Laws for the Protection of the German Blood and Honour (Nuremberg Laws), clear parameters were set for the formal identification of all those deemed to be non-Aryan or partially non-Aryan.

Some organizational and statistical information: In 1925, the national census established the presence in Germany of some 565,000 identified members of the Jewish *Gemeinden* (communities, in fact corporations in public law and therefore not comparable to the voluntary congregational system of synagogues extant in the United States and Canada). By 1933, their number had diminished to about a half a million and, according to the 1939 census, to 215,000, not inclusive of 185,000 Jews added to the total in consequence of the Austrian *Anschluss* of March 1938.

As noted, the anti-Jewish decision makers of Germany considered "Jewish" to be a racial quality (today we would speak of "ethnicity"), hence Christians or religious dissenters of Jewish descent are necessarily included in these statistics. Nazi authorities in September 1935 cited figures that reflected a total of 450,000 religiously identified Jews plus 300,000 people of Christian or of no religious affiliation with two Jewish parents ("full Jews") plus another 750,000 "*Mischlinge*" of half or even of quarter Jewish descent.[8]

As early as August 1933, it was therefore essential for these "non-Aryan" Christians to found their own organization in order to be represented with governmental authorities. Thus a "Reich Association of Christian-German Citizens of Non-Aryan or of not purely Aryan Descent" (*Reichsverband christlich-deutscher Staatsbürger nichtarischer oder nicht reinarischer Abstammung*) was established in Berlin under the leadership (the term "*Führer*" was expressly used in order to disassociate any perception of democratic elections) of one Gustav Friedrich. He died on 31 October 1933, succeeded by a Committee of eight, of whom lawyer Richard Wolff soon assumed leadership.

This *Reichsverband* clearly enunciated that its endeavours were "thoroughly legal and that they certainly do not comprise resistance or opposition against any measures of the Reich government". Indeed, "All decision-making official authorities are continuously informed and they approve of our endeavours". The *Reichsverband's* spokesmen proclaimed that non-Aryan Christians had always done battle against "Un-Germanness", against everything which during the Weimar Republic era collected itself in the way of un-German spirit, against overly clever intellectualism, pacifism, and, of course, communism. The *Reichsverband* praised Adolf Hitler for saving the German *Volk* from Bolshevism, thus: "No one against whom there exists even the slightest doubt as to his political ideology or activity would be accepted for membership. An additional collateral for the quality of our membership is furnished by the fact that the lists of members are submitted to the Gestapo (Secret State Police) for vetting."[9]

As of the beginning of the Hitler era, German Jewry existed as an impeccably well organized community, one sharply divided on ideological lines. The Integrationist camp was substantially dominated by the *Central-Verein*, the students' "*Kartell-Convent der Verbindungen deutscher Studenten jüdischen Glaubens*", active on all university campuses, the war veterans, called *Reichsbund jüdischer Frontsoldaten* (Reich Union of Jewish Combat Soldiers), and the Association for Liberal Judaism (*Vereinigung für liberales Judentum*), representing the religiously Liberal (Reform) Jews. To the right of these anti-Zionist organizations the Union of Nationally-German Jews (*Verband nationaldeutscher Juden*–VNJ) held prominent sway. Founded in March 1921 by lawyer Max Naumann, it was forcibly dissolved upon a decree of the Secret State Police in November 1935. The VNJ characterized itself as an association of "Germans of Jewish Stock, who, while fully declaring their descent, regard themselves so inextricably united with Germanness and German culture that they cannot feel and think other than German." Militantly anti-Zionist, the VNJ accepted as members only those who had not resigned from "Judaism". Therefore, VNJ members were not necessarily required to hold membership within the Jewish *Gemeinden* because in some German states, particularly in Prussia, one was legally entitled to resign from *Gemeinde* membership and still declare Judaism as one's religion. Max Naumann and his organization opposed the *Central-Verein*, because its leadership was insufficiently specific on the issue of Germanism, for which reason the VNJ regarded the *Central-Verein* as an "in-between" association, hence not fully anti-Zionist. In late 1933, a rather short-lived political movement arose from among the membership of the Liberal/Reform Jews: "Renewal Movement of the Jewish Germans" (*Erneuerungsbewegung der jüdischen Deutschen*). Its leadership proclaimed absolute opposition to Zionism and against those who were inadequately committed to Germany.

Also the Zionist organizations in Germany were well established. With the advent of the Third Reich, the State Zionists (*Staatszionisten*) came to the fore and began to assume decision-making powers. Led by a former chairman of the Berlin Jewish Community, Georg Kareski, the State Zionists were in league with Vladimir Jabotinsky's Zionist-Revisionist views on the nationally-Jewish *state* ambition of Zionism, and therefore dissatisfied with mainstream Zionist approaches towards a mere "Jewish National Home". Moreover, the State-Zionist Organization was itself supportive of an extreme rightist, oftentimes fascist attitude respecting the nationally-Jewish state in Palestine, which was to be established, by force of arms if necessary. Not surprisingly, Georg Kareski, an overly ambitious communal politician, cooperated with the Secret State Police in trying to assert his leadership over the central organizations of German Jewry, and thus within the Berlin *Gemeinde* and the Reich-Representation of German Jews (*Reichsvertretung der deutschen Juden*), subsequently re-named Reich Association of Jews in Germany (*Reichsvereinigung der Juden in Deutschland*) by order of the Nazi authorities, since the latter rejected the designation of Jews who deemed themselves to be "German".

Georg Kareski, then fifty-seven years old, was granted the opportunity on Christmas Eve 1935 to present the views of his State Zionist ideology in *Der Angriff*, the Berlin newspaper of Joseph Goebbels, Reich-Minister for Propaganda and Peoples' Enlightenment. *Der Angriff* treated Kareski as an interviewee on the issue of the Nuremberg Laws of 15 September 1935. Throughout addressed as "*Herr Direktor* Kareski" (he served as executive director of "*Iwria*", a small loans bank), he entirely concurred, as a Zionist ideologue, with the premises of these laws for the "protection of the German blood and honour". An extract of this interview would so indicate.

Question: You are aware, *Herr Direktor* Kareski, that our *Führer* and Reich-Chancellor expressed anticipation for the reasoning of the Nuremberg laws, that by this one-time secular solution possible there can be created a level on which it may be possible for the German *Volk* to find an accommodative relationship to the Jewish *Volk*. You, as leading personality of the State Zionist movement, have always stood for a sharp separation between German and Jewish folkdom on the basis of mutual respect.

Answer: That is correct. For many years I have regarded a clean delimitation of the cultural concerns of two cohabitating Peoples as a condition for a conflict-free cohabitation and I am for such a border, which pre-conditions respect for the realm of an alien folkdom, and I have long advocated such.

Question: As well knowledgeable, *Herr Direktor* Kareski, of National-Socialist ideology, you are aware that according to German perception, the matrimonial community of two humans is a lofty ethical task as well as a cultural element of first rank. The prohibition of mixed marriages therefore is also as to cultural regards, aside from its race-political significance, an important aspect. What have you to say to this from the Jewish-folkist point of view?

Answer: The immense significance of healthy family life needs no explanation from the Jewish side. If the Jewish People for two millennia after the loss of its independence as a state maintained itself to this day in spite of the lack of a united settlement community and linguistic unity, there are two factors for this:

Its (the Jewish People's) race and the strong position of the family in Jewish life. The loosening of these two ties during the past decades was also on the Jewish side the subject of serious worry. The interruption of the dissolution process in wide Jewish circles, as such is furthered by mixed marriage, is therefore to be unconditionally welcomed by the Jewish side. For the creation of a Jewish state in Palestine these two factors, religion and family, retain decisive significance.[10]

Needless to say, while the Zionist-separatist attitude was welcomed by the authorities in command and in charge of Germany during the Third Reich, the (majority) Jewish positions of integrationist (assimilationist) view engendered full rejection. The best example for this Nazi differentiation and preferential treatment of the Zionist protagonists was in the compulsory dissolution of Max Naumann's VNJ in late November 1935. It was not for long, however, that even the State-Zionist leadership, notably Georg Kareski, left for Palestine where, incidentally, Kareski had to defend himself against charges leveled against him because of his cooperation with the Secret State Police of Germany. He was acquitted of these charges.

On the other side of the ideological fence, during 1933 and 1934 and well into 1935, the majority of Germany's Jews unsuccessfully attempted to impress Hitler's government by asserting full support of his "National Revolution". Basically, German-Jewish leadership optimistically anticipated a typology of Fascism in Germany in which Jews would be assessed as to their political stance and to the degree of their unconditional fealty to the National-Socialist state. In that regard there seemed to be ample analogy with the situation of the Jews in Benito Mussolini's Italy, where no less than 25 percent of the Italian-Jewish population of some 50,000 had joined the Fascist Party, and where some appreciable number of these Jews enthusiastically were in the very front ranks of Italian Fascism. (Italy's "Race Laws" of March 1938 terminated this relationship.)[11]

A significant number of German Jews lulled themselves into believing that a differentiation was going to be made between those whose ancestors were born in Germany and the others who essentially had immigrated from eastern European areas including the Austro-Hungarian Empire's Polish provinces. As well, this "old line" German-Jewish community regarded adherence to the Zionist viewpoint as an un-German alien-minded attitude and as emotional disaffection from Germanism. Little did these "national-German" Jews comprehend that, neither to Hitler himself, nor to those who shared his ideological perceptions, were there distinctions to be made among the Jews, or even as to those who or whose ancestors had abandoned Judaism entirely.

Max Naumann, founding and ideological genius of the VNJ, was bitterly opposed to the central *Reichsvertretung der deutschen Juden*, inasmuch as it comprised Jews organized in Zionist groupings. Indeed, with the advent of Adolf Hitler and particularly with his seizure of power, tens of thousands among the German Jews strengthened the membership of Germany's Zionist Organization. Naumann succeeded in enlisting most notably the *Reichsbund jüdischer Frontsoldaten*—the Jewish War Veterans —or at least its founding genius and leader, Captain (and doctor of Engineering Science) Leo Löwenstein, to join a very short-lived "Action Committee of the Jewish Germans" (*Aktionsausschuss der jüdischen Deutschen*) in April 1933. This Action Committee also included two expressly anti-Zionist youth movements of the period: the Black Pennant (*Schwarzes Fähnlein*) and the German Advance Guard, Adherence of German Jews (*Deutscher Vortrupp, Gefolgschaft deutscher Juden*). Within two months, this Action Committee fell apart, but during its brief existence the Action Committee announced its intentions of coordinating itself fully into the building of the new German Reich, stressing its deter-mination to counteract any attempt by foreign intervenors into intra-German affairs. Its leadership proposed to coordinate with German officialdom in order to completely terminate the "hate campaign" against National-Socialist Germany.

In point of fact, the National-Socialist government was wholly unconcerned with these overtures and it rejected out of hand any such coordination with Jews of whatever ideological colouring. On the contrary: Nazi ideology could not tolerate any viewpoint whose advocates proclaimed their membership in the German *Volk*; Nazis rejected out of hand any kind of assimilatory endeavours by Jews as such. The Secret State Police was actually capable and desirous of working on behalf of Zionist attempts to settle German Jews in Palestine and to otherwise see to the segregation and ghettoization of the Jews as an entirely separate type of *Volk* and community.

In consequence, there was nothing but rejection of the endeavours that Leo Löwenstein launched on behalf of his *Reichsbund* of Jewish Combat Soldiers. On 23 May 1933, he wrote to Hitler that his *Reichsbund* had been apprized of an Upper Silesian Jew, Bernheim, who appealed to the League of Nations in order to demand discussion of alleged violations concerning the German-Polish treaty on minorities. Bernheim had asked for minority national status for Upper Silesia's German Jews. The *Reichsbund* stridently opposed any kind of "solution of the Jewish Question" which would result in the German Jews being conducted out of the association of the German nation. Professing undying loyalty to the German Nation and the German *Heimat* "for which we staked our lives and to which we profess ourselves to the very last breath", Löwenstein emphasized though that such profession to Germany and Germanism is aligned in "unimpeded union with our upright solidarity to Jewish tradition and the Jewish stock (*Stamm*)."[12]

Once the German Jews and those of Jewish descent were excluded from military conscription and service in the German armed forces, the *Reichsbund* directed further letters and resolutions to Hitler, in which requests were made to grant young Jewish men right and honour of service in the German armed forces, "if necessary in separate Jewish military formations". As could have been anticipated, Nazi newspaper commentators gleefully made sport of these submissions and characterized them as trying to form a "Jewish Foreign Legion" for which the National-Socialist State had absolutely no use whatever.[13]

Going beyond the parameters even of the *Reichsbund*, Max Naumann's VNJ submitted lengthy remonstrations in which he asked for the imposition of a Commissariate of Jewish Affairs, in which absolutely loyal "Germano-Jews" (*Deutschjuden*) were to adjudge the Germanism or lack thereof of all Jews. Moreover, Naumann demanded that all Jewish worship services be conducted entirely in the German language. The consequence of these proposals, dated from the beginning of September 1935, that is, immediately prior to the issuance with much fanfare of the infamous Nuremberg Laws, was that they were filed away and perhaps were instrumental in the arrest and confinement of Max Naumann by late November 1935.

The leading personality of German Jewry was Rabbi Dr. Leo Baeck, then a man of sixty (deported to Terezin in 1943, he survived the Holocaust years and died in November 1956). Liberal-religious and a non-Zionist, he occupied the very highest offices in Germany's Jewish representative organizations. Grand President of the *B'nai B'rith* and the first president of the Reich Representation of German Jews, during World War I he served as chaplain with the German armed forces. In his official capacity he published the central statement against the Nazi government's contention that the German Jews were enemies of the state:

> The national German revolution which we are witnessing contains two non-separable directions, namely the struggle to surmount Bolshevism and Germany's renaissance. What is German Jewry's position to these two directions? Bolshevism, particularly in its Atheists Movement, is the most embittered enemy of Judaism, extirpation of the Jewish religion is in its programme. A Jew who converts to Bolshevism is an apostate. Germany's renaissance is an ideal and a longing among the German Jews. It would have been fair to determine individual misdeeds and bring them to the knowledge of appropriate authorities. Instead, false friends were persuaded into serious and regrettable errors. As political antagonists of the new German power wielders and in order to create difficulties for them, Leftist circles throughout the world used Germany's Jewry like a shield in front of them during their attacks. They attempted by way of irresponsible and untrue reports to damage their political enemies, the National-Socialists, who govern.[14]

Truth be told, neither Rabbi Baeck, nor any other prominent German Jew, or person of Jewish descent, was able to influence or impress Adolf

Hitler and his governing clique. The Nazi rulers regarded Jews as an alien and undesirable body within what they had artificially constructed as some "Aryan" racial society. Hitler was totally disinterested in both Judaism as a religion and the complaints and statements of rabbis that Jews who had "converted" to Communism were deemed to be apostates. Anti-Jewish ideologues, were certainly familiar with the talmudic interpretations of Judaism, according to which even apostate Jews continued to be Jews. Moreover, since even those Jews who had converted to Christianity, or whose parents and even grandparents had done so were deemed to be "non-Aryans", Hitler remained unconcerned with attempts to shift this issue onto the "religion" track. Jews in other countries, especially so in the United States, scheduled mass meetings to protest actions taken against the German Jews. Leading lights in this campaign to alert American public opinion were Rabbi Stephen S. Wise, founder and president of the World Jewish Congress, and Samuel Untermeyer, a distinguished American jurist and statesman. Their demands for the boycott of German merchandise was forthwith countered by a Day of Boycott against all Jewish-owned shops and businesses in Germany. On 29 March 1933 the *Reichsvertretung der deutschen Juden* and the Board of Directors of Berlin's Jewish *Gemeinde* (then numbering some 170,000) issued an outraged proclamation as follows:

> The German Jews are profoundly shocked by the Call to Boycott of the national socialist German workers party (sic! it ought to have been capitalized). Because of the transgressions of a few for whom we are not responsible, shall we, German Jews, who with all our heartstrings feel ourselves bound to our German homeland, be prepared for economic destruction? In all the wars of the fatherland, German Jews have offered their blood sacrifices for such ties. During the Great War, of 500,000 German Jews, 12,000 gave their lives. In the areas of peaceful work we have done our duties with all of our strength. The Horror and Boycott campaign (against Germany) in foreign lands the Jewish organizations of Germany have combatted with utmost efforts,

and successfully so. They have done all that was in their power to do and shall continue to do so. Nevertheless, now the German Jews, as the alleged guilty ones, are to be economically destroyed. We appeal to the German People, to whom justice has always been its highest virtue.

The reproach that we caused damage to our (German) people appends most profoundly on our honour. For the sake of truth and for the sake of our honour we solemnly take exception to this accusation. We rely on the Reich-President and on the Reich-Government that it will not remove from us justice and existence in our German fatherland. We repeat in this hour the profession of our belonging to the German Volk, to whose rejuvenation and ascent our collaboration is our most sacred duty, our right and our most passionate desire.[15]

The VNJ reflected a considerably larger section of German Jewry than its limited membership would have suggested. Moreover, the VNJ comprised hardly any Jews who adhered to religious orthodoxy (as against being "nationally Jewish" they regarded themselves as "nationally German."). That consideration led to its establishment in early 1921, not any kind of allegiance to the right-reactionary *Deutschnationale Volkspartei*, whose leadership eventually joined forces with the National-Socialists. Nevertheless, these *nationaldeutsche* Jews were largely of the moderately conservative, political Right as substantially organized in the *Deutsche Volkspartei*, led by Gustav Stresemann.

Having noted the lack of Orthodox religionists in its ranks, it may be recognized that even among the "ultra" Orthodox adherents of Agudas Jisroel, an international body of "Torah-True" Jews founded in 1912, pejorative comments were constantly passed against East-European Jews. Thus, Jakob Rosenheim, the chairman of the Secessionist-Orthodox community in Frankfurt, and in fact, the founding genius of Agudas Jisroel, testified as to derogatory designations leveled against co-religionists who were less than Germanic in their exercise of Judaism. And indeed from among the ranks of both the Secessionist (*Austritts*) Orthodox and the Community (*Gemeinde*) Orthodox there emanated protestations of abject and devoted support to Nazi absolutism.[16] This support of Hitler as dictator substantially may have derived from Orthodoxy's intrinsically non-democratic understanding of Divinely-unfolding history and events. Jewish Orthodoxy, at least in Germany, seemed to be considerably more intensively worried about the free exercise of democracy and personal liberties that endangered Orthodox dogmatics than it was of political absolutism. Thus Orthodox spokesmen expressed considerably greater concern, not to say obsessive fears, that Hitler might veer away from his hardline policy of rejecting persons of Jewish ancestry irrespective of religious persuasion. These Orthodox leaders worried about the introduction of reappraisals by Nazi ideologists such that relinquishment of Judaism and acceptance of baptism into Christianity would exempt or somehow privilege these apostates from Judaism. In fact, Hitler had never considered such nineteenth century typology of differentiating between communicants of Judaism and Jewish converts to Christianity. "Can we imagine what the reaction among Germany's Jews would be, were apostasy from our holy religion and Christian baptism to entitle to full or even partial access into and by the National-Socialist Germany?" asked Orthodox-Jewish officialdom, only to respond that: "There would be the most massive flight from our holy Jewish religion." These Orthodox-religious leaders need not have been unduly alarmed because the opportunity never arose, nor was it seriously ever contemplated among the National Socialists. The elite of German-Jewish religion Orthodoxy, comprising notably its southern-geographical component, for instance Jakob Rosenheim, Elie Munk and Isaak Breuer in 1933 and 1934 wrote to Hitler personally, emphasizing its lifelong battle against Marxism and Atheism, against Liberalism and moral corruption, and fervently offering to travel to the United States in order to fight the "anti-German Horror campaign" among their co-religionists. It is doubtful that these remonstrations were ever submitted to the *Führer* himself; more probably the Reich-Chancellery executive officers filed them away for posterity and for the benefit of historians.

In retrospect, it may appear that the majority German-Jewish population as well as those who had left Judaism, but who nevertheless were regarded as Jews, seemed incapable of grasping evident realities. In actual fact, some 295,000 German Jews decided and were able to emigrate from their homeland in Germany. Unhappily, hope sprang eternal, hope that Adolf Hitler would recognize an asset in the Jews of Germany, that they posed absolutely no danger to him; on the contrary, that they were dedicated to working for the good and welfare of the Reich. Emigration from Germany always required countries prepared to receive these emigrants. What with the economic disaster following the October 1929 economic depression, to all intents and purposes that economic depression had not been surmounted well into the 1930s.

Few were the prophets, if indeed any, who could have anticipated Adolf Hitler's murderous plans for the physical extermination of just about all Jews (or of Jewish descent) within his grasp.

Excepting the January 1940 deportation of the west-Pomeranian Jews from the Stettin area to the charnel ghettos of Poland, deportations to the death camps and the starvation conditions of the ghettos did not begin until October 1941. Until that time the Nazi government encouraged the German Jews (no longer referred to as such, but as "Jews in Germany") to leave the *Deutsches Reich* by any and all means. Permission to emigrate was summarily withdrawn by the end of September 1941. In any event, it had become virtually impossible to obtain immigration visa or permits by that time or to provide the financial means requisite for emigration.

In hindsight, it is evident that all efforts to conciliate Adolf Hitler and his governmental or party apparatus were entirely futile. It becomes easy therefore to condemn or to deprecate the leadership of the German Jews for their endeavours to arrange some kind of *modus vivendi* with a government officially committed to anti-Semitism. After the facts and the mass murder of the Holocaust, questions are asked as to the will to resist at that time. While it is true that there was no kind of organized resistance movement among Germany's Jews or among its appointed leadership, there were no psychological bases for such opposition in the minds of these Jewish Germans, schooled and socialized in concepts of obedience to Authority. Moreover, there were no conditions that could have encouraged the formation of an organized resistance to the Nazis' deportations from Germany and into the East-European death camps.[17]

Within the limits of their then understanding of government and of historical precedent, Germany's Jews could but act in a manner that was appropriate to their experiences and their perceptions. Most tragically, those actions and inactions resulted in their destruction.

Reporting Nazi Murder: The Einsatzgruppen Reports

Ronald Headland

...I emphasize and state again that I never approved of the shooting of the Jews, and that it was against my innermost heart that I was put in this position in the war. I never ordered the shooting of the Jews and never gave an execution order, so help me God! I have committed no crimes and am filled with no feelings of guilt. [1]

...Today I can confirm that *Einsatzkommando* 3 has reached the goal of solving the Jewish problem in Lithuania. The only remaining Jews are labourers and their families... I wanted to also put the working Jews and their families to rest, but the armed forces declared war on me and issued the prohibition: "These Jews and their families must not be shot..." I regard the Jewish actions of *Einsatzkommando* 3 as virtually completed. The remaining working Jewish men and women are urgently needed, and I imagine that they will still be needed after the winter. I am of the opinion that the male working Jews should be sterilized immediately to prevent any procreation. A Jewish woman who nevertheless becomes pregnant is to be liquidated... [2]

THESE EXCERPTS from two separate documents were written eighteen years apart, by the same man. The first was written on 21 June 1959 in a prison cell in Ludwigsburg Germany. The second was part of a report, dated 1 December 1941, a report which summarized the killing operations carried out in Lithuania to that point by *Einsatzkommando* 3.

The author of this report had been the leader of this *Kommando*. The man was Karl Jäger, certainly one of the most efficient mass murderers in modern history. The 1959 document was a farewell letter that Jäger wrote while undergoing interrogation as part of preliminary criminal proceedings of a German court. Jäger, in spite of his claims of innocence, was unable to face the mounting evidence that was being collected. Shortly after writing this letter he committed suicide in his cell.

We shall return later to Jäger's report. The purpose in beginning with these two documents is not so much to point out the obvious untruth of postwar statements of men like Jäger, who, in the face of clearly murderous documents with their own signatures on them, still denied their guilt. Rather, the purpose is simply to establish immediately the perspective of this paper. The subject is mass murder, and the perspective is that of the killers—Germans and their collaborators. Bear in mind that we will see through German eyes only, the eyes of the perpetrators. I will be concerned with what the Germans did, and what they wrote about what they did.

Jäger's report was one of more than two hundred and fifty extant *Einsatzgruppen* reports. These reports were top secret and were supposed to have been destroyed so as to not fall into enemy hands, but as was the case in many other German agencies, too many copies of these reports had been made and distributed. It was impossible to destroy them all. One virtually complete set survived and came to light after the war. For the most part, the surviving reports were compiled and edited in Berlin, and were based on material sent in regularly from the east by the various *Einsatzgruppen*. Page after page of these reports detailed in succinct, impersonal, language the systematic killing of Jews, communist officials, Gypsies, and others, in the eastern territories occupied by the Germans. No other documents among the thousands that were unearthed offer such an extensive and precise day-by-day account of mass killing, written by the killers themselves, while the killing was actually taking place. Confronting us on the pages of these reports is the uniquely Nazi phenomenon of acts of such barbarity as to require absolute secrecy in order to carry them out, on the one hand, and, on the other, the strange desire to record the murderous events in writing.

I believe the *Einsatzgruppen* reports are important in two fundamental respects. First, they are crucial for what they tell us directly about what happened on the eastern front—the unfolding of the operations, the statistical record, and so on. And secondly, they are important for what they tell us indirectly, for the most part inadvertently, about the process of mass killing itself, and the men who carried this out. Therefore, in the following discussion I will examine briefly some aspects of both of these perspectives, the direct and the indirect.

Before discussing the reports, a few words about the *Einsatzgruppen*. Who were they? How did they come into being, and how were they organized?

In the late winter and spring of 1941, as part of the preparations for the planned attack on the Soviet Union, a series of negotiations took place between the German army and Heinrich Himmler's Security Police. These negotiations led to written agreements which delineated the relationship that was to exist between Himmler's police units, known as *Einsatzgruppen* (literally, action groups), and the army commands within whose area the *Einsatzgruppen* were to operate.[3] The final agreement stipulated that the *Einsatzgruppen Kommandos* were to operate on their own responsibility under Himmler's authority in the rear army areas. There was no mention of killing as such. The agreement stated that the *Einsatzgruppen* were to carry out "executive measures concerning the civilian population."[4]

During May and June of 1941 the leaders and rank-and-file members of the *Einsatzgruppen* assembled in the towns of Pretzsch and the nearby villages of Düben and Schmiedeburg in Germany. It was here that the *Einsatzgruppen* were organized into the four groups: *Einsatzgruppe* A, B, C, and D. Each *Einsatzgruppe* was subdivided into functioning units called *Einsatzkommandos* and *Sonderkommandos*. Each *Einsatzgruppe* was attached to a specific army group. *Einsatzgruppe* A was to operate on the northern front in the Baltic States and in the western part of White Russia; *Einsatzgruppe* B was to operate south of *Einsatzgruppe* A in White Russia; *Einsatzgruppe* C was to operate in the northern and middle Ukraine; *Einsatzgruppe* D was to operate in parts of the southern Ukraine, the Crimea, and later, the Caucasus.[5]

Altogether the four *Einsatzgruppen* numbered about three thousand men. *Einsatzgruppe* A, the largest *Einsatzgruppe*, had a total strength of 990 people as of October 1941.[6] The *Einsatzkommandos* and *Sonderkommandos* generally varied in size, some having up to approximately 170 men, while others had as few as 70 or 80 men.[7] These *Kommandos* could if necessary be further broken down into smaller groups, known as *Teilkommandos*, often consisting of only a few men. Therefore, several units from one *Einsatzkommando* would be operating in a number of places at the same time. Each *Kommando* had all the requirements to carry out their tasks—motorcycles and other vehicles, drivers, technicians to repair the vehicles, administrative officials, liaison officers with the army commands, clerical staff, teletype operators, mobile kitchen staff, interpreters, as well as experienced Security Police officials.

The Einsatzgruppen were under the direct operational control of the *Reichssicherheitshauptamt* (Reich Security Main Office), or RSHA, in Berlin. A labyrinth of departments and subsections headed by Reinhard Heydrich, the RSHA had been created in 1939 just after the start of the war. The RSHA combined two things: the *Sicherheitspolizei*, or Security Police, and the *Sicherheitsdienst*, or Security Service. The Security Police was itself a combination of two police agencies, the Secret State Police, or Gestapo, and the Criminal Police. The Security Service was the intelligence-gathering arm of the party. Working alongside the *Einsatzgruppen* in the east were members of the *Waffen SS*, the military units of the SS, as well as battalions of the *Ordnungspolizei*, or Order Police, the regular German police. These other police units took part in mass shootings with, and at times, separately from, the *Einsatzgruppen*. They usually worked with the *Einsatzgruppen* in large-scale operations, for example, the killing of more than 33,700 Jews at Babi Yar in Kiev in two days at the end of September 1941.[8] In addition to these other German police units the *Einsatzgruppen* also recruited collaborators from amongst the civilian population in the east, who actively took part in the killings. Furthermore, units of the German army itself at times participated in the slaughter.[9]

The leaders of the four *Einsatzgruppen* and the various *Kommando* leaders were drawn from the Security Police and Security Service departments of the RSHA. Most had joined the Nazi Party and the SS during the 1930s and during this period had risen through the ranks of the Security Police or one or other of the police organizations. It is noteworthy that the *Einsatzgruppen* leaders were generally quite young— in 1941 most were in their mid-thirties and early forties. They were essentially intellectuals. Almost all were well educated. Several had doctorates. Many had studied law, while others had pursued careers in architecture, medicine, education, and business. Otto Rasch, the first leader of *Einsatzgruppe* C, had attained two doctorates, a Doctor of Jurisprudence and a Doctor of Law and Economics. Rasch had practiced law and had been the mayor of Wittenberg.[10] His successor as leader of *Einsatzgruppe* C, Max Thomas, had been a physician and had left his medical practice to devote himself to the SS and the Security Police.[11] The leader of *Einsatzgruppe* D, Otto Ohlendorf, was a brilliant economist. Ernst and Erwin Weinmann were brothers. Ernst Weinmann had been a dentist and had also been the mayor of Tubingen, and later he became commander of the German Security Police in Serbia. His brother Erwin had been a doctor before becoming a *Kommando* leader in *Einsatzgruppe* C.[12] One *Kommando* leader named Klingelhöfer had been an opera singer.[13] Another man, whose name had originally had been Szymanofsky, had changed his name to the more German name of Biberstein. Before becoming a *Kommando* leader Biberstein had studied theology and had been a Protestant clergyman.[14]

These were the kind of men who led the *Einsatzgruppen*. With their proven leadership abilities and their personal ambition they became skillful mass murderers. The *Einsatzgruppen* were virtually independent of the German civil administration and the army in the rear areas on the eastern front. This position was strengthened almost immediately in July 1941 when Himmler was given full power to carry out so-called "security police" measures in the areas under civil administration.[15] The result of this personnel mix, organizational structure and jurisdictional authority of the *Einsatzgruppen*, as well as the extreme mobility of the *Kommandos*, was that the *Einsatzgruppen* became one of the most powerful killing machines in human history.

On 22 June 1941 the German armed forces attacked the Soviet

Union. Immediately the *Einsatzgruppen* troops followed behind the advancing German armies. Immediately the *Einsatzgruppen* secured the territory, capturing the civilian population within their grasp. Immediately the shootings began.

The *Kommandos* carried out their task in essentially the following way: Jews, and other victims, would be taken in groups on foot or in trucks to remote places where pits had been dug to accommodate the number of intended victims. The Jews were then generally forced to remove all their clothes and were then shot in the neck or the head, either beside the pits or lying down in the pits. When the pits were filled the bodies were covered with earth. Often the killings were carried out in public, as reprisal actions, to terrorize the local population and to prevent them from engaging in acts of sabotage or from supporting the Russian partisans.

The onslaught of the *Einsatzgruppen* marked the beginning of the organized and deliberate physical annihilation of the European Jews. Within six weeks more than 62,000 victims had perished under the *Einsatzgruppen* firing squads.[16] By the end of 1942 the death toll had reached well over one million.[17]

But this global statistic of the dead is a problem. It does not in itself convey the sense of the relentless day to day killing process. Like the number six million it is too vast, too abstract. We really cannot picture it.

To illustrate more concretely this gradual accumulation of victims and at the same time to provide an example of the direct statistical evidence of mass killing, one *Einsatzgruppen* report will be examined— "Operational Situation Report 148" (*Ereignismeldung UdSSR* 148), dated 19 December 1941. It must be kept in mind that there is nothing particularly special about this report. It is typical of the 195 Operational Situation Reports issued between June 1941 and April 1942. Operational Situation Report 148 contains reports relating to *Einsatzgruppe* B only, and since the *Einsatzgruppe* B reporters were not always precise in their reports as to when their actions took place, the time frame of these killings is not absolutely clear. In fact, no specific dates are mentioned at all. A comparison with other reports where the time frame is indicated more clearly would suggest that the events described in this report probably occurred within a period of approximately a week to ten days. What follows is not the entire report, but simply a summary of the essential information.

OPERATIONAL SITUATION REPORT 148
Measures Against Criminals and Looters

In several locations, 35 Russians and Jews were described as having committed certain crimes, including looting, arson, prostitution, and embezzling. These 35 people were shot.

In Mogilev, in a special action in a labour camp, 150 Jews were shot for being actively rebellious.

In the woods near Mogilev, 127 Jews were shot for not wearing their badges and for not having the required papers.

In a transient camp near Mogilev, 196 Jews and communist officials were shot.

In Bobroisk, "confidential messages" from informers stated that the Jews were not wearing the star, had refused to work, had connections with partisans, and had displayed a provocative attitude toward the German forces. These actions threatened the "public security and order". The result: 5281 Jewish men and women were shot. Bobroisk and vicinity were declared "free of Jews" (*Judenfrei*).

In Paritischi, 1013 Jews, both men and women, were shot.

In Rudnja, 835 Jews were shot.

In Gomel, 52 Jews were shot. Agents reported that the Jews had helped the partisans. The result: in Gomel, Rogatschow and Kormu, 2365 Jews, men and women, were shot.

In Klinowitschi and Tschorikow, 789 Jews, men and women, were shot.

In Ljubawitschi, 492 Jews were shot.

In Borissow, 146 Jews in jail were shot. They had been arrested for loitering and endangering the public security.

In Kritschow, to maintain public security and order, 1213 Jews were shot.

For the same reason, in Roslawl and Schumjatschi, 510 Jews were shot.

Also in Schumjatschi, in an orphanage, 16 mentally ill Jewish and Russian children were shot.

In Witebsk, during an "evacuation" action in the ghetto there, 4090 Jews were shot.[18]

Remember that this is just one report, one *Einsatzgruppe*. The total number of victims in this one report: 13,094. One can therefore see a bit more clearly how the numbers of people shot could reach such a high level by the end of 1942 alone.

That is an example of the direct statistical evidence. What about the indirect evidence? What insights into the killers and the killing process itself do the reports provide us indirectly? Obviously this is a complex subject, one that cannot be dealt with in any definitive way in a short paper such as this. Therefore, I will confine myself to two areas only relating to this subject: first, the language of the reports, the language of justification and coverup; and second, the self-praising tone of the reports, which attempts to place the *Einsatzgruppen Kommandos*, and hence their leaders, in the best possible light.[19] Both these phenomena play important roles in the process of mass murder.

The *Einsatzgruppen* began a program of murder that by the end of the Second World War had claimed the lives of, among others, one third of the Jews of the world. The reports reflect necessary steps in a killing operation of this magnitude. To decide to destroy the Jews of Europe is one thing; to carry this out, quite another. In this regard German leaders faced many technical and organizational problems. Above all, they faced the difficulty of getting ordinary men to perform extraordinary tasks. The killers had to cope with the shootings on a daily basis, they had to make acceptable to themselves the horrific acts they were perpetrating against defenceless men, women and children.

A process of mass murder, in order to be carried out on such a scale, inevitably involves the need for the dehumanization of the intended victims. This is an absolutely essential ingredient. In the minds of the men pulling the triggers the victims first have to be seen as being guilty of some crime. It is evident that in Operational Situation Report 148, along with the numbers of persons killed, there is almost always some "reason" or "reasons" given to explain and justify the shootings. Jews are accused of alleged criminal acts—looting, rebellious behaviour, not following various German regulations, or helping the Russian partisans. The *Einsatzgruppen* reporters often went to great lengths to come up with justifications for their work. Other reports mentioned that the Jews were a danger because they could spread epidemics, or that the Jews spread false rumours and hate propaganda, or that they terrorized the local population with "usury", or that they were "unreliable elements". Jews could be shot on the mere "suspicion" that they had committed some crime. In Operational Situation Report 148 we saw that the Jews could be shot for the crime of loitering.

The use of these "reasons" by the *Einsatzgruppen* reporters was a way of providing themselves with a "legal" basis for the killings. With an eye to the future, and a possible, (though unlikely) occasion when they might be held accountable, these explanations rationalized the killings and covered them in a shroud of legality. The reports maintained the executions were simply counter measures against unlawful acts of Jews, communists, partisans, and other dangerous elements. The implication was that the shootings were legal.

In itself the very act of reporting mass murder in the way it was done to some degree legitimized it for the readers. The reports did not deal exclusively with the killing operations, but also reported on a variety of other areas of concern to the Security Police and the Security Service. This juxtaposition of mass killing with other subjects helped to place mass murder within the realm of "normal" behaviour. The killing of thousands simply became one subject among others to be reported on. Therefore, in the reports right alongside the annihilation of the Jewish population of whole cities or regions, one also finds ordinary discussions of educational, economic, and social policy. The shootings, in the reporters' words and minds, were reduced to a function of routine policework.

In addition to the use of justifications the reporters often used code words or euphemisms to cover up the act of murder, and this, too, became a requisite part of the process. It was, of course, inconceivable that the *Einsatzgruppen* could continuously present what they were doing as murder or mass killing. Other terms had to be used. These reports were highly secret. Since they were not meant to be seen by outsiders and since the *Einsatzgruppen* bureaucracy did not really have to justify its actions or employ euphemisms, then why did it do so? It did so in order to conceal the act of killing, as Holocaust historian Raul Hilberg has put it, "not only from all outsiders but also from the censuring gaze of its own conscience".[20] As a result, the reports often simply described the shootings as actions, or special actions, special treatment, cleansing action, liquidation, severe measures, rendering harmless, overhauling, and similar innocuous phrases to make the reality of mass murder more palatable to the killers.[21]

Euphemisms could, to some extent, put reality out of mind. If one did not think too hard about it, the self-deception worked. Members of the *Kommandos* were, of course, ordered not to talk about what they were doing to outsiders, and it was generally considered bad form to discuss the killings amongst themselves. The use of euphemistic language concerning the Jews was not confined to the *Einsatzgruppen* reports, but was a part of private conversations and letters of individuals, as well as correspondence within all institutions of the Third Reich. Its use by the *Kommandos*, however, was extremely necessary, since for them the killing was an immediate daily reality. In the *Einsatzgruppen* reports one encounters a pathetic effort to find plausible reasons for mass murder and to distance the reader from the reality of what was happening. Yet it is precisely this constant and mindless repetition of the same clumsy explanations and formulaic code words over and over again that robs the attempts at justification and coverup of any real believability.

But the picture was even more complex than this. On paper the Jews had to be called criminals in order to justify the measures against them. Nazi ideology, by its very nature, however, viewed the Jews in a much more radical and profound way, in a way, in fact, that went well beyond the more usual concepts of criminality that, for the most part, were being advanced in the reports. Reflecting Nazi dogma, the reports constantly depicted the Jews as the instigators and controllers of

Bolshevism. The Jews were said to be the wielders of power whose control over society and government had to be destroyed. As well, Jews were seen as racially inferior beings. They were seen as the absolute enemy not only of Germany but of humanity itself. Ultimately, the Nazi view accused all Jews of one fundamental crime—that of having been born.

This idea was central, it lay behind all others. Guilty of this overriding, fundamental crime, the Jews were to be destroyed. And this idea, too, surfaced directly in the reports. Therefore, side by side with the efforts to disguise or routinize the *Einsatzgruppen* activities, cited above, one also finds throughout the reports completely unambiguous statements about the intended complete destruction of the Jews. (This has been seen already in the report by Jäger mentioned earlier.) Jews are shot with no attempt whatsoever at justification. In another example, Operational Situation Report 194, dated 21 April 1942, the *Kommandos* of *Einsatzgruppe* B listed shootings they had carried out in the previous month of March. Beside the category "Russians", one finds the usual brief explanations. Beside the categories "Jews," and "Gypsies", no explanations are given, simply the numbers killed.[22]

Here then is yet another characteristic feature of the reports—the stark contradiction between the crude facade of "legality", and the obvious implementation of mass murder based on ideology. Perhaps this contradiction did not go unnoticed by the *Einsatzgruppen* editors, yet it likely was not a cause for too much concern. One does not generally search Nazi documents for demonstrations of profound logic, and these reports are no exception. Other inconsistencies abound. For example, the alleged legal basis for the killings continued to be put forward long after it was apparent to anyone reading the reports that, regardless of anything else, the staggering number of victims alone rendered quite preposterous any connection between these killings and normal punishment for criminal activity. As late as mid-December 1941 one could read in a report the following example of Nazi thinking: "Since the Jewish population, despite severe punishment continually disturbed the desired pacification of the occupied regions, the severest measures will have to be continued against them."[23] Again, it was the Jews who were to blame for what the Germans were doing to them.

In addition, in many reports a necessary part of the rationalizing centered on the frequent blaming of both Jews and retreating Soviet soldiers for "inhuman atrocities."[24] The *Einsatzgruppen's* own horrific deeds in this respect were, of course, in no way comparable with the acts of the despised enemy. It is important to remember that, however conventionalized the legal justifications were at the time, after the war, while on trial at Nuremberg, many of the *Einsatzgruppen* leaders advanced the same reasons as part of their defence. They repeated the claim that their actions were retaliation for the "criminal" activities of the Jews and others.[25] By the same reasoning some leaders maintained the killings were really no different than the allied bombing of German cities where thousands of German civilians had been killed.[26]

The killings went on throughout 1941 and 1942. Reports continued to be drawn up, sent to Berlin, compiled, typed, copies made and forwarded to designated recipients, extra copies filed away. The process did not stop. Both the shootings and the bureaucratic paperwork continued.

Incidentally, quite by accident, I discovered something else about this bureaucratic paperwork. My book on the *Einsatzgruppen* reports contains several appendices that give a complete listing of the reports, their numbers, the dates they were issued, and other information.[27] While examining the list of the Operational Situation Reports I noticed a small but revealing detail concerning the dates of these reports. I noted that from 23 June until 26 October 1941 the reports were issued every day, seven days a week. Starting three days later, on 29 October 1941, the reports then came out regularly three times a week, on Monday, Wednesday and Friday, and this pattern continued uninterrupted until Monday, 22 December 1941. The next report would normally have appeared two days later, on Wednesday. But this Wednesday was 24 December, that is, the day before Christmas. Like any factory or business enterprise, the bureaucracy in Berlin, which for six months with absolute regularity had compiled reports dealing with mass murder, closed up shop, and took a break of a week and a half for the Christmas holiday. The reports were resumed on 2 January 1942.

The observance of a holiday by these men in Berlin underlines the extent to which the massacre of human beings was brought down to the level of routine office work. The reports on the killings were like a commonplace inventory of shoes or umbrellas, and, like all commonplace inventories, this one too could be put aside so that the Berlin officials could enjoy the holiday with their families.

A further aspect of the self-deception was the fact that nowhere in the reports is there one word about Jewish suffering or that of other victims. On one level this was to be expected. In official Security Police reports there was no place for Jewish suffering. As with the use of euphemisms, the total absence of any reference to the appalling nature of the actions was essential in putting reality out of mind. In the reports then, the real nature of the actions, the brutal horror of the killings, were refined out of existence. One can only try to imagine the terrible agony of the victims. Any suffering that is mentioned is not that of the victims, but of the killers. Reports made reference to the difficult task, the "heavy mental burden" of the men who had to carry out the shootings.[28] In this vein, under cross-examination at his trial at Nuremberg, Otto Ohlendorf stated that "there is nothing worse for people spiritually" than to have to shoot defenceless people. The prosecuting attorney immediately countered this by saying that there is "nothing worse than being shot when you are defenceless."[29]

Salient in the reports was the effort made to constantly present the operations of the Security Police in the most favourable light. The *Kommandos* were doing their job smoothly and effectively. Anything that would detract from this impression was omitted, for example, any sign of weakness or reluctance on the part of the men in carrying out the shootings. Therefore the reports themselves only hint at this problem of the psychological stress on the killers. Beyond the reports, however, there is much evidence of various kinds indicating that this problem was a real one for some members of the *Kommandos*. We know that some men had nervous breakdowns during the operations. We know the consumption of alcohol was often a necessity for the men to participate, as were the *Kommando* leaders' frequent pep talks and instruction concerning the political rationale for the task to be undertaken, as well as comradely fireside encounters to help the men forget the unpleasant work of the day. Recently the American historian Christopher Browning examined in depth one battalion of the *Ordnungspolizei*, Reserve Police Battalion 101, which murdered thousands of Jews in Poland during 1942 and 1943. Browning concluded that at varying stages of the battalion's first killing assignment in the village of Józefów in Poland, some ten to twenty percent of the members of this unit refused to take part in the shootings or took evasive action of some kind.[30] While no statistics of comparable precision exist for the *Kommandos* of the *Einsatzgruppen*, it is certain that the problem existed for men in these groups as well. Although the difficulty was there, at no time did it ever prevent a shooting operation from being completed. There were always enough men willing to do the shooting. Often even men who were reluctant to begin with, once they took part in the shootings, became inured, and continued to participate without further misgivings. The problem of the mental stress was there, however, and although it ultimately did not change anything, it was an element in the total picture. In the case of killing women and children the problem at first was especially acute,[31] and it led to the development of the mobile gas van, which was originally introduced on Himmler's orders in order to kill women and children in what was considered to be a more "humane" form of execution—more humane for the killers and supposedly for the victims as well.

Not only is Jewish suffering absent in the reports, but there is also no detailed description of the preparations for and the actual circumstances surrounding the shootings, with one exception—and here we return to the report by Karl Jäger. Jäger's report does offer some indication of the preparations involved in carrying out the shootings. Jäger was proud of his *Kommando's* ability to kill thousands of Jews. In this excerpt from his report, one is struck by the self-serving boastfulness, as Jäger describes how the problems surrounding the killing operations could be overcome by, as he puts it, careful organization.

The implementation of such actions is in the first instance an organizational problem. The decision to free each district of Jews necessitated thorough preparation of each action as well as acquisition of information about local conditions. The Jews had to be collected in one or more towns and a ditch had to be dug

66

at the right site for the right number. The marching distance from collection points to the ditches averaged about three miles. The Jews were brought in groups of 500, separated by at least 1-2 miles, to the place of execution. The sort of difficulties and nerve-scraping work involved in all of this is shown by an arbitrarily chosen example:

In Roskiskis 3208 people had to be transported 3 miles before they could be liquidated. To manage this job in a 24 hour period, more than 60 of the 80 available Lithuanian partisans had to be detailed to the cordon. The Lithuanians who were left were frequently being relieved while doing the work together with my men.

Vehicles are seldom available. Escapes, which were attempted here and there were frustrated solely by my men at the risk of their lives. For example, 3 men of the *Kommando* at Mariampole shot 38 escaping Jews and communist functionaries on a path in the woods, so that no one got away. Distances to and from actions were never less than 90-120 miles. Only careful planning enabled the *Kommando* to carry out up to 5 actions a week and at the same time to continue the work in Kovno without interruption.[32]

On 6 February 1942, two months after Jäger's report was issued, Walter Stahlecker, the head of *Einsatzgruppe* A, asked three of his *Kommando* leaders, including Jäger, to send to him the total number of executions by category carried out by their respective units. Apparently Stahlecker received no answer from the other two leaders, but on 9 February 1942 Jäger sent a one-page hand-written reply. Jäger stated that as of 1 February 1942 his *Kommando* had killed 138,272 people. The breakdown by category was meticulously recorded by Jäger as follows: 136,421 Jews, 1064 communists, 56 partisans, 653 mental patients, 44 Poles, 28 Russian prisoners of war, 5 Gypsies, and 1 Armenian. Of the total number of persons killed 55,556 were women, and 34,464 were children.[33] This was the legacy of just one of the eighteen *Kommandos* that made up the four *Einsatzgruppen*.

Mentioned earlier was the effort of the *Einsatzgruppen* to constantly present themselves in the most favourable light. Throughout the reports this boasting quality surfaced time and time again. The point here was to leave the impression that the members of the Security Police were getting the important job of killing Jews and others done properly. One early report, for example, stated that the "liquidations were brought into smooth running order and are being carried out daily at an increasing rate". The report then asserted that "the carrying out of the necessary liquidations is guaranteed under any circumstances."[34] Another report boasted that in Janowitschi 1025 Jews were subjected to "special treatment" solely by a *Kommando* leader and twelve men.[35]

The boasting was not limited to discussions of the killing, however. The problems of terrible weather, poor roads, as well as the "heavy" burden of the killings, were also presented as difficulties that were solved by the hard-working Kommandos. Furthermore, throughout the reports one finds constant criticism of other German agencies in the east, mainly the civil administration and the German army, and this criticism, coupled with continuous implicit and explicit self-praise, was made to serve the interests of the *Einsatzgruppen* leaders.

It is clear from their reports alone that a good part of the motivation of these men to kill was their personal ambition and their concern for advancing their careers within the Security Police. To what degree personal feelings of anti-Semitism determined the actions of these men (of course, one could not hope to find a greater demonstration of anti-Semitic hatred than the *Einsatzgruppen* reports) is not easy to tabulate in any precise quantitative way.[36] No doubt such attitudes were present, but after the war most of these men naturally tried to distance themselves as much as possible from what they had done. On trial for their lives, they could not admit they had personally hated the Jews. If they were in fact asked about their personal views—something that was infrequently done by court interrogators—they usually denied they were anti-Semitic. They admitted that they were aware of the anti-Semitism of others, or they usually went as far as to suggest that the Jews within Germany had acquired too much economic power. Whatever their personal attitudes may have been, they certainly carried out their mission with astounding ruthlessness. For our purpose here it is important to acknowledge the significance of the self-serving nature of the reports. It is noteworthy that both the zealousness of the leaders in realizing their task, and the self-promotion that was ubiquitous throughout the reports apparently paid off. After serving their terms as either *Einsatzgruppe* or *Kommando* leaders, most of these men returned to Berlin to take up positions of leadership in the various departments of the RSHA.[37]

In summary, the *Einsatzgruppen* reports, these "messages of murder," as I have called them, offer evidence of great historical value. Beyond the numbing statistical record that they present, these reports illustrate how rationalizing, normalizing and distancing mechanisms are a necessary part of the implementation of mass murder. Moreover, the *Einsatzgruppen* reports, which were originally meant to report objectively on events in the occupied Soviet territories, soon became a means of furthering the self-aggrandizement of the *Einsatzgruppen* leaders. These distancing mechanisms and the motivational pull of racial ideology and careerism not only helped to make this murderous undertaking possible, but also enabled it to unfold smoothly.

Finally, a brief word about what happened to the *Einsatzgruppen* leaders. After the war at least seven of the leaders committed suicide before being brought to trial.[38] Four others died in prison or while their trial was underway.[39] Of the twenty-two defendants tried in the original *Einsatzgruppen* leaders' trial held at Nuremberg in 1947/48 (Case 9, United States of America versus Otto Ohlendorf et al.), twenty-one were found guilty of crimes against humanity and/or war crimes. Of these twenty-one men, fourteen were sentenced to death, two men were given sentences of life imprisonment, three men were given sentences of twenty years, and two men were given sentences of ten years. Of the fourteen leaders sentenced to death, only four were eventually executed. They were hanged in Landsberg Prison in June 1951.

As time passed, all the other death sentences were reduced to terms of imprisonment, and gradually all the terms of imprisonment were also reduced. The consequence of these reductions was that by 1958, barely thirteen years after the war, all surviving *Einsatzgruppen* leaders from the original trial were free men.[40] Such was the fate of the men who had wrought terrible destruction, a fate so different from that of their many victims.

Arab Nationalists and Nazi Germany, 1939-1945

Avraham Sela

The Attraction of German Nationalism[1]

THE HISTORICAL RECORD of Arab nationalists' relations with Nazi Germany during the years under discussion is, for the most part, one of mixed motives: a strong attraction to German nationalism and militarism combined with *realpolitik*. Arab political elites were captivated by German authoritarianism, romantic and militarist nationalism, and populism. The challenge posed by Nazi Germany to the existing international order in Europe, and directly to British and French hegemony, won a sense of admiration among Arab political elites and a desire to establish contacts with Berlin through its official representatives in the Arab states. These were mainly Fritz Groba in Baghdad and Jidda, and Franz von Pappen in Ankara.

Obsessed with pan-Arab nationalism and the struggle for liberation from British and French rule in the inter-War period, Arab political leaders and pan-Arab ideologists became fascinated with the example of German nationalism and, with the exception of anti-Semitism, adopted its basic premises and historical arguments. From the mid-1930s on, Nazi nationalist ideology and its para-military youth movement served as a role model for the rising middle class urban elite in the Arab countries, who combined a strong claim for social and political change with militarist nationalism and xenophobia. Hence the rise of movements such as the Syrian National Party (*al-Hizb al-Qawmi al-Suri*) in Syria and Lebanon, the Young Egypt Society (*Misr al-Fatah*), the Phalange Party (*Hizb al Kata'ib*) in Lebanon, and the Youth Movement (*al-Futuwwa*) in Palestine. From Egypt to Iraq and Lebanon, Scout movements attempted to imitate the

Italian and German examples of para-military youth movements.[2]

The establishment of the Phalange by Pierre Jumayyil, a young Lebanese-Maronite, a pharmacist by profession, can attest to this influence. Jumayyil visited Berlin in 1936 as the captain of his country's football team and was deeply impressed by the Nazi youth movement, the Hitler *Jugend*. Upon his return, he established the Phalange as a sport youth movement combining symbols and values of Fascism and totalitarian nationalism derived from German, Italian and Spanish examples. The main themes adopted by the Phalange were God, homeland, and family. The movement, whose main source of support was the Maronite middle and lower-middle classes in the major cities, was organized on an authoritarian basis with a strong Lebanese nationalist character.

German nationalism not only appealed to Arab political culture but also intensified the ongoing processes of political and social radicalization. From an Arab viewpoint, Germany was an ideal ally since she had not been identified with imperialism in the Arab region. Moreover, Germany's geographic distance and absence of claims for influence in the Mediterranean rendered it preferable to Italy, whose conquest of Libya and claims for hegemony in the Middle East tarnished her image—in spite of the appeal of Fascism—and generated a gap of suspicion and animosity among Arab nationalists.

As a rule, support for Germany was prevalent and discernible at the public level through the various Arab nationalist movements, while official circles tended to be more cautious. With very few exceptions, such as Amir Abdallah of Transjordan, Arab political elites manifested, from the mid-1930s to the end of 1942, a tendency to use Germany as a source of political and military support. In Iraq, and to a lesser extent in Egypt, high-ranking military officers endeavoured to establish close military and political collaboration with Nazi Germany, particularly during the critical period for Britain's stature in the Middle East in the years 1941-1942. In Syria, the National Bloc headed by Shukri al-Quwatly was the main proponent of Nazi Germany and agitator against the Syrian government. This agitation reached its peak in April 1941 amidst growing cooperation between Vichy France and the Germans.

Some leading Arab figures in power as well as in the opposition, including some of those most identified with Britain, such as Iraq's Nuri al-Sa'id, and Saudi Arabia's King Ibn Sa'ud, had some flirtation with Nazi Germany. Essentially, however, their position toward the Axis, like the majority of Arab leaders, can be best defined as sympathetic neutrality. Indeed, with the exception of the Mufti of Jerusalem, al-Haj Amin al-Husaini (see below), Arab nationalists' relations with Nazi Germany were marked by careful political calculations of self-interest and self-preservation.[3]

The Quest for Arms

Particularly salient were Arab efforts to purchase weapons from Germany as an expression of national sovereignty and independence. Although nominally independent, Iraq and Egypt were entirely dependent on Britain for arms supply in accordance with their treaties which had prohibited purchasing military materiel from other countries. Saudi Arabia, too, was dependent on Britain.

Already during the Arab revolt in Palestine (1936-1939), attempts were made by Arab Palestinian and Arab nationalist supporters to obtain German arms supplies for the Arab rebels. Yet these efforts, conducted in extreme secrecy, resulted in very small quantities of weapons being transferred to the rebels in Palestine through third parties (Iraq, Saudi Arabia, or the Templar colonies in Palestine). Financial support for the rebellion was also very limited and fell far behind the rumours and intelligence reports of the period. Realizing that supplying arms to Arab countries linked to Britain might aggravate its relations with Britain, Germany turned down Iraqi and Saudi Arabian requests for arms supplies until 1938.

It was only after Munich, however, when the question of Anglo-German relations lost its significance for Berlin, that Germany agreed to enter into substantial negotiations with Arab nationalists over arms supplies and other spheres of collaboration. In May 1939, leading figures of the Third Reich, including Adolf Hitler himself, received King Ibn Sa'ud's emissary, Khalid al-Karkani, whose visit was principally aimed at purchasing arms. A few weeks after the beginning of hostilities in Europe, a German-Saudi arms deal was signed, but was never implemented.

British Counter-Pressures

It should be noted that the appeals to Germany made by Arab leaders such as Ibn Sa'ud or Nuri al-Sa'id did not reflect a tendency to break all ties with Britain and replace them with German alliances. Their approach was marked by caution, insistence on preserving maximum freedom of action, and a desire to maintain cooperation with Great Britain. These leaders, however, represented only one type of Arab attitude toward Germany. Nuri al-Sa'id and the royal Hashemite dynasty in Iraq were by that time strongly challenged by militant army officers who would form the hard core of the anti-British nationalist revolt of April 1941 in which the Mufti of Jerusalem, al-Haj Amin al-Husaini, played a leading role.

The growing anti-British sentiment among high-ranking military officers in Iraq and Egypt can be explained against the background of growing British pressures on these nominally-independent govern-ments—once the war broke out—to declare war against Germany according to the treaties between these states and Britain. These treaties also committed the Arab signatories to contribute forces to the war effort. Yet, with the growing public sympathy to the Axis in these countries, even the governments most strongly identified with Britain would not dare to declare war against the Axis Powers, let alone contribute forces to the Allies' war effort. The governments of Egypt and Iraq contented themselves with cutting off diplomatic relations without actually declaring war against Germany.

In Iraq, the issue of declaring war against the Axis Powers aroused a tense political debate within the military echelon and the general public, both of which were united against Britain; this tension was one of the causes for the ensuing nationalist Iraqi revolt against Britain and the Hashemite regime. Egypt refused to declare war against Italy, while Iraq declined to cut off relations with the Mussolini regime.

Nuri al-Sa'id and the Palestine Problem

In August 1940, Prime Minister Nuri al-Sa'id embarked on an attempt to barter an Iraqi declaration of war against Germany and a contribution of a division-size force to the Allies' war effort in exchange for a more explicitly pro-Arab British policy in Palestine. Nuri suggested the establishment of a national government in Palestine as a step toward independence under the domination of its Arab majority. Nuri proposed far-reaching plans for the resolution of the Palestine problem within an Iraqi-led Fertile Crescent federation, including Transjordan and Syria, after the liberation of the latter from Vichy rule. The Iraqi statesman let it be understood that his proposals had been accepted by the Arab-Palestinian leadership, including the Mufti. Hence, he argued, if the British Government would go along with his proposals, the Arab Higher Committee headed by the Mufti would endorse the White Paper of May 1939, which had been previously turned down by the Palestinian leadership.[4]

The alleged Palestinian approval of Nuri's proposals was to be used a few years later as evidence that the Arab Higher Committee had effectively accepted the White Paper and that it was Britain's obstinacy that prevented an agreement. Nuri al-Sa'id's suggestions had indeed been discussed with the Mufti and some of his aides then in Baghdad. These discussions included Colonel S.F. Newcombe, a British official and representative of the Arab propaganda bureau in London with whom this affair had become identified in the historical literature. Palestinian historiography has made much of the British rejection of the Newcombe/Nuri suggestions in justifying the Mufti's position, arguing that it was only after he became desperate about Britain's policy on Palestine that he was left with no other choice but to turn to Nazi Germany for support.[5]

The Iraqi proposals to Britain represented an effort to mitigate the Mufti's fierce and influential anti-British propaganda which undermined the legitimacy of the Hashemite regime. The Mufti had arrived in Iraq in October 1939 as a political fugitive and was received by the Iraqi political elite as a national hero. Within less than two years, he managed to become a major factor in Iraqi domestic politics due to his close connection with a group of high-ranking Iraqi military officers—the Golden Square—who represented extreme nationalist attitudes and constituted the hard core of opposition power within the Iraqi army.[6]

Anti-British Revolt and Agitation 1941-1942

Two historical events stand out in the context of the Arab national quest for independence from British influence through collaboration with Nazi Germany. In both cases Britain was obliged to resort to the use of force in order to defend its imperial interests in the area. Both events left an unmistakable imprint on Arab nationalist attitudes to Britain for years to come, staining pro-British Arab politicians as collaborators guilty of betraying the Arab national cause.

The first and most serious challenge to British interests in the Middle East was the Iraqi nationalist revolt and seizure of power in April 1941. Although militarily repressed within less than two months, the short-lived revolt led, among other things, to the pogrom (*Farhud*) against the Jews of Baghdad in May 1941, the most significant anti-Jewish manifestation by Muslims in modern Middle Eastern history. The Iraqi revolt reflected the growing disagreement and tension between Britain and its Iraqi allies, on the one hand, and nationalist army officers and political parties, on the other. The British pressure to dismiss Rashid 'Ali al-Kailani for a more moderate Iraqi Prime Minister eventually exacerbated resentment and led to the colonels' revolt in April 1941.[7]

The second event had to do with the growing militant support for Nazi Germany among Egypt's political and military elite during the last months of 1941. Already in June 1940, Egyptian army officers headed by 'Aziz 'Ali al-Misri, the Chief of Staff, had been involved in plotting a revolt against Britain with Germany's assistance. The growing anti-British sentiment was encouraged by the presence of Rommel's Afrika Corps in the Western Desert and by an impression of British weakness. This culminated in al-Misri's attempt to cross the front lines by airplane, probably to establish direct contact with Rommel, an attempt that was foiled by the British. In February 1942, when Britain's pressures on King Faruq to replace 'Ali Mahir's government with one under the premiership of the pro-British Wafd leader Nahhas Pasha remained unheeded, the king was forced to accede to British demands under threat of British tanks surrounding his 'Abdin Palace.

German Policy
Germany's Middle East policy was primarily determined by European-based strategic considerations. During its early years in power, the Nazi

regime ignored Arab nationalist appeals for cooperation, including those of the Mufti. Germany's Arab policy until 1937-1938 had been motivated by her hope to reach an understanding with Britain; thus, any policy which would trigger tension between the two powers was to be avoided. Initially, Nazi Germany had recognized the Middle East as an Anglo-French sphere of influence.

Germany left the arena for Italy to bear the brunt of entanglement with Britain through arms supplies and financial support to Arab political movements, as well as military interference in Ethiopia. Only in 1938, after concluding that cooperation with Britain was unrealistic, did Berlin seek to consolidate its foreign policy in the Middle East on the basis of cooperation with Italy, Britain's main rival in the Eastern Mediterranean. It was not until 1939, however, that the Germans started broadcasting propaganda to the Arab world from Berlin; until then, Germany was content with Italian broadcasts emanating from Radio Bari.

The absence of consideration of Arab interests in German Middle East policymaking was saliently expressed by the regime's policies on German Jewish emigration to Palestine. Until 1939, Germany continued to allow its Jewish citizens to transfer part of their property abroad (in the form of German commodities) in accordance with transfer (ha'avarah) agreements with Jewish organizations in Germany. In fact, the Nazi regime was so eager to rid itself of Jews that it allowed the establishment of preparatory camps for Jewish emigrants to Palestine.

This policy, which was in effect supportive of Zionist goals, could not be ignored by Arab nationalists. Yet it seemed to have little or no impact on the Mufti, whose interest in establishing close cooperation with Germany remained unaffected. This interest continued to be guided by Hitler's deep hostility to Jews and to Britain.

Germany's tendency to refrain from involvement in the Middle East was reinforced by the growing collaboration between Hitler and Mussolini after 1937. The two leaders agreed that Italy was to be the paramount power in the Middle East, while Germany's interests were to be focused in central Europe. Each party would act to promote the other's goals.

Germany also sought to avoid the unnecessary resentment of France, which ruled Syria and Lebanon as well as the North African Arab countries. In addition, Germany was cautious not to arouse Turkish resentment by promoting the Mufti's proposals, hoping that this country would eventually join the Axis Powers.

The Role of the Mufti

The Mufti's record of collaboration with Nazi Germany stands out not only when compared to the *realpolitik* approach manifested by other Arab leaders. It is astounding that, while most Arab nationalists turned their backs on Germany once the conduct of the war began shifting in the Allies' favour, the Mufti's political collaboration with the Nazis intensified even as the war approached its end and there remained little doubt that Germany had in effect lost the war.

Shortly after Hitler's assumption of power the Mufti, al-Haj Amin al-Husaini, paid a visit to the German Consulate-General in Jerusalem and sent his congratulations to the new Chancellor of Germany. Apart from his immediate efforts to halt the immigration of German Jews to Palestine, the Mufti defined his goal as an all-out war against the Jewish community in Palestine (the *Yishuv*) and world Jewry.[8] In 1937, after all his efforts to establish a dialogue with the German government through its representatives in Jerusalem and Baghdad had remained unheeded, the Mufti sent an emissary to Berlin with a specific proposal which he had tried to advance ever since 1933, namely, a political proclamation by Germany recognizing the independence of all Arab states, including Palestine, and expressing support for their right to unite and resolve by themselves the question of Jews living in the Arab countries. The German authorities, however, refused to meet the Mufti's messenger, for the above-mentioned reasons.

In mid-1940, the Mufti, then in Iraq as a political exile, reopened communications with the German government, presenting himself as the head of a Pan-Arab movement (*Hizb al-Umma*), he suggested that Palestine, which had been "fighting the democracies and international Jewry," was "ready at any time to assume an active role and redouble her efforts . . ." The Mufti expressed his hope that Germany's final victory would result in the Arab peoples' independence and unity, linked to

Germany by a "treaty of friendship and collaboration."[9] In later contacts at the end of the year, the Mufti and the Iraqi nationalist government demanded immediate financial and military support for the ensuing anti-British revolt of which the Mufti had been the architect and spiritual leader.

Yet, even at this stage, despite advanced preparations for its invasion of Russia (Operation Barbarossa) and the importance the German General Staff gave to collaboration with the Arabs, Germany adhered to its earlier approach, which was to favour links with Arab states rather than with an obscure pan-Arab or pan-Islamic movement. Even when the German authorities were willing to receive the Mufti's emissaries for talks, they refused his request for a political understanding. Nonetheless, in March 1941 the German Foreign Ministry transmitted to the Mufti's emissary, Uthman Kamal Haddad, a written declaration in Hitler's name, although over the signature of the Deputy Foreign Minister. Not only was the declaration classified and not to be released for publication, but its substance was far from satisfying to the Mufti. The German document recognized the independence of those Arab states that had already achieved it, and the right to independence of those Arab countries still struggling to achieve it.

The Iraqi nationalist revolt erupted without the Germans' knowledge and against their opinion in terms of its proper timing—as they had been entangled in conquering Greece and Crete. Although notified in advance by the Mufti about the approaching nationalist revolt in Iraq, Germany did not have sufficient time to complete the needed preparations for extending military assistance to the rebels through Syria, still under Vichy rule. During the short-lived Iraqi revolt, German military support for the rebelling Iraqi forces was meager because Syria was immediately taken over by British forces. Although the Mufti was informed about the Germans' need for further preparations, he played a major role in encouraging the Iraqi political and military leadership to execute the revolt sooner rather than later. The Mufti joined with the Iraqi army's strongmen (the Golden Square) in opposing Prime Minister Rashid 'Ali al-Kailani's views on the timing and tactics of the revolt. When the revolt began, Kailani was willing to accept a proposal for a cease-fire with the British forces. But the Mufti and the Golden Square turned down the proposal, eventually foiling any possibility of a compromise with the British.[10]

In October 1941, two weeks after his arrival in Italy, the Mufti was met by Mussolini who reportedly expressed his hostility to the Jews and Zionism. Henceforth, the Mufti continued in his efforts to obtain a public German-Italian statement acknowledging the right of the Arab countries to independence and unity. This he failed to achieve. Hitler, despite his meeting with the Mufti on 28 November 1941, turned down the Arab leader's request for a written declaration, secret or public. In April 1942, the Mufti and the exiled Iraqi Prime Minister, Rashid 'Ali al-Kailani, received identical official letters from the German and Italian governments in which the latter endorsed the Arab countries' independence and unity. Yet these letters also were to remain secret.[11]

Until 1942, the Middle East had not been considered by Berlin as strategically essential. Italy, on the other hand, was interested in concentrating the Axis war effort in the Mediterranean basin, thereby enhancing its own aims in that region. Following Britain's repression of the Iraqi nationalist revolt of April 1941, Mussolini welcomed the Mufti in Rome in June of that year and endeavoured to use Haj Amin's position for convincing Germany to look upon the Middle East as the primary battleground for defeating Britain.

In Germany, the Mufti met with Hitler and was treated as an official guest, along with other Arab nationalist exiles of the Iraqi revolt such as al-Kailani and Fawzi al-Qawuqji. (The latter would become the commander of the Syrian-based Army of Deliverance in the Palestine war of 1948.) The Mufti's collaboration with Nazi Germany reached its zenith in 1943-1944. In spite of the growing evidence of Germany's ensuing defeat, the Mufti developed close relations with the SS apparatus and intensified his efforts on behalf of the Nazi regime. According to the written testimony of Dieter Wisliceny, one of Adolf Eichmann's senior aides in charge of implementation of the Final Solution, the Mufti paid a visit to Eichmann sometime in late 1941 or the beginning of 1942. This meeting was followed by a visit of some of the Mufti's aides to the concentration camp of Sachsenhausen, as well as their participation in

SS courses. As far as can be determined from documentary evidence, it was the only visit of non-Germans and non-SS individuals to a concentration camp. This led to growing collaboration between the Mufti and Himmler in which the former undertook a good-will mission aimed at resolving problems that the Germans encountered with Muslim populations under their control.[12] The Mufti also undertook efforts to draft Muslims from Yugoslavia and the Caucasus into special Muslim army units within the Wehrmacht, as well as to create a Waffen-SS volunteer division recruited from among the Muslims of Bosnia and Herzogovina. The latter played some part in the destruction of Yugoslav Jews. Haj Amin was also involved in an effort to establish an independent Arab force under German auspices which would serve as the nucleus of an independent and unified Arab state in the aftermath of the war.[13]

In May 1943 the Mufti moved his office to the SS headquarters in Berlin. This would provide him with stronger influence and a close contact with the Muslim populations under the Third Reich through the SS machinery. At the end of the year he began developing an ideology endorsing a Muslim-German alliance which was to culminate in a joint conference to endorse this ideology and redefine anti-Semitism so as to exclude the Arab peoples from that designation.[14]

The Mufti's collaboration with the SS also took the form of a constant effort to bring about German attacks against the *Yishuv* as well as the Zionist leadership. Yet his main efforts, from 1943 till the end of the war, were devoted to preventing Jewish emigration from Hungary, Rumania, Italy and Bulgaria, by appealing to their governments and urging them to send these Jews to Poland, that is, to the death camps, instead. This effort reflected the Mufti's ideological view that the Arab-Jewish conflict was all-encompassing, with Europe's Jewry constituting the main reservoir of potential emigrants to Palestine. Furthermore, Zionist activity in the United States and Britain, as well as political developments in Palestine, provided ample evidence that the Arab-Jewish struggle for mastery in Palestine would be renewed with the end of the war.[15]

Postwar

Arab nationalist sympathy for Nazi Germany was undoubtedly motivated by strong nationalist sentiment mingled with resentment against Britain and its stooges, Arab and Zionist alike. Indeed, as the *farhud* (pogrom) in Baghdad demonstrated, this nationalist sentiment could be easily turned against the Jews. In the loaded atmosphere of the late 1930s and early 1940s, Arab nationalism was dominated by the desire for Britain's defeat. In this atmosphere, the distinction between Jews and Zionists vanished, largely as a result of the growing role of the Palestine issue in Arab politics.

At the close of World War II, the Mufti's role in the Iraqi anti-British revolt, and mainly his overt record of collaboration with Nazi Germany, rendered him anathema to the Allied governments. Arab rulers, although officially welcoming the Mufti because of his strong popularity among the Arab masses, were uncomfortable with the Mufti's record which hindered their efforts to reestablish cooperation with the Allies and to blur any record of their own contacts with Nazi Germany. No doubt, Western public and official support for the Zionist aim of establishing a Jewish state in Palestine was significantly influenced by the Holocaust. Equally significant was the Mufti's role during World War II in determining the Allied Powers' unfavourable position toward the Palestinian-Arab cause between 1945 and 1948, the crucial years of the Palestine Question.

In addition, the Mufti's central role in the anti-Hashemite revolt of 1941 was to turn him into *persona non grata* for the Iraqi government in the postwar years. This underlay Baghdad's hostile attitude toward the Mufti's efforts to re-establish himself as the leading authority of the Palestinian Arabs after his return to the Middle East in June 1946, and to supervise preparations for the ensuing war following the British decision to relinquish the Mandate for Palestine. These bitter residues among Iraqi leaders would, at this most vulnerable moment for the Palestinian Arabs, become a fateful factor in undermining the Mufti's desperate efforts to lead the Palestinians to independence, paving instead the road to the Palestine disaster (*al-Nakba*).

The Holocaust and the Arab-Israeli Conflict

Neil Caplan

THE PAIRING TOGETHER of two such complex and emotion-laden topics as the Holocaust and the Arab-Israeli conflict would appear, to some, as an invitation to needless controversy. Indeed, such was the initial reaction of several prominent Montrealers in 1994 when they learned that the organizers intended to include this subject among the First Annual CEGEP Holocaust Symposium's panels.

Some objections reflected the perennial concern about trivializing the Holocaust by offering inappropriate parallels, making tendentious comparisons, or deducing fallacious lessons from that unique event in human history. Some counselled avoidance of this topic because both Arabs and Jews have used and misused the Holocaust in the ongoing propaganda battles that have accompanied the Arab-Israeli conflict since 1948.

Although these observations are indeed correct, they did not result in the cancellation of this scheduled topic. The intertwining of the Holocaust and the Arab-Israeli conflict is an historical fact, and is surely worthy of serious scholarly analysis.

Pre-1948 Origins

Arguments and counter-arguments linking the Holocaust and the Arab-Israeli conflict were already well developed during World War II. Between 1917 and 1948 the British ruled the area known as Palestine under a League of Nations Mandate. Under the impact of Zionist immigration, the territory's Arab majority began to decrease with the corresponding increase of the country's Jewish minority, which grew from under 10 percent of the population in 1917 to around 33 percent in 1947.

One of the main aspects of the struggle between the two communities for prominence, and eventually for independence, was the question of immigration. Jewish immigrants from Europe (and elsewhere) came in waves, and one of the most dramatic upsurges occurred in the years immediately following the rise to power of Adolf Hitler, surpassing 61,000 in 1935.

Year	Jewish Immigration to Palestine	Palestine Jews	Total Palestine Population	Jewish Percentage of Total
1930	4,944	164,796	921,699	17.9
1931	4,075	174,606	966,761	18.1
1932	9,533	192,137	1,007,274	19.1
1933	33,327	234,967	1,074,388	21.9
1934	42,359	282,975	1,144,001	24.7
1935	61,854	355,157	1,241,559	28.6
1936	29,727	384,078	1,300,139	29.5

SOURCE: *A Survey of Palestine*, prepared in December 1945 and January 1946 for the Information of the Anglo-American Commission of Inquiry, vol. I (London: HMSO, 1946), 141, 185.

This sudden and massive increase in the Jewish population (during the same period, Jewish immigration to the United States varied between a meager 2300 and 6200 per annum) was one of the contributing factors to the outbreak of the 1936-1939 Arab Revolt in Palestine. One reaction of Arab nationalist circles to the perceived threat of the Jews taking over Palestine was the alliance which al-Haj Amin al-Husaini, Mufti of Jerusalem and the recognized leader of the Palestinian-Arab national movement, sought to make with the Third Reich.[1]

In the late 1930s and early 1940s, Zionist leaders and spokesmen lobbied intensely among Western politicians and diplomats for the need for a sovereign Jewish state to serve as a refuge for those seeking to flee the horrors of Nazi Europe. In May 1942, an emergency Zionist conference held at the Biltmore Hotel in New York passed resolutions calling for immediate mass immigration to rescue European Jews and the postwar creation of a Jewish "commonwealth" in an undivided

Palestine.[2] As Rabbi Abba Hillel Silver, the rising star among American Zionist leaders, argued:

> We cannot truly rescue the Jews of Europe unless we have free immigration to Palestine. We cannot have free immigration into Palestine unless our political rights are recognized there. Our political rights cannot be recognized unless our historic connection to the country is acknowledged and our right to rebuild our national home is affirmed. The whole chain breaks if one of our links is missing.[3]

Arab reaction to such appeals was to seek to detach the struggle for Palestine from the European Jewish question as much as possible.[4] At a conference in Alexandria, Egypt, in the fall of 1944, the foundations of the League of Arab States were laid down and resolutions were passed repeating earlier Arab calls for "the cessation of Jewish immigration, the preservation of Arab lands, and the achievement of independence for Palestine." While declaring their regret over "the woes which [had] been inflicted upon the Jews of Europe by European dictatorial states," Arab delegates to the conference added that

> the question of these Jews should not be confused with Zionism, for there can be no greater injustice and aggression than solving the problem of the Jews of Europe by another injustice, i.e., by inflicting injustice on the Arabs of Palestine. . . . [5]

In their well-known meeting aboard a warship in the Red Sea in early 1945, American President Franklin D. Roosevelt tried in vain to convince King Ibn Saud of Saudi Arabia to support the opening of the doors of Palestine to provide a refuge for Jewish survivors of Nazi Europe. The Arab monarch insisted stiffly that the European Jewish tragedy would have to be solved by the nations of Christian Europe.[6]

The Refugee Question

During the 1950s and 1960s, many Jews around the world looked back on an almost supernatural link between *tekumah*, the Zionist Redemption (rebirth of Israel in May 1948), and *shoah*, the Holocaust tragedy of 1933-1945. For some, it was expressed in the dichotomy between defenceless, passive diaspora sheep who had been herded to their slaughter and new, proud, combative *sabras* (native-born Israelis), around whom a militant mystique was being built.[7] Others looked upon the new independence of Israel as a welcome intervention—whether divine or by the international community—somehow compensating the Jewish people for the recent devastation and historic injustices of which they had been victims. As Prime Minister Shimon Peres commented in his *Yom ha-Shoah* (Holocaust Remembrance Day) address in April 1996, "[t]he establishment of the State of Israel is the Jewish people's victory over Nazi Germany."[8] The causality of the relationship between the Holocaust and the birth of Israel continues to be the subject of much rhetoric, polemics and serious scholarship.[9]

The primary connection between the Holocaust and the emerging Arab-Israeli conflict after 1948 took shape in the interlocking tragedies of Jewish and Palestinian Arab refugees. Between 1947 and 1949, during and after the fighting in Israel's War of Independence, two processes were at work, producing complications that would last for generations to come: (a) during that fighting, almost 700,000 Palestinian Arabs fled or were expelled, leaving behind homes and property which the new state of Israel, seeking to alleviate an acute housing shortage, turned over to many of the hundreds of thousands of Jews pouring into Israel at the same time; (b) the huge influx of Jewish refugees ingathered in the first years of Israeli independence burdened as well as bolstered the new state, since most of the refugees, including many from the Arab lands, had been forced to leave their own homes and wealth behind.[10]

While many Israelis at the time hoped that this phenomenon would be treated as an "exchange of populations" and thus resolve the conflict quickly, the "Arab refugee problem" resisted political solutions and has persisted until today. This situation provided evidence to the Arab argument that innocent Palestinian Arabs were being made to pay for the Holocaust, to pay for the sins of Europe.

As late as 1967, the eminent historian and "non-Jewish Jew," Isaac Deutscher, captured well this Arab interpretation in an allegory:

A man once jumped from the top floor of a burning house in which many members of his family had already perished. He managed to save his life; but as he was falling he hit a person standing down below and broke that person's legs and arms. The jumping man had no choice; yet to the man with the broken limbs he was the cause of his misfortune. If both behaved rationally, they would not become enemies. The man who escaped from the blazing house, having recovered, would have tried to help and console the other sufferer; and the latter might have realized that he was the victim of circumstances over which neither of them had control.

But look what happens when these people behave irrationally. The injured man blames the other for his misery and swears to make him pay for it. The other, afraid of the crippled man's revenge, insults him, kicks him, and beats him up whenever they meet. The kicked man again swears revenge and is again punched and punished. The bitter enmity, so fortuitous at first, hardens and comes to overshadow the whole existence of both men and to poison their minds.[11]

The Israeli responses—that a *de facto* transfer of populations had occurred during 1948-1950; that Jewish immigration mostly benefitted, rather than crippled the local Arab population; that the Arab sufferer did more deadly things than merely swear revenge—did little to win over Arab opinion or quell Arab resentment on the issue.

The promulgation of Israel's Law of Return in 1950[12]—allowing automatic Israeli citizenship to any Jew applying for it—was also a belated answer to a hostile or indifferent world which had not offered sufficient refuge or sanctuary to Jews fleeing for their lives. This Law, too, became entwined in the package of unresolved grievances which increased Arab bitterness. Since Israel had clearly rejected any massive return of Palestinian-Arab refugees as envisaged by most interpretations of United Nations General Assembly Resolution 194 of 11 December 1948,[13] Arabs and their supporters accused the new Israeli government of acting in a racist, discriminatory manner in defiance of the international community.

Uncomfortable Undercurrents in Israel

While the rebirth and survival of the new Jewish state in the late 1940s and early 1950s was celebrated in Zionist and Jewish circles, an uncomfortable undercurrent was present in the day-to-day encounters between Holocaust survivors and the "new Israelis." This was illustrated by Israeli journalist Tom Segev:

> Holocaust survivors imposed on earlier immigrants a past that many had not yet succeeded in putting aside, and their disdain of the survivors often reflected a desire to distance themselves, to deny what they themselves were. The survivors forced the Israelis to realize that the vision of the "new man" was not to be. Most came as refugees, not as visionary Zionists. . . . Each new arrival was a reminder that the Zionist movement had been defeated in the Holocaust. . . . Not only was the *yishuv* not able to come to the rescue, but it now found itself in a position where its existence and future depended on the willingness of the Holocaust survivors to settle in the country and fortify its army against the Arab threat.[14]

According to Segev, there were four basic assumptions that united Holocaust survivors and Israelis during the 1948-49 war and the difficult early years of the state:

1. The Holocaust had proven once again that the only solution to the Jewish problem was an independent state in Israel.
2. The rest of the world—literally every nation—was hostile and had done nothing to save the Jews during the Holocaust.
3. The phrase "Holocaust and Heroism" contained two words of equal moment, "two flames burning in one heart," producing the ideological basis for the memorial culture that developed over the years.
4. The less everybody talked about the Holocaust the better.[15]

This collective Israeli silence on the Holocaust was broken only by the Kastner affair of the mid-1950s,[16] and, more decisively, the Eichmann trial of 1961.[17] During the 1960s Israelis belatedly started to come to grips with the Holocaust, with major emphasis on the question of resistance versus passivity in the face of the Nazi onslaught. Kibbutz Yad Mordechai, named after Mordechai Anielewicz, martyred resistance fighter in the Warsaw ghetto, became legendary for its own valiant (but ultimately futile) resistance against the advancing Egyptian army in May 1948. After being recaptured from the Egyptians and rebuilt in 1949, Yad Mordechai became well-known for both its educational displays commemorating the 1948-1949 battles and its stark, ultra-modern museum which "recounts Israeli history within the wider context of the Jewish tragedy in modern times."[18]

Israel's Role in International Affairs

Going beyond sentiment in the consciousness of the Israeli-Jewish public, political leaders in Israel have taken upon themselves an active and interventionist international role on behalf of the Jewish victims of the Holocaust. One of the tangible and symbolic signs of Israel's view of its role with regard to the Holocaust was the requirement (absolutely compulsory until 1994) that every foreign dignitary on an official visit to the country would begin with a stop at the country's Holocaust memorial, Yad Vashem. The intended message was: "After you see this you will understand what makes us tick and why we must be ever vigilant about precious Jewish lives in an uncaring world environment." In the words of a leading scholar, the dominant "attitudinal prism" of Israel's foreign-policy makers was a decidedly *Jewish* one, in which they had "a searing consciousness of the Holocaust" and perceived the state of Israel "as the logical, necessary and rightful successor to the collective interests and rights of the few who survived" and as "the voice, the representative, and the defender of Jews in distress everywhere."[19]

Examples of Israeli leaders taking up *Jewish* concerns as *Israeli* responsibilities in Holocaust-related matters include the negotiation of reparations payments from West Germany in the 1950s, and the capture and trial of Adolf Eichmann in 1960-1961. The historic importance of the latter, for David Ben-Gurion, lay not in the punishment that would be meted out to the senior Nazi official, "but the fact that the trial [was] taking place, and [was] taking place in Jerusalem."[20] The Prime Minister wanted the trial to be used to validate the very *raison d'être* of Israel as the world's only Zionist-Jewish state by (a) reminding the international community of its shameful responsibility for the Holocaust, and (b) educating the young generation of Israelis who were at risk of ignoring important lessons of Jewish vulnerability in the absence of a strong Jewish state.

1967: The Holocaust that Didn't Happen

Students of Middle Eastern history know that the June 1967 Arab-Israeli war, nicknamed the Six-Day War to underline its brevity, represented a stunning Israeli military victory which resulted in the expansion of Israel's borders southward through Sinai to the Suez Canal, eastward to the Jordan River, and northeastward onto Syria's Golan Heights. What is less well-known is the fact that, among Israelis and Jews at the time, the June 1967 war—when considered in the context of the anxious anticipation during the preceding month of May 1967—is sometimes referred to as "the Holocaust that didn't happen."[21] Daily news reports during May showed Israel blockaded and threatened by Egyptian and Syrian troop buildups. Israelis and Jews around the world grew nervous at the escalation of sabre-rattling rhetoric about Arab armies overrunning Israel emanating from Cairo and Damascus. When, on 5 June 1967, Israel launched a preemptive strike against the Egyptian Air Force, some pointed to this move as evidence that the Israelis, unlike their diaspora Jewish cousins, aunts and uncles who became victims of the Holocaust, would not remain passive in the face of any threat to their existence.

A decade later, Israeli Prime Minister Yitzhak Rabin provided a similar positive lesson of the Holocaust tragedy by his decision to launch a commando raid on Entebbe Airport in Uganda. The purpose was to rescue hostages being held by German terrorists working with the Popular Front for the Liberation of Palestine. Particularly disturbing—with its echoes of Nazi selections during World War II[22]—as the reported separation of Jews and Israelis from the other passengers aboard the hijacked French Airbus. The daring and heroism displayed in the Entebbe raid were regarded by many Israelis and non-Israelis alike as proof of a newfound Jewish security and pride. The message, loud and clear, was: thanks to a vigilant and militant Israel, Jews would no longer be defenceless prey as they had been in the Holocaust.[23]

During this period, the well-known Israeli journalist Amos Elon had much to say about the importance of the Holocaust in forming the Israeli psyche. "The holocaust remains a basic trauma of Israeli society," he wrote in his best-selling book, *The Israelis: Founders and Sons*.

> It is impossible to exaggerate its effect on the process of nation-building. . . . The Nazi holocaust caused the destruction of that very same Eastern European world against which the early pioneers had staged their original rebellion, but to which, nevertheless, Israel became both outpost and heir.[24]

When it came to Israel's unresolved conflict with the Arabs, Elon noted that there was a "latent hysteria in Israeli life that stems directly from" the Holocaust, whose "lingering memory" made "Arab threats of annihilation sound plausible." There was, he wrote, "an obsessive quality in such preoccupation; inevitably some Israelis, at certain times and places, have found it unduly morbid, burdensome, and even contrived."[25]

Israeli Connections: The Begin Years
The decade following the replacement of the long-entrenched Labour party by a right-wing Likud government under Menachem Begin in June 1977 saw an increasing use of Holocaust rhetoric in Israeli political discourse, both at home and abroad. The "obsessive quality" of the Holocaust "preoccupation" described by the liberal-minded Elon became one of the hallmarks of the Begin approach. During the signing ceremonies for the Israel-Egypt Peace Treaty on the White House Lawn in March 1979, the Israeli Prime Minister felt obliged to set the joyous occasion of Egyptian-Israeli peace into a wider and more sombre context. It was, he declared, not exactly the happiest, but the *third* happiest day of his life (after Israel's independence on 14 May 1948 and the reunification of Jerusalem in June 1967). On this occasion, he felt obliged to "bring back to memory" the *Shir ha-Ma'alot* (Song of Degrees) which he had learned in his parents' home before it was destroyed...

because they were among the six million people, men, women, and children, who sanctified the Lord's name with their sacred blood, which reddened the rivers of Europe from the Rhine to the Danube, from the Bug to the Volga—because, only because they were born Jews, and because they didn't have a country of their own, neither a valiant Jewish army to defend them, and because nobody, nobody came to their rescue, although they cried out: save us! save us! *de profundis*, from the depths of the pit and agony[.][26]

Such usage of the Holocaust as an argument in foreign affairs was exactly what Elon had earlier decried as

not always [being] in good taste; foreigners have on occasion resented it as emotional blackmail. There are instances when such resentment is justified—here [in Israel] as elsewhere the language of politics is debased.[27]

During the early 1980s, other liberal and left-wing Jews in Israel and America—among them A.B. Yehoshua and Leon Wieseltier—denounced what they considered the misuse and abuse of the Holocaust and of Auschwitz as metaphor by their own leaders.[28]

Another explicit use of the Holocaust in Israeli foreign policy was Prime Minister Begin's justification of the highly risky bombing, by the Israel Air Force, of the Osirak nuclear reactor in Baghdad in mid-1981. In a statement to the press, Begin explained that Saddam Hussein might have produced a number of nuclear bombs to use against Israel within two, three or four years. If the Israelis had not taken this preemptive action, he argued,

then this country, and this people, would have been lost, after the Holocaust. Another Holocaust would have happened in the history of the Jewish people. Never again, never again. Tell so [sic] your friends, tell anybody you will meet, we shall defend our people with all the means at our disposal. We shall not allow any enemy to develop weapons of mass destruction turned against us.

Responding to the consensus that Israel had acted in defiance of international law, Begin added: "I hope that in the days to come all men and women of good will, wherever they live, will understand our motives: it was an act of supreme, legitimate self-defence."[29] Re-reading these words after the 1990-1991 Kuwait/Gulf crisis and war—during which the Iraqi leader threatened to incinerate half of Israel[30] and raised the horrific spectre of Jews being gassed, post-Holocaust, by long-range missiles within the supposed safety of the Jewish state[31]—adds some poignancy to the maverick Israeli attitude of June 1981.

It is impossible to discuss connections between concern for Israeli security in the Arab-Israeli conflict and the Holocaust without referring to the passionate cry, "Never Again," popularized by the late Rabbi Meir Kahane, first in the diaspora through the Jewish Defense League and later in Israel as leader of the extremist Kach Party and member of the Knesset. The theme of a strong and militant Israel ensuring that "never again" would Jewish victims passively accept their fate was accompanied by another call: "No Jewish Guilt!" Defending the behaviour of the Israel Defense Forces against Palestinian rioters and stone-throwers during the *Intifada*, Meir Kahane invoked the Holocaust in a paid advertisement in the *New York Times*:

> And if the only way to survive is to take the lives of people who attack us, we have no choice. I wonder how many mourned and protested the killing of German civilians during World War II bombings of Berlin, Hamburg and Dresden? No guilt. There is nothing ethical about dying nor anything moral about another Holocaust. There is nothing immoral in winning and nothing necessarily noble in a loser. . . .

Arguing that the best way to end the Arab-Israeli conflict was to remove all Arabs from Israel and "let them live with their brothers and sisters in any of the 22 Arab states," the Kach leader's statement continued:

> And let us not fear the world. Those who stood by during the Holocaust and when Israel faced destruction in 1948 and 1967

have nothing to tell us. Faith in the G-d of Israel and a powerful Jewish army are the only guarantors of Jewish survival. Let us not fear the world. Far better a Jewish State that survives and is hated by the world, than an Auschwitz that brings us its love and sympathy.[32]

Nazification of the Enemy

In the ongoing interplay of Israeli and Arab propaganda claims and counterclaims, the Holocaust issue has never been far from current events. Even in Egypt, a country which has been at peace with Israel since 1979, Holocaust denial is still respectable in some intellectual circles, while editorial cartoonists attacking Israeli leaders too often resort to anti-Semitic motifs and stereotypes.[33] Some Arab and Palestinian intellectuals have fallen prey to the seductive logic of Holocaust denial because of its corollary of the de-legitimization of Israel. Classic Holocaust-denial literature makes sense to some of Israel's Arab enemies because of its claim that the Holocaust is a fiction created by a worldwide Zionist conspiracy in order to strengthen Israel by extracting financial reparations from Germany while mobilizing world sympathy for the Jewish state in its battles against the Arabs.

Other elements in the propaganda wars have included the mutual nazification of one's foes. Article 22 of the 1968 National Covenant (or Charter) of the Palestine Liberation Organization (PLO), in the course of defining Zionism, referred to its "essentially fanatical and racialist" nature and described its methods as being "those of the Fascists and the Nazis."[34] Some of the counter-arguments offered by Zionists and Israelis have focused on the wartime record of the exiled Mufti of Palestine, who had offered his support for spreading the Nazi message to the Muslim and Arab worlds. For many Jews and their supporters, Hitler's all-out war against world Jewry and the Arab nationalist struggle against Israel became intimately linked. After the creation of the Jewish state, some Israeli propagandists compared the repression of Jews in Iraq to "the worst excesses of the Nazi regime."[35] During the 1950s and 1960s, Israeli (and European) cartoonists and editorialists likened Gamal Abd al-Nasser, the charismatic pan-Arab nationalist leader, to Adolf Hitler. During the

1970s and 1980s, PLO leader Yasser Arafat was demonized in similar fashion.

In the wake of Israel's battlefield victories over Arab armies in 1948-1949, 1956, 1967, and 1973, Arab propaganda often depicted the Israelis as behaving towards them as the Nazis had behaved towards the Jews of Europe, with political cartoonists frequently twisting the Star of David into the shape of a swastika. This motif reached its height in the 1982 portrayals of Menachem Begin and Ariel Sharon as cruel Nazis in their treatment of Lebanese and Palestinians during Israel's invasion of Lebanon. The contrasting vision which the Israeli Prime Minister held of his Operation Peace for Galilee was that it was a war in which valiant Jewish soldiers were rescuing helpless Lebanese Christian civilians from Muslim Nazi killers. Similarly, the Israel Defense Forces' (IDF) siege and attack of PLO headquarters in Beirut was seen as a reenactment of the 1945 bombardment of Hitler's Berlin bunker.[36]

Arab nazification of the Israeli enemy became even more frequent and insidious during the Palestinian *Intifada* between 1987 and 1991, when the international media portrayed an apparently all-powerful Israeli army beating and shooting unarmed, protesting civilians. Detention camps for Palestinian prisoners were likened to Nazi concentration camps. By depicting Israeli leaders and soldiers as engaging in cruel and Nazi-like behaviour against stone-throwing youths and innocent bystanders during the *Intifada*, Palestinians and their supporters waged a media war against the Israelis which played successfully on Israeli and Jewish post-Holocaust traumas which were still pertinent fifty years after the horrors of World War II.[37] Such Arab use of Holocaust rhetoric in the Arab-Israeli conflict has been especially troubling and painful for Jews, given the latter's deep-rooted conviction that the IDF was fighting defensive wars for the very survival of a besieged nation against enemies who seemed to want to complete the job that Hitler started.

Conclusion: The *Intifada* and Beyond

In the preceding pages, we have seen how Israelis in particular feel about, and are affected by, the Holocaust, and how this has had a major impact on how their leaders conduct foreign policy, especially vis-à-vis relations with the Palestinians and the Arab states. Menachem Begin's blatant use of the Holocaust, together with the criticism it unleashed, offer striking proof of the accuracy of Amos Elon's stress, made a decade earlier, on the Holocaust as helping to explain

> the fears and prejudices, passions, pains, and prides that spin the plot of public life [in Israel] and will likely affect the nation for a long time to come. . . . If, in Israeli eyes, the world at large has tended to forget too soon, Israelis hardly give themselves the chance. The traumatic memory is part of the rhythm and ritual of public life.[38]

In Elon's analysis, the Holocaust

> accounts for the prevailing sense of loneliness, a main characteristic of the Israeli temper since Independence. It explains the obsessive suspicions, the towering urge for self-reliance at all cost in a world which permitted the disaster to happen. . . . The trauma of the holocaust leaves an indelible mark on the national psychology, the tenor and content of public life, the conduct of foreign affairs, on politics, education, literature, and the arts.[39]

Much can be written about variations in the use of the Holocaust among Israel's political parties. It may be briefly noted here that the return to power of the Labour Party in June 1992 was accompanied by an interesting shift in the leadership's rhetoric about Israel's place in the world. After renewing the impetus to the peace process started by his Likud predecessor at Madrid in October 1991, Prime Minister Yitzhak Rabin reviewed his first year in office (two and a half months before the surprise announcement of the September 1993 accord with the PLO) and expressed his determination to overcome all obstacles. "The train that travels towards peace," he added,

> has stopped this year at many stations that daily refute the time-worn canard—"the whole world is against us." The United States has improved its relations with us. . . . In Europe, our dialogue

with the E[uropean] C[ommunity] has been improved and deepened. We have been inundated by visiting heads of state—and we have responded to them with friendship and with economic and other links. We are no longer "a People that dwelleth alone."[40]

Indeed, in the two years following the Madrid conference, 34 countries established (or re-established severed) diplomatic relations with the Jewish state, while in December 1991 "a completely different correlation of forces at the United Nations" voted to revoke the infamous 1975 "zionism equals racism" resolution.[41] Reflecting the new spirit of international acceptance, Rabin's appeals to his countrymen began to incorporate some of the discourse previously confined to peace activists and liberal spokesmen such as former Foreign Minister Abba Eban, who had for years been arguing that Israelis should stop thinking like outnumbered and beleaguered ghetto fighters, but should rather visualize themselves as strong and secure enough to take some calculated risks for peace.[42] One manifestation of this new approach is that visiting foreign dignitaries are no longer obliged to stop at Yad Vashem, although most continue to make the recommended pilgrimage.

But deeply-ingrained attitudes, perceptions and self-images are not changed overnight. It is too soon to assess just how lasting and how profound these changes may be, and much depends on the changing degrees of safety and vulnerability of Jews in all the lands of their dispersion. While it does seem as if some Israelis may be ready to modify their worldview somewhat along Labour's open and liberal lines, others cling to the cautious and defensive attitude reflected in Likud leader Benyamin Netanyahu's arguments against returning to Israel's pre-1967 "Auschwitz borders."[43]

Despite the record of frequent misuse of the Holocaust in the context of building or destroying arguments about the Arab-Israeli conflict, there are important reasons for seeking a deeper understanding of the connections between these two highly-charged subjects. Even if we were to accept the hypothesis that it might be best if we could somehow manage to keep discussions of these topics separate from each other, it would not eliminate the fact that both Arabs and Jews *do* dwell, in different and conflicting ways, on connections between the two issues. Careful analysis of the links between the Holocaust and the Arab-Israeli conflict remains a legitimate and worthy task of the serious scholar.

The Genocide of Sephardi Jews:
The Impact on a Community

Yossi Lévy

THE TOPIC OF THE HOLOCAUST and the effect it had on the Sephardim is not one which is very easy to deal with. The Shoah had important consequences on the Sephardim, just as it had on the other Jewish communities of Europe. In order to understand these consequences, I will first give a brief background on the history of the Sephardim. Second, I will discuss the influence of Fascism and Nazism in the areas where Sephardim were living before the war, then deal with the Shoah, per se. Finally, I will finish with a few words and poetry from authors who have written on the Holocaust from a Sephardi point of view. In the course of this paper I will focus, in particular, on the contribution of Primo Levi, an Italian Jew, to the literature of the Holocaust.

To understand the history of the Sephardim, we have to remember one very important date: August 1492. After uniting their kingdom, Queen Isabel and King Ferdinand of Spain issued an edict which gave the Jews who were living in the newly-united Kingdom of Spain the choice of being converted to Christianity or leaving the Kingdom. The expulsion of the Jews from Spain (*Sepharad* in Hebrew), where they had lived since the 6th or 7th century, had several consequences. First, it brought about the conversion of many Jews to Christianity. Second, it scattered the Jews who refused to convert or wanted to return to their faith to other countries around the Mediterranean, especially North Africa, but also Italy, the Balkans, Greece, Turkey and Pa lestine, and even northwards to Holland, Germany, (especially Hamburg and then Vienna), Britain, and westward to North and South America.

This Sephardi diaspora was quite large. Almost all the countries of the Mediterranean, Europe and North and South America had communities of Sephardim or Marranos (people who were converted to Christianity but kept some of the history and the memory of their Judaism). The Sephardi immigrants had an influence on the Jewish populations already residing in those countries, leading to some cultural conflict with the native Jewish communities which received them, especially in the Mediterranean region.

Between the 16th and 20th centuries, many historical changes took place in the Sephardi communities. In Europe, their integration was linked to the development of modern nation-states. In the Middle East and North Africa, Sephardi Jews were accorded a specific status called *dhimmi*, i.e., under the protection (and domination) of their Muslim rulers. In many countries, they were unable to achieve the status of equal citizenship and thereby kept their specific culture and language much longer than was the case in other countries where they were able to borrow many elements from the host cultures.

The situation of the Sephardi communities changed drastically with the rise of Fascist and Nazi policies before the Second World War. Anti-Semitic policies linked to these movements were put into place in many countries around the Mediterranean region. Furthermore, with the development of the Zionist question, the intercommunal tensions in the Muslim countries dominated by the colonial powers were sharpened. The conditions of the Sephardim differed according to the country. In Italy, with the ascension to power by Mussolini and the Fascist party, anti-Semitic rhetoric, quite inoffensive at first, become part of a racist programme after 1936, when Italy became linked to Hitlerian Germany. Fascist literature in Italy presented the Jews and Zionism as the major dangers confronting humanity. The Jews were considered at the same time capitalists and parasites and bolsheviks with a knife in their teeth. In such conditions, the Jews had to disappear to make room for the Aryan race. As early as 1937, the Italian state enacted discriminatory laws against Jews, who were forbidden to teach, to marry non-Jews, and were put under economic and civil restrictions. Faced with this situation, the Italian Jews did not rebel. Some tried to convert to Christianity as a way of not being considered Jewish, while others sought to emigrate. One film which expresses very well the powerlessness of the Jewish middle and bourgeois class of Italy is *The Garden of the Finzi-Contini*, which provides a nuanced portrayal of the community's reactions to Fascism and the humiliations forced upon its members.

These policies were also applied in Libya, conquered by Italy at the beginning of the 19th century. At the beginning of the Fascist era, anti-Semitic rules were not applied in Libya, but the pressures increased and, in 1938, racist legislation was adopted, provoking a crisis of confidence in the local Jewish community. The Jews were confronted with tensions and problems on two fronts: Italians had enacted laws against Jews living in the country, while the Muslims of Libya were trying to fight against the Italian occupation. As the economic situation worsened, Jews were attacked many times during the 1920s and 1930s in Benghazi and Tripoli, the principal towns of Libya.

In Yugoslavia the situation was different. Anti-Semitism there was less oriented towards the Sephardim than towards the Ashkenazi population, which was associated with the Austro-Hungarian Empire. In Greece, anti-Semitism was more violent. There were pogroms in Salonika between 1932 and 1934, but after a *coup d'état* in 1936 the status of the Jewish minority in Greece improved. Bulgaria, which had lost the province of Thrace and other regions after the First World War, applied the same policies to the Jews as did the Germans, presenting them as people supporting both capitalism and bolshevism, while an international organization called the *Organisation révolutionnaire macédonienne* (Macedonian Revolutionary Organization) used terror and intimidation to extort money from them.

In Turkey, anti-Semitism was not able to take root. Turkey was the first country to accept Jews after their expulsion from Spain, and subsequently allowed them to become a real part of Turkish society. Even though there was a fascist movement in this country, there was no specific attack against Jews, which was not the case in other Muslim countries like Iraq or Egypt, where nationalist movements were influenced by fascist movements and tried to raise tensions against Jews.

Turning to the North African countries, we can also see differences. The most important country, Algeria, was from 1830 considered as a *département* of metropolitan France. At the end of the century, the Jews of Algeria were considered French and had French nationality. Anti-Semitism in Algeria, which was influenced by the extreme right in France and then by Nazism and Italian Fascism in the 1930s, gained ground among the *pieds noirs* (French settlers) in Algeria. In 1921 the town of Oran elected an anti-Semitic party to its municipal council, and in 1934 (with the election of the *Front populaire* in France) a pogrom took place in Constantine. In reaction against this anti-Semitism, Jews joined groups such as the *Ligue internationale contre le racisme et l'antisémitisme* and established political contacts with Muslim reformist movements. In Tunisia and in Morocco, Fascist and Nazi influence was felt in the Muslim nationalist movements. Extreme-right movements like the *Croix de Feu* developed an anti-Semitic campaign during the 1930s which took hold in the Moroccan Muslim nationalist milieu and provoked incidents between the two communities.

While we have seen that the development of fascist ideologies and politics in all regions led to tensions affecting the resident Jewish communities, those tensions and the strength of anti-Semitic policies varied according to local conditions and circumstances. This would also be the case when we look at the Holocaust itself; each country would react according to its own situation, with the result that the Shoah in the Sephardic world was not a single experience, identical from country to country. While the experiences of the Sephardic Jews varied from country to country, and produced differences in terms of the reaction of the Sephardic world to the Shoah, from the perspective of the Germans there was to be no distinction between any particular type of Jews. All Jews, Sephardic or Ashkenazi, were to be murdered.

Let us begin with the North African Sephardic communities where the Shoah was avoided for complex reasons linked primarily to questions of logistics. Far from Europe, these countries would have had difficulties in deporting the Jews. But each country had its specific situation. Morocco was a French protectorate which was not totally under the control of the French government. While the French government enacted anti-Semitic laws, the King of Morocco, Mohammed V, chose to protect the Jews against deportation. The three countries of North Africa under the control of the French Vichy government did, however, develop a corpus of laws to discriminate against Jews in the economic, professional, education and political spheres. Jews were not allowed, for example, to go to French schools. Although they had to go to separate schools, they did not have to wear the yellow star. Work camps were opened throughout French North Africa for Jews who were foreigners and for some native Jews, particularly in Tunisia. Jews joined the resistance movement against the French regime and against the Nazis who occupied some places, like Tunisia. Many Jews participated in the movement to liberate Algeria from the Vichy government. Another factor was the early arrival of American troops in North Africa in 1942 and 1943, effectively precluding the implementation of Nazi plans of mass murder. But, even after the landing of the American troops and the annulment of racial laws in 1943, the Jews of Morocco and Algeria continued to be subjected to laws of exclusion and were interned in detention camps.

It is interesting to see that, in spite of very close ties between Nazi Germany and the Franco regime, Spain did not put into effect any laws against Jews. The Jews who were living in the Spanish enclaves of Morocco did not suffer from discriminatory laws. Many refugees who were conscious of this privileged situation went to Spain where they were able to enjoy legal protection. Faced with the Nazi challenge, Spain, perhaps because of the first edict of expulsion four and a half centuries earlier, was not ready to be marked, for the second time in history, as being part of a barbaric "solution" to the Jewish "problem." It is also worth noting that the Vichy government was not at all happy with the position of Franco's government towards the Jews, since it created a troubling parallel with its own position on the Jews. We have to note also that the Vichy government developed its own internal anti-Semitic dynamic and policies without being coerced by the Nazis.

In Tunisia, the German occupation lasted until 1943, and was accompanied by more severe maltreatment of the Jews, who were sent to forced-labour camps and were subjected to multiple forms of discrimination. Mass killings, however, were not carried out against the Jews of Tunisia, largely because of the problems of transporting the victims to the European killing centres. There were not enough German troops to implement this solution and, furthermore, many Italian soldiers were not very interested in following the orders to deport the Jews. Thus, the majority of the Jews of Tunisia were saved.

For Sephardim in European countries, the situation was much worse. In Italy, the Fascist regime took its time in deporting its Jewish citizens, but after 1943, in the zone where the Nazis were in control, around 8,000 Italian Jews were placed in concentration camps and deported to Auschwitz; two-thirds of those people would die in Auschwitz and other camps. But in the zones under the control of Italian soldiers (for example in France, Greece and Yugoslavia), the Jews were, for the most part, protected by the Italian army. Thus, in Dalmatia protection of Jews was ensured by the Italian army, but after the invasion by Germany, they were murdered except for those who had been evacuated by Tito's troops and those who went on to work with the Yugoslavian resistance in this region.

In other parts of Yugoslavia, the German occupation in 1941 brought about the death of more than two-thirds of the Jewish population, around 60,000 persons out of a total of 75,000 Sephardi and Ashkenazi Jews. In Croatia, many concentration camps were built, as Croat Fascists were ready to lend a hand to the mass murder of the Jews. Only people who had no more than one Jewish parent, or Jewish spouses in mixed marriages, were safe. In Bosnia-Herzegovina, the Muslim population followed the lead of Haj Amin al-Hussaini, the exiled Mufti of Palestine, and even created a local SS Battalion which participated in attacks on Jewish buildings prior to the mass deportations. Thus, the final solution was applied differently in disparate regions of Yugoslavia, according to the relative strength of the Fascist movement and of Nazi influence.

Bulgaria, aligned with Germany, began to introduce anti-Jewish legislation at the very beginning of the Second World War. In Macedonia, which was controlled by Bulgaria, and in Thrace, Jews—mostly Sephardim—were deported to Treblinka where they were killed. But many were saved by the intervention of Bulgarian politicians who were helped by members of the Orthodox Church. Nevertheless, under the pressure of the Nazi authorities and in spite of its protestations, the government prepared for the expulsion to the provinces of the Jews of

Sofia, the capital of Bulgaria. This step preceded deportations to the death camps, but the King of Bulgaria, Boris III, refused to sign this order and the Jews were sent instead to labour camps. In 1944, anti-Jewish restrictions were abolished and, with the rise to power of the Communists and the entry of the Red Army into Bulgaria, the possibility of Nazi deportations was removed. In the end, Bulgaria saved the great majority of its Jewish population (47,000 out of 50,000), many of whom emigrated after the war to Israel.

In Greece, the occupation by German and Italian troops brought about the deportation of a large majority of the Jewish population of Jenina, Epirus and Salonika. These towns were occupied by German forces. After sending the men to forced labour and taking money from the community, the Nazis put discriminatory rules into effect and deported 95 percent of the population; approximately 45,000 people were sent to Auschwitz and Birkenau.

The tiny Jewish community on the Island of Rhodes, which is in the Dodecanese, was not spared the deportations. At the beginning, it was the Italians who implemented the anti-Semitic policies, but when the Nazis occupied the island in 1944, they deported all its Jewish population, around 2,000 people, to Auschwitz; the great majority of these people did not survive their ordeal in the camp. Jews were also deported from Crete.

In Holland, the small Sephardic community at first asked to be granted the status of Aryans, in order to escape annihilation. But these Jews were subjected to the same rules as the other Jewish communities, and the majority died between 1942 and 1943 in the camps of Auschwitz, Sobibor and Theresienstadt. Many Sephardim living in the south of France and in Lyon were sent off to camps, but many also participated in the resistance.

While all these communities came under Nazi rule, we can see that the reaction of the different Mediterranean and European countries towards the murder of the Jews was not totally the same. The Bulgarians, for example, were able to save many of their country's Jews despite an anti-Semitic tradition and the important influence of the Church. While Franco was a Fascist, he nevertheless refused to hand over Spanish Jews to the slaughter. We can also see that, when there was resistance against the policies of the Germans, it was possible to save Jews. But in places where the Germans themselves intervened directly, saving local Jews was much more difficult. We can conclude from this rapid overview that there was no single policy, and there were different reactions and levels of resistance towards these policies from one country to the next. What is tragic is that the Jews from the Balkans, from Greece, and so on, who died in the camps, took with them Sephardic language and Sephardic traditions.

What was the reaction of the Jews in the field of literature and creativity during the Shoah and afterwards? Here we find many interesting things. First, we have a traditional rewriting of some of the events in Jewish history to explain or to narrate the Holocaust. The two most important narrative matrices are the *hagadah* (telling) of Passover, recounting the exodus of the Israelites from Egypt under Moses, and the Purim story, in which a symmetry is established between Haman's plans for exterminating the Jews in ancient Persia and Hitler's final solution in Germany. In Tunisia, we find poetry which takes the form of the *Kinot*, which is a traditional Jewish lamentation, updated to express the conditions of the Jews under Nazism.

Parallel to these traditional literary forms we can see the development of modern poetry, in many languages—Judaeo-Spanish, French, Spanish, Greek—in which Sephardi survivors have expressed their experiences. Many of these poems have been gathered by a scholar originally from Rhodes, Isaac Jack Lévy, who has written a very beautiful book called *And the World Stood Silent: Sephardic Poetry of the Holocaust*, which includes an anthology of poems. In his analysis of this poetry, Lévy notes that "the primary duty of the writers is to retain their own identity through the remembrance of fallen brothers and sisters, [and] through literary recomposition, the book's message is to give expression to the Holocaust in order to prevent the recurrence of more such catastrophes for Jews and gentiles alike." [1]

Another important theme is linked to religion and the role of the Divinity in these events. Lévy writes that "while the Sephardi poets denounce the guilty, they also praise and immortalize those who, at the cost of their lives and of their families, came to the aid of the condemned." [2]

Let us examine four of these poems. Although naturally something is lost when the poems are translated into English from French and Spanish, one can still experience some of the feeling of the originals. The first poem, "Ecological Attila," is by Henriette Asseo, a professor at the École Normale Supérieure in Paris and a descendant of Salonika Jews. With the use of repetition and the accumulation of images the poem builds to a climax in the final two lines.

> . . . on the piles of the pieces of the corpses of my people
> on the heaps of the corpses of my people
> in Maidanek and Auschwitz
> in Birkenau and Treblinka
> only green
>
> > grass.

The second poem is called "The Prayer of the Persecuted Jew," and is by Marcel Chalom, who was born in Turkey. Here, too, the images pile up on each other as the poet desperately longs for a world "with no quarrels and no wars," a world "where the mothers/Will raise their children/with no fear," a world which "Will only know one utterance: /I love you!"—a world where the poet wants spring "To fill all the moments/of the year. . ."

The third poem is by David Haïm from Salonika, and is called "Seven Days Locked Up." The title refers to the time during which Jews were confined "in boxcars for animals" on the trip to the death camps. The poet addresses both his mother, who was fortunate to die in her own country, not in Auschwitz, and his father, who in fact did come with his brother "to the crematorium of Auschwitz." In the final verse the poet speaks to his family members:

> Father and mother, brothers and sisters,
> may you all be supplicants
> to the Master of the world
> to grant me health
> and remove me from these camps
> to recite for you the Kaddish!

From this example we can see that poetry gives the sense of the tragedy but also the maintaining for many of a religious response towards this event. But it is also true that some poets did not accept the event and refused to put it in theological perspective. To illustrate this, I would like offer as a last example a poem by Avner Perets, who was born in Jerusalem but whose family members, from Salonika, were murdered during the war. The poem is called "Cast Into the Fire." The poet asks the Jewish victims who have been cast into the oven, "Who is the God/that will save you/from the catching fire?" And in the next verse he bitterly answers this question as follows:

> Your god whom you served
> in centuries of gold,
> in centuries of darkness,
> will not save you
> from the catching fire.

The Malahe a-sharet descend from heaven and accompany the victims into the burning fire. "And the Ancient of Days/will remain silent."

Other authors who offered important expressions of the experience of the Holocaust in this region include Giorgio Bassani, the well-known author of *The Garden of the Finzi-Contini* and Carlo Levi, who wrote *Christ Stopped at Eboli* which describes his experience under Fascism. Another author, Liliane Atlan, whose family is originally from Salonika, has written many plays which deal with the Holocaust, exploring human relations and tensions in the camps. But the most important of all is Primo Levi, whom many consider one of the century's preeminent writers on the Holocaust. Levi died several years ago under ambiguous circumstances—perhaps suicide, perhaps an accident. Among his many books, the two most important are *Survival in Auschwitz* and *The Saved and the Drowned*,[3] in which Levi observed the workings of the concentration and extermination camp system like an anthropologist. He placed himself in the position of an ethnographer and really tried to describe, to understand, and to give witness to this system. These books analyze all the dimensions of the *Lager* (concentration camp) system—from the divisions between people, the economic workings of the camps, the relationships between people, the acts of brutality and the altruistic acts he witnessed.

At the beginning of *Survival in Auschwitz*, Levi says that the book had "not been written in order to formulate new accusations; it should be able rather to furnish documentation for a quiet study of certain aspects of the human mind."[4] What is very interesting is his use of the term "quiet study" in order to express this relation towards the Holocaust. A second theme which is central to Levi is that, even if the camp is an extreme experience, this experience is a source of learning about human nature. "We are convinced," he wrote in *Survival in Auschwitz*, "that no human experience is without meaning or unworthy of analysis and that fundamental values, even if they are not positive, can be deduced from this particular world we are describing. We would also like to consider that the *Lager* was pre-eminently a gigantic biological and social experiment."[5]

For Primo Levi, we must learn from the Holocaust; extreme experience is part of human experience. This vision of the gigantic biological and social experiment led Primo Levi to conclude that the *Shoah* was a unique event. As he writes in *The Saved and the Drowned*:

> The Nazi concentration camp system still remains a *unicum*, both in its extent and its quality. At no other place or time or time has one seen a phenomenon so unexpected and so complex: never have so many human lives been extinguished in so short a time, and with so lucid a combination of technological ingenuity, fanaticism, and cruelty.[6]
>
> . . .
>
> We must be listened to: above and beyond our personal experiences, we have collectively witnessed a fundamental, unexpected event, fundamental precisely because unexpected, not foreseen by anyone.... It happened, therefore it can happen again: this the core of what we have to say. It can happen, and it can happen everywhere.[7]

I think that is the essence of what Primo Levi has put forward: not only the fact that it happened but that it is an event that can be repeated.

From this brief overview of the experience of Jews from the Sephardic world, we can appreciate that this experience has given birth to much work which is not well-known, but which I think is part of a rich Shoah literature currently being gathered and preserved by Sephardim. Although we have singled out mainly works in the field of literature, there are people like Isaac Lévy working on a book of paintings, painters and artists which will soon to be published. We can also see that there are many common experiences shared between survivors from both the Ashkenazi and Sephardi worlds. Yet there are, I think, differences between the two Jewish communities; for example, in the ways their experiences have been linked with religious themes, and how those experiences have been translated into the specific languages and idioms of Ashkenazim and Sephardim.

Anti-Semitism in Quebec and Canadian Popular Culture: Adrien Arcand and Ernst Zundel

Stanley Asher

IN THE WAKE of the narrow defeat of the separatist forces in Quebec's October 1995 referendum on sovereignty, the nationalist camp showed signs of a revived xenophobia bordering on racism. Many prominent, and not-so-prominent, Quebec political figures, from Premier Jacques Parizeau down, searched for roots of the defeat in the "ethnic" minorities' refusal to show proper gratitude for living in Quebec.

Within weeks of the referendum-night remarks by the Premier about "*le vote ethnique et l'argent*", more specifically racist complaints surfaced. Raymond Villeneuve, retired from his career as FLQ terrorist, stated publicly what many observers of the Quebec scene may have suspected privately, that the Jews of Quebec, along with two other ethnic groups, the Italians and the Greeks, were the real culprits. Villeneuve stopped just millimetres short of saying that these "*ethnies*" (the new buzz word in Montreal) were traitors.

Adrien Arcand

The racist overtones of the Quebec political scene in the late 1990s are reminiscent of the years between the world wars, when Montreal's newspapers included a number of overtly anti-Semitic weeklies. These were all founded and edited, in succession, by Adrien Arcand, a shadowy figure in Montreal journalism who turned out vicious hate literature in the guise of political satire and commentary. Arcand's activities spanned the period from the onset of the depression in 1929 to the beginning of the Second World War.

Perhaps the most accessible and detailed account of Arcand's early years can be found in Lita-Rose Betcherman's pioneering work, *The Swastika and the Maple Leaf*, which devotes several chapters to his education (McGill, paradoxically), his first local journalistic assignments (*The Montreal Star*) and, particularly interesting, the roots of his anti-Semitism.[1] Others have written on this topic, notably David Rome, Montreal Jewry's most respected historian, whose recent passing has left a huge gap in the community. Rome researched and produced a multi-volume history of anti-Semitism in the years between the world wars.[2] Both Rome and Betcherman recall the Jewish School Commission Bill of 1930 in the Quebec legislature. Whereas the purpose of this proposed legislation was to deal democratically with Jewish children's rights to public education in Quebec, Arcand "maintained that there were only two minorities in Canada—the English in Quebec and the French in the rest of the country. By alleging that Jews were not entitled to minority status ...Arcand was able to refute Jewish claims for equal treatment under the law."[3]

Local, national and international politics all figured in Arcand's rise to power. His satirical weekly, *Le Goglu*, had received financial backing from Montreal's flamboyant mayor-to-be, Camilien Houde, and in turn Arcand campaigned for Houde in the elections of 1930. When Houde recanted and condemned Arcand's anti-Semitism publicly, Arcand turned against his former ally.

The next politician to receive praise from *Le Goglu* was R. B. Bennett. Betcherman notes that publicity in *Le Goglu* helped the Federal Conservative Party win 24 seats in Quebec. On the international level, Arcand's support for Mussolini did not go unnoticed by Montreal's growing Italian community. Throughout this time the paper, edited and for the most part written by Arcand, descended to the crudest of anti-Semitic cartoons, jokes and polemics.

This flurry of activity came to the attention of the National Socialist (Nazi) Party in Germany only months before it assumed power in January 1933. A certain Kurt Ludecke spent several months in Canada at the end of 1932. Part of Ludecke's work, self-appointed at that time, was to contact Arcand. Betcherman refers to Ludecke's memoirs, *I Knew Hitler*, in which the German agent recounts his amiable meeting with Arcand.[4]

As the Great Depression hit North America, *Le Goglu* became *Le Miroir*. With the coming to power of Hitler and the Nazi Party in 1933, the new paper, again edited and written by Arcand, welcomed the German Chancellor to world politics with a full-page spread.

By 1934 Arcand, emboldened by the success of the Nazis, was now producing articles for yet a third paper, *le Patriote*, which advanced an even more anti-Semitic agenda. In further imitation of his idols in Berlin, Arcand established *le Parti National Social Chrétien*, which blended the "best" elements of Mussolini's and Hitler's racial doctrines. The party sported blue shirts, and by 1937 was importing quantities of virulent anti-Semitic propaganda from Nazi Germany. Arcand's local paper underwent a fourth name change and was now called, quite openly, *le Fasciste canadien*. Whereas the source of the earlier work of Arcand, from 1929 to the mid-thirties, had been his own fertile imagination, much of the newest paper's rantings were now direct translations from German-language speeches of the Nazi Party hierarchy.

As the world came perilously closer to war, Arcand found opportunities to expand his realm of influence. In 1937 he arrived in Toronto, a city that had had its share of anti-Semitic incidents during the decade (such as the Christie Pits riots of 1933). In Europe, appeasement was the prevailing wind of the west, and in Britain Sir Oswald Mosley had become prominent. Arcand received suggestions from Mosley on how to bring fascist candidates into the local Toronto elections.[5]

By 1938 Arcand's name received grudging attention from the American media. Both *Life* and *The Nation* sent reporters and photographers to the Montreal headquarters of the Canadian Fascist Party. In the case of *Life*, Arcand and his followers enjoyed a three-page spread as the issue's lead story, which was accompanied ironically by lesser coverage of a federal Conservative Party rally. *Life* treated Arcand with a healthy dose of cynicism, but *The Nation*'s reporter was eerily respectful, noting Arcand's professed knowledge of Yiddish.[6]

While Arcand had brazenly incorporated the swastika into the newspaper's masthead during the mid-1930s, he realized by the summer of 1938 that associating directly with the Nazis was becoming a liability. Two conspicuous changes appeared in the propaganda materials that

Vol. I — No 36
MONTRÉAL, 11 AVRIL 1930

Rédaction et administration :
987 blvd Saint-Laurent, Montréal.
Tél. LAncaster 1967

5c **5c**

LE GOGLU

JOURNAL HUMORISTIQUE

Circulation nette: 2ième française en Amérique   *"Rions bien nous mourrons gras"*
<small>(ÉMILE GOGLU)</small>

QUEBEC LIVREE AUX JUIFS

Révélation des détails se-crets et inédits sur la plus grande trahison de notre histoire.

Enyoupinons la province !

Sathanase David est créé Chevalier de la Glorieuse Gousse (d'ail).
Pour sauver Parasol Plante.

NE BOUCHARD EST HEUREUX.

(De notre correspondant secret)
Québec, 10 avril.—La population a peut-être appris avec une légère surprise que notre correspondant...

"POURVU QUE LA FIERTE JUIVE SOIT SATISFAITE"

SATHANASE DAVID et HARENG BOUCANE TASCHEREAU, devant les députés juifs Cohen et Bercovitch: "Grâce, grâce, nos bons amis ! Prenez toute la province, tous nos droits, toute notre fierté, mais de grâce gardez-nous le vote juif de Montréal, notre seul espoir de garder notre Clique au pouvoir. Au diable la fierté canadienne, mais nous vous promettons de satisfaire à la fierté juive, à n'importe quel prix."

VICTOIRE! VICTOIRE! VICTOIRE!

Enfin, la Clique qui rongeait et saignait Montréal depuis vingt ans est écrasée par le vote le plus gigantesque qu'une population honnête ait jamais donné. Le maire Houde a pris une majorité presque fantastique, ses échevins sont en grande majorité au pouvoir, DesRoches devient un insignifiant dans une...

M. BOURASSA ET LES JUIFS

En marge d'un déclaration du député de Labelle aux Communes. — La prétention que les Juifs ont des droits n'est pas défendable en ce pays.

Droit national et droit des gens.

Nos lecteurs nous excuseront d'interrompre momentanément notre étude sur les problèmes connexes au Bill David des écoles juives pour reproduire l'article suivant, paru dans le "Miroir" de dimanche dernier, tout particulièrement pour le bénéfice des milliers de lecteurs éloignés qui ne reçoivent que le "Goglu".

[...]

C'EST FACILE DE VENDRE A BON MARCHE

La jolie Canadienne est attirée chez le Juif par les prix alléchants affichés dans la vitrine. Elle croit faire un bon marché et épargner plus que chez le boucher canadien-français. Mais a-t-elle remarqué de quelle façon le Juif tient son pouce sur la balance au moment de la pesée? Arrivée chez elle, elle constatera que, si elle a une balance, elle a peut-être gagné un quart sur la pesée. Dans ces conditions-là, c'est facile de s'enrichir tout en vendant bon marché.

Adrien ARCAND

Ça ne prendra pas partout, cette année

[...]

LES PRESCRIPTIONS DU DROIT CANON A L'EGARD DES JUIFS

Un évêque d'origine juive, Mgr Gohn, ancien professeur de droit canon — écrit Mgr Delassus à la page 46 de son livre "La question juive" — a résumé les prescriptions du droit canon (les ordonnances de la Sainte Eglise) au sujet des Juifs.

"Au dire du savant évêque, elles n'ont pas été abrogées.

"I—Les Juifs ne peuvent avoir des esclaves chrétiens, ni employer des chrétiens pour le service de leur maison ou de leur famille. Il est interdit aux chrétiens d'accepter un emploi permanent rémunéré chez les Juifs.

"II—Il est spécialement interdit aux chrétiennes de s'engager comme nourrices chez les Juifs.

"III—Les chrétiens ne peuvent recourir, en cas de maladie, aux services des médecins juifs, ni accepter des médicaments préparés par des mains juives.

"IV—Il est interdit, dans tous les cas, aux chrétiens, SOUS PEINE D'EXCOMMUNICATION, d'habiter dans la même maison ou dans la même famille que les Juifs.

"V—On doit veiller à ce que les Juifs n'arrivent pas dans la vie publique à occuper des fonctions qui leur donnent une certaine autorité sur les chrétiens.

"VI—Il est interdit aux chrétiens d'assister aux mariages des Juifs et de prendre part à leurs fêtes.

"VII—Les chrétiens ne peuvent inviter les Juifs à dîner, ni à accepter les invitations qui leur sont faites par les Juifs."

Voilà en quelques mots la substance de la législation de l'Eglise catholique à l'égard des Juifs.

(Cité par l'abbé Antonio Huot, dans une conférence sur la question

Arcand continued to pour forth: the swastika was replaced by the logo of a flaming torch, and the party's name was toned down to the National Unity Party.

When Britain and Canada declared war on Germany, Arcand abruptly lost his respectability and was forced to continue his work subversively. Continue he did, and in the spring of 1940 he spoke before an audience of six hundred people who had come to hear Father Fabien, a priest notoriously sympathetic to Arcand's views.[7]

The end of Adrien Arcand's activities came shortly after Mosley had been arrested in Britain on 23 May 1940.[8] Canada's leading fascist was seized, arrested, and interned for the duration of the war in New Brunswick. Four years after his release, he tried to return to public life by running for parliament. He must have realized, however, that the shocking news of the Holocaust would have prevented him from ever again achieving any prominence. No less important a supporter than Quebec Premier Maurice Duplessis provided Arcand, in his postwar years, with some translation and editing work.[9]

Ernst Zundel

In his final years, Adrien Arcand's life intersected with that of a young German immigrant, recently arrived in Canada. Ernst Zundel was nineteen when he settled in Montreal. Within a few years he married a Québécoise, with whom he had two children. Teachers at what was then Sir George Williams University remember young Zundel taking courses in political science, but his political leanings were unclear until he met Arcand shortly before the latter's death in 1967.

Arcand found a kindred soul in Zundel, eager to learn about the old Fascist's past glories in prewar Montreal. Soon Zundel became part of the network of neo-Nazis who were beginning to proliferate in Germany and elsewhere. When Arcand died, Zundel delivered the funeral oration and inherited Arcand's massive library of propaganda and Nazi materials, reputed to be most comprehensive collection of its kind in Canada.

Zundel plied his trade as a printer in the sixties and early seventies in Toronto, and remained relatively unknown, though he had been a candidate in 1968 for the leadership of the Liberal Party of Canada, getting not a single vote to Pierre Elliot Trudeau's thousands. By the mid-seventies, however, Zundel began to flex his neo-Nazi muscles with several published items. One demanded the release of Rudolph Hess from Spandau Prison. Others appeared in various fringe publications in the United States. In one of them, the *White Power Report*, Zundel was listed on the masthead as an editorial writer.[10]

The 1980s were a busy decade for Ernst Zundel. After he reprinted a scurrilous pamphlet, *Did Six Million Really Die?*, he was confronted by Holocaust survivor Sabina Citron, a Toronto resident who was able to get Zundel's postal privileges denied. This was not a stumbling block to the determined Zundel, however; he simply moved his mailing address across the border to Buffalo, New York. Canadian laws were sufficiently lax to enable Zundel to return to his Toronto mailing address in less than a year, when a postal review board reversed the original decision.

Various Jewish organizations pressed the matter further, and on 7 January 1985 a trial began in the county court of Toronto,[11] on a charge of spreading "false news." After eight weeks, Zundel was convicted, sentenced to fifteen months in jail, and shortly afterward freed on bail. A condition of his bail, which he never honoured and for which he was never condemned, was that he cease his neo-Nazi activities. A new trial in 1988 found him guilty again; this time his prison sentence was nine months. The pattern of bail and violation of bail agreement was repeated.

Zundel's next recourse was an appeal to the Supreme Court of Canada. In 1992 that judicial body reversed the previous convictions on the grounds that the "false news" law was not constitutional.[12] This decision left Zundel free to continue his activities, none of which he had ceased throughout the five-year series of litigations. In 1995 his request for Canadian citizenship again brought him onto the pages of Canadian newspapers.

When his Carlton Street house/office/media-centre was firebombed in May 1995, his activities were only temporarily curtailed.[13] He soon resumed producing videotapes, some of which are shown on public access cable television stations in such areas as Rochester, New York. There, as elsewhere, his followers, with financing from Germany, use the principle of free expression to place his programs in the context of German culture.

5c

MONTREAL, 25 OCTOBRE 1930
Vol. II — No 12

LE

Rédaction et administration :
927 Blvd Saint-Laurent, Montréal.
Tél. LAncaster 1907

5c

GOGLU

JOURNAL HUMORISTIQUE

Circulation nette: 2ième française en Amérique   "Rions bien nous mourrons gras"
(ÉMILE GOGLU)

M. HOUDE A PEUR DES JUIFS

Il refuse toujours de se prononcer sur le principe du Bill David, n'en condamnant qu'un détail technique.

Ménagements continuels.

Les Juifs ont raison, les Canayens ont tort, et il ne faut pas faire d'antisémitisme, suivant M. Houde.

CRAINTE ET FINASSERIE

M. Houde a peur des Juifs.

Il a plus peur des Juifs que des Canadiens-français.

Et il faut être aveugle pour ne pas s'en apercevoir.

L'anti-sémitisme fait rage dans le monde entier: en Allemagne, au Mexique, en Autriche, en Arabie, en Turquie, en Palestine, en Amérique du Sud, en Roumanie, en Pologne, etc. Le mouvement commence à s'agiter en France, aux Etats-Unis et même en Russie, où les chrétiens sont traités comme du bétail par une poignée d'agitateurs juifs. Probablement que tous ces pays ont tort et que seuls les Juifs ont raison.

Québec est le coin du globe le plus exploité par les Juifs; on leur a donné nos richesses naturelles, on leur a laissé prendre notre commerce, nos plus beaux sites, on a saboté nos lois pour leur faire plaisir, on en a fait les égaux des enfants de la province. Mais nous n'avons pas droit de nous défendre contre le Juif envahisseur, l'ennemi mortel de nos traditions et nos principes. Non, nous avons tort, car M. Houde ne veut pas que nous fassions d'anti-sémitisme. Tous les pays du monde se défendent en ce moment contre la puissance israélite qui cherche à les étreindre. Mais Québec doit se laisser faire, car M. Houde l'exige.

On comprendra l'attitude de M. Taschereau, car ce sont les libéraux qui ont fait venir les Juifs en ce pays, qui leur ont donné le droit de vote, des chartes de compagnies, des lois de faveur suivant la mentalité juive, qui les ont élevés au niveau d'une minorité officielle. Mais on comprend difficilement l'attitude si libérale du chef "conservateur". Il n'y a qu'une explication: c'est que M. Houde a peur des Juifs. Il devrait pourtant savoir que le Canayen n'a pas peur du Juif. Un Canayen peut se faire tromper et se faire emplir par un Juif, mais il sait le reprendre [...]

lations, les finasseries de M. Houde dans la question juive.

Il laisse passer sans personnellement rien dire le Bill David, bien que les évêques donnent l'alarme au point de vue religieux, national et financier.

Quand des Juifs vont se plaindre à lui de la campagne déclenchée par nos journaux, il nous condamne et déclare que les Juifs forment une "minorité ayant droit à toute la protection de nos institutions", elle [...]

Juifs votent en bloc contre lui; ils doivent trop de reconnaissance aux libéraux.

Quand il paraît assuré que le gouvernement va ravaler sa loi des écoles juives, forcé par nos journaux et la colère du peuple, M. Houde recule aussi, malgré sa déclaration de principe, et annonce — mais trop tard — qu'il va combattre le Bill David. Il profite de sa reculade pour condamner encore notre anti [...]

Voyez vos ménagements ! Il ne veut pas dire que le Bill David est mauvais, anti-national et anti-canadien. S'il en était convaincu, il le dirait. Mais non, il ménage Israël dans l'espoir d'avoir son vote, n'ayant [...]

* * * * *

mandes bien que nos presses aient fonctionné jour et nuit sans arrêt, de mardi matin à samedi soir. Aucun journal, quotidien ou hebdomadaire, n'a encore enregistré une telle augmentation pour un même numéro. De son côté, le "Miroir", le journal du dimanche par excellence, continue sans jamais fléchir son ascension vers des sommets nouveaux et commande toujours l'appréciation de l'opinion saine de notre race. Cette [...]

ECOLE

L'ENFANT DE PRÉDILECTION DES DEUX CHEFS RIVAUX

C'est à qui, de M. Taschereau et M. Houde, ferait le plus agréable minoucheries à l'écolier juif, qui a coûté plus d'un quart de million d'argent des catholiques, l'an dernier, alors que le petit Canadien-français des campagnes est si négligé. C'est à qui ferait le plus pour avoir le vote juif. Pour ce qui est de M. Taschereau, ça ne comprend facilement. Mais on a été tout surpris de voir M. Houde approuver le principe du Bill David, puis condamner le Bill sur un détail technique, craignant de dire s'il est bon ou mauvais, puis condamner à deux reprises la campagne anti-sémite des goglus pour la reprise de notre commerce, notre argent et notre industrie dans notre pays. Quand aurons-nous un chef patriote qui ne craindra pas les Juifs ?

Le PATRIOTE

Journal hebdomadaire
paraissant le jeudi

5 SOUS

Rédigé en
collaboration

VOL. I — No 19   MONTREAL, 7 SEPTEMBRE 1933   1725 rue St-Denis — Tél. HArbour 8216

Le Juif, être dégoûtant, rêve de dominer le monde

Son Talmud lui enseigne qu'il est permis de faire du mal aux non-Juifs, qui sont "des chiens sans âmes". — Les auteurs juifs admettent que la juiverie est la race la plus sale, la plus corruptrice et la plus pervertisseuse du monde. — Race qui n'a jamais été déiste et qui a assassiné tous les envoyés de Dieu. — Il faut s'en défendre comme de la peste et l'arrêter dans sa conquête.

LE BOYCOTT! LE BOYCOTT! LE BOYCOTT!

Dans son livre "The Way to Zion", le Juif Kurt Munzer a écrit: "Nous, les Juifs, avons souillé le sang de toutes les races. Nous avons tout rendu fou, pourri, décomposé, putréfié".

Un autre Juif, le Dr Oscar Lévy, a écrit: "Nous, les Juifs, avons fait la Grande Guerre. Nous, les Juifs, ne sommes que les séducteurs du monde, ses incendiaires, ses assassins. Notre dernière révolution n'est pas encore faite. C'est nous qui avons inventé le "mythe" du peuple-choisi."

Et on pourrait citer à ne plus finir les journaux et livres juifs qui affirment qu, les Juifs sont les auteurs de toutes les guerres depuis deux siècles, de toutes les révolutions, du trafic clandestin des narcotiques, de la traite des blanches, de la contrebande du mauvais alcool, des livres démoralisants, des films pervertisseurs, qu'ils sont l'âme et le mobile de la franc-maçonnerie, du communisme, du socialisme, du libéralisme, de l'anti christianisme, qu'ils sont les grands exploiteurs de l'usure, du vol, du recel, de l'incendie criminel, des spectacles malsains, etc., etc. Et toutes ces opinions ne sont pas celles de diffamateurs, d'insulteurs, de propagandistes fanatiques, ce sont des affirmations faites par les Juifs eux-mêmes, par une foule d'auteurs juifs qui ont exposé les raisons de l'antisémitisme et ont essayé d'améliorer leurs congénères afin de leur épargner les conséquences finales de leur abominable corruption.

AVEC LES SIRES QU'ON SCIE

Toujours, jamais . . .

Heureusement que le systè me Robot n'existait pas lors du passage de la Mer Rouge, car autrement tous les Youpins s'y seraient noyés. Et quel bon débarras pour nos agents de la circulation.

Des Juifs qui se moquent de nos règlements de vitesse, en veux-tu en voilà: L. E. Ludman, M. Ship, (pas celui de Jonas). Charles Feldman, Nathan Grostein A. L. Goldig, iger, (pas ceux de 1932), Silver Lazarre, (que n'est-il au tombeau), S. Plotskin, Ivali Winsberg, Jos Bremner et madame H. Passmore, (quant à nous, elle peut bien tout passer), etc.

Et la liste s'allonge sans fin

Bill Federooka s'enivre avec Alfred Oram.

Un agent crie: "Aux rames" et les deux Israélites sont pin cés.

LA GALERIE DES ASSASSINS

YANKEL YOUROVSKY

Voici des assassins les plus déboutants de l'histoire: le juif Yankel Yourovsky. Ivrogne, vicieux et débauché. Depuis le 4 juillet 1918, il gardait la famille impériale russe à la maison Ipatief (Ekaterinbourg, dans l'Oural), aide de son adjoint juif Nikouline et de dix prisonniers de guerre austro-hongrois choisis parmi les bourreaux ordinaires de la Tchrezvytchaika tramification de la sanguinaire "commission contre la contre-révolution" que commandait Filznoble juif.

Pierre Gilliard, précepteur du tsarévitch et qui échappa miraculeusement au massacre, raconte que, dans la nuit du 6 au 17 juillet 1918, un peu après minuit, Yourovsky pénétra dans les chambres occupées par les membres de la famille impériale, les réveilla, ainsi que leurs domestiques, et leur dit de se préparer à le suivre. Le pretexte qu'il leur donne, fut qu'on doit les amener, qu'il y a des émeutes dans la ville. On descend. Yourovsky marche en tête, suivi de Nikouline, puis le prince Alexis, l'impératrice et ses quatre filles Anastasie, Olga, Marie et Tatiane), le Dr Botkine et trois serviteurs, Anna Demidova, l'haritonof (chef de cuisine) et Troup (laquais). Les prisonniers s'arrêtent dans une pièce du rez-de-chaussée, qui leur est indiquée par Yourovsky...

la plupart des prisonniers. Le petit Alexis gémit faiblement. Yourovsky l'achève d'un coup de revolver. La grande-duchesse Anastasie n'est que blessée et se met à crier à l'approche des meurtriers; elle succombe...

...sous les coups de baïonnette. Anna Demidova elle aussi, a été épargnée grâce à la grosse masse de l'argent dans laquelle elle se cache. Elle se lance de côté et d'autre et, poursuivie par...

Le Patriot, 7 September 1933
Bibliothèque nationale du Québec

These television shows have also been shown in Germany, whose laws forbid the production of Holocaust denial material, but apparently not the rebroadcast of foreign tapes dealing with this subject.

The only permanent casualty of the fire in his studio, which he milked in the media for all it was worth, was the cessation of his weekly radio broadcast, "The Voice of Freedom." This half-hour show, taped on what sounds like crude equipment in his Carlton Street headquarters, was easily accessible to listeners throughout eastern North America on shortwave station WRNO, New Orleans, at 7355 kilohertz. This station continues to broadcast other neo-Nazi programming, including *National Vanguard*'s "American Dissident Voices," which in the summer of 1996 was still spewing forth anti-Zionist, anti-Israeli and classic anti-Semitic hate propaganda, drawing for inspiration and actual source material from the *Protocols of the Elders of Zion* and Henry Ford's *Dearborn Independent*.

Hate Propaganda as a Teaching Tool

Ernst Zundel has sent requests to Jewish media and community spokespeople to debate him openly on the issues of the Holocaust.[14] He denies being a "denier," but simply wants to "question" such facts as the existence of Auschwitz as an extermination camp, and the authenticity of Anne Frank's diary. During a 1995 shortwave broadcast, for example, he claimed the diary was a fraud, written in ink not invented at the time of the war.

The mainstream reaction of the Jewish community of Canada has been to attempt to use the courts to silence Zundel and his ilk, and to ban the written and video materials produced by neo-Nazi and other fascist groups. My own views on this issue are mixed. When I deal with Arcand and Zundel in my college course on the Holocaust, I am reluctant to distribute copies of either sets of material. This reluctance is partly a result of unwillingness to spread their propaganda further, even unwittingly. On the other hand, students have to know, in my opinion, that in the so-called free world, now as well as then, these dangerous aberrations existed and continue to exist. My personal solution is to place them on transparencies and display them on screens, larger than life, strictly for explanation and analysis only.

Rather than ignoring Arcand's and Zundel's writings, it is my belief that they should be examined closely and analyzed, and even used in teaching the Holocaust. Students and teachers would learn much from the exercise of refuting the lies in this material. Arcand's entire body of "journalism" is available on microfilm from several library sources. A convenient one is in the David J. Azrieli Holocaust Collection at Concordia University. Zundel's work is available from his Carlton Street headquarters. Library indexes have extensive bibliographic listings of the recent controversies surrounding Holocaust denial and hate propaganda in its printed, visual and electronic forms.[15]

Le Patriote, 24 August 1933.
Bibliothèque nationale du Québec

Two Composers Respond to the Holocaust: *Arnold Schoenberg's* A Survivor from Warsaw *and Dmitri Shostakovich's* Babi Yar Symphony

Robert Frederick Jones

ON 16 MAY 1943, Jürgen Stroop, the German SS and Police Leader charged with carrying out the destruction of the Warsaw ghetto, reported to his superiors that there were no Jews left in Warsaw. They had all been killed or deported to death camps.

One and a half years earlier, in September 1941, special police troops attached to the invading German army rounded up nearly 34,000 Jewish residents of Kiev and, over two days, machine-gunned them to death at Babi Yar, a ravine just outside the city. Over the next twelve months the killings continued. In total, about 100,000 people were killed at Babi Yar, at least 90 percent of them Jews.

In the history of the Nazi regime these two events are major, but unfortunately typical, atrocities. In the history of music they acquire special significance in that they were the seeds from which grew two of the most powerful works by two of the twentieth century's most important composers. It is these two works, Arnold Schoenberg's *A Survivor from Warsaw* and Dmitri Shostakovich's *Symphony No. 13* (subtitled "Babi Yar"), that form the subject of this essay. Although these two masterpieces are certainly strong enough to stand on their own without commentary, it is hoped that the present discussion, placing them in their biographical and historical contexts, will result in increased appreciation.

Arnold Schoenberg, one of the most influential composers of the twentieth century, was born in Vienna in 1874. At the age of eight, he began taking violin lessons. Inspired by reading a biography of Mozart he began to compose. His father died when he was fifteen and he was forced to quit school and get a job as a bank clerk in order to support his family. He continued to compose. When he was twenty-two, the bank where he was working went out of business, and Schoenberg was delighted to be able to devote himself to music. After this date (1895) his stylistic evolution was astounding.

His compositional career can be loosely divided into three periods. In the first, he began in a somewhat conservative (for the time) Brahmsian style, quickly mastered the more advanced Wagnerian style, and pushed its progressive harmonic tendencies to the limit. *Verklärte Nacht* (*Transfigured Night*, 1899), for strings, and the gigantic oratorio *Gurre-Lieder* (*Songs of Gurre*, 1900, orchestration completed in 1911) are typical works from this period.

His "second period" began in 1908. In that year, in the midst of a profound crisis in his emotional life, he began to compose music which dispensed with a sense of key. Complex harmonies that traditionally could only be used in contexts in which they resolved to more stable harmonies were now used without preparation or conventional resolution. For the next six years Schoenberg was in a period of intense creativity producing a series of masterpieces in what is generally called the "atonal" style: the one-character opera *Erwartung* (*Waiting*, 1909), the *Five Pieces for Orchestra* (1909), *Pierrot Lunaire* (1912, a cycle of twenty-one pieces for reciter and chamber ensemble), and many others.

The outbreak of World War I in 1914, the deteriorating living conditions in Vienna during the war, and the severe problems of the immediate postwar years (food shortages, epidemics, financial crises, and so forth) resulted in a reduction in Schoenberg's compositional output. In the next few years he struggled to develop some way of bringing a sense of rational order to the atonal style, with its virtually unrestricted and infinite possibilities.

By 1923 he had developed the "12-tone method" of composition. To oversimplify what is involved in writing a 12-tone piece: the composer chooses a particular ordering of the twelve different notes of the chromatic scale (with each of the twelve notes used only once) and then uses this series as the basis of a composition. All of the melodic and harmonic material is derived from the basic series and various systematic transformations of the series. For the remaining twenty-eight years of his life, Schoenberg used this method in most of his works. Among his 12-tone compositions are his *Violin Concerto* (1936), *Piano Concerto* (1942), *Third and Fourth String Quartets* (1927 and 1936), the first two acts of an unfinished opera *Moses and Aron* (1932), and *A Survivor from Warsaw* (1947).

So far we have surveyed Schoenberg's musical development as though it occurred in a vacuum, ignoring what one writer has called "the world beyond the manuscript paper." In order to understand more fully the road that led to *A Survivor from Warsaw*, we must return to the composer's childhood and trace aspects of his spiritual development.

Schoenberg's parents were of Jewish origin: his father was a thoroughly secularized freethinker and his mother, whose family included several generations of synagogue cantors in Prague, was more devout. Both of these strains seem to have influenced his personality. When he was sixteen, he wrote a remarkable letter to a cousin who had criticised "all the nonsense in the Bible." He wrote:

> ... now I must oppose you, as an unbeliever myself, by saying that nowhere in the Bible is there any nonsense. For in it all the most difficult questions concerning Morals, Lawmaking, Industry and Medical Science are resolved in the most simple way, often treated from a contemporary point of view; in general the Bible really gives us the foundation of all our institutions (except the railway and the telephone).[1]

In 1898, at the age of twenty-four, Schoenberg formally converted to Christianity, and was baptised and confirmed in the protestant Lutheran church. Writers on Schoenberg have "explained" this conversion in various ways. Some have taken it at its face value as motivated by conviction; others have seen it as the result of social pressures or simply as a shrewd career move. In favour of Schoenberg's sincerity in this matter we should note that the cultural and political institutions of the Austro-Hungarian empire in which Schoenberg lived were dominated by Catholicism. Jews converting for the sake of better career opportunities became Catholics not Lutherans.

Skimming quickly over twenty years, during which Schoenberg manifested mystical, theosophic and Swedenborgian inclinations, we pass to an incident that happened in 1921, and which precipitated a change in his attitudes. In that year, he and his wife went for their usual summer holiday in the Austrian resort town of Mattsee and found that Jews were no longer permitted to rent accommodation there. In the postwar period, overt anti-Semitism was increasing on a massive scale. This was the case not only with incipient Naziism in Germany; all over Europe and America anti-Semitic movements among people of all levels of intellect were finding increasing support. In the light of this trend Schoenberg began to reconsider his Jewish origins. Over the next twelve years such incidents accumulated as Adolf Hitler, about whom Schoenberg was warning his friends as early as 1923,[2] gradually rose in prestige and power. After Hitler's election as chancellor of Germany in 1933, Jews (or rather, persons defined as Jews by the government's race laws) were forbidden to hold official positions. Schoenberg, who had been head of the composition department at the Berlin Academy of the Arts since 1925, found himself without a job, and with his music banned from performance in Germany. He left the country, and, four months later in Paris, he formally rejoined the Jewish faith, stating at the time that it was the outward sign of a conversion that had happened inwardly some years before.[3]

Later that year he sailed to the United States, where he was to live for the rest of his life. After a year in Boston, he moved to Los Angeles, where he became a professor of composition and theory at the University of California.

What has only recently come to light is the extent to which Schoenberg was involved at this time in a massive effort to organize an international society to raise money from Jews outside Germany for the purpose of, in effect, paying off the Germans to permit the emigration of German Jews.[4] He foresaw, with sometimes uncanny prescience, that the Nazi regime was headed inexorably in the direction of trying to solve the "Jewish problem" by mass murder. Little came of Schoenberg's efforts at fundraising and prophecy, and he soon was forced to concentrate his efforts on supporting himself and his young family. Nevertheless, he continued to follow events in Europe and to deepen his identification with Judaism.

After the war ended, he supported the establishment of the state of Israel and, in the last year of his life, was proud to accept the position of honorary President of the Israel Academy of Music in Jerusalem. Many of his last works are concerned with Jewish themes: there is a setting of Psalm 130 for a cappella choir (dedicated to the state of Israel), an unfinished work for chorus and orchestra entitled *Israel Exists Again*, and a series of texts which he called *Modern Psalms*, meditations on a wide-ranging series of subjects including prayer, atheism, the ten command-ments, Jesus, children, sexuality, and the atomic bomb. The last music he composed was a unfinished setting of one of these *Modern Psalms*, and the last words he set to music were *"Und trotzdem bete Ich ..."* (And nevertheless I pray ...).

We turn now to *A Survivor from Warsaw*. From what we have already learned about Schoenberg's character, it is not difficult to imagine the shattering effect that the revelations of the full extent of the Nazi atrocities against the Jews would have on him. In 1947 he received a commission for a short work for orchestra and used that opportunity to pour forth his feelings in a musical form.

The work is entirely composed using the 12-tone method. All the harmonies and melodic material is derived from the series:

A# B E C Ab G D F C# F# A D#

In the present context a detailed analysis of how the series is used is not relevant. First of all, Schoenberg always insisted on the irrelevance of finding the rows in his compositions, asserting that he wrote "12-tone *compositions*" not "*12-tone* compositions";[5] and secondly, the work is of such powerful dramatic intensity that considerations of compositional technique seem to be almost irrelevant.

By the time Schoenberg came to compose *A Survivor from Warsaw* he had been composing 12-tone music for nearly twenty-five years and was as thoroughly at home using it as Bach was at writing fugues. One of my teachers was the violist Eugene Lehner, who played in the premieres of

Schoenberg's Third and Fourth String Quartets and who had known the composer over a period of many years. He described how he arrived once quite early for a rehearsal at Schoenberg's house. Schoenberg said that he was very busy and asked Lehner if he would mind waiting while he went on with his work. Schoenberg sat down at his desk and began rapidly putting down notes on manuscript paper. Lehner thought at first that, as Schoenberg was writing so quickly, he must be copying something. He strained for a closer look. No other music was on the desk. He then thought that he must be composing, but there were no tables of the various row forms. When Schoenberg finally stopped working Lehner asked him what he had been doing. "Composing," was the reply. "But where are the charts of the tone rows?" Schoenberg pointed to his head. "They're in here."

A Survivor from Warsaw is scored for reciter, unison male chorus, and a fairly large symphony orchestra with an extensive percussion section. The narrator represents the Survivor as he recalls incidents in a Nazi death camp after the destruction of the Warsaw ghetto. The text is by Schoenberg. It is mostly in English, but with some quotations in German. It is based on Schoenberg's conversations with survivors, and with reports that he had read. The climax represents an occasion at which prisoners were being counted off to be sent to the gas chamber and they all began to sing the *Shema Yisroel*, the statement of faith from the biblical book of Deuteronomy that begins with the great commandment to love God: "Hear, O Israel, The Lord is our God, the Lord is one. Thou shalt love the Lord thy God will all thy heart, and with all thy soul, and with all thy might."[6] At this point the English text spoken by the narrator gives way to the original biblical Hebrew sung by the chorus.

For virtually all of his life, Schoenberg lived in a society in which freedom of artistic expression was respected. His compositions might be received with incomprehension, hostility, contempt, or neglect, but—with the exception of the few months he lived in Hitler's Germany—he was free to compose in any way he felt, and to have his works played by anyone who cared to play them.

With Dmitri Shostakovich the situation was very different. Born in 1906, he was only eleven when the Bolsheviks seized power. Thus all of his creative life was spent under the Soviet communist regime. According to communist doctrine, the artist is considered a government employee whose purpose is to further the goals of the revolution. In practice, this meant that decisions as to what works got played, where it was played, how many people got to hear it, even what styles and subject matter were acceptable or unacceptable, were decided by committees headed by party bureaucrats, whose decisions were often swayed by external pressure from above. This also meant that if artists strayed too far from what was currently acceptable, they could be jailed, sent to work camps, even killed. The fact that Shostakovich was able to produce such a large body of artistically significant compositions under such conditions represents a triumph of the human spirit over adversity.

In the past, western commentators have tried to find a consistent viewpoint in the Soviet policies on aesthetic matters. More recently, since the fall of the communist system in Russia, we have come to realize the extent to which these policies were influenced by external factors: power struggles in the highest regions of the administration or even the mere whims of the men at the top. Crudely put, artistic policy could be changed simply to get rid of someone you wanted to get rid of, and the implications for all the other artists affected by the decision were quite simply side-effects. We shall see an example of this later.

The one consistent thread running through Soviet thought on artistic matters is that the artist must serve the needs of the people. This doctrine, however, could be (and was) interpreted in many different ways. Shortly after the revolution, the view was put forward that revolutionary art was the only proper art for a revolutionary society. An attempt was made at this time to allow only music composed by Soviet composers to be performed, on the grounds that all earlier music was tainted by its reactionary social origins. (An exception was allowed for Beethoven, who was considered sufficiently revolutionary.) This view did not last for long and in the 1920s there was a bitter power struggle between two groups of composers: those who felt that all musical resources should be available to the composer, and those who thought that only uplifting art that could be immediately understood by the masses was to be tolerated. To a large extent, the views of the latter group prevailed. Certain words came to be used as code words to describe the unacceptable: "bourgeois", "elitist", "anti-social", "decadent", and the all-purpose pejorative word, "formalist". A "formalist" artist is one who is concerned only with form, not with content. The positive ideal of Soviet aesthetics was expressed in the term "Socialist Realism", a rather vague and flexible concept that in practice implied a very conservative artistic vocabulary, and a tendency to allow only positive, uplifting, happy endings.

Dmitri Shostakovich was from the first the prize example of the new Soviet artist. His First Symphony, an astonishingly original masterpiece composed in 1925 when he was only eighteen years old, rapidly made him recognized throughout the world as a major artistic figure. For the next ten years, he developed the modernist tendencies of his style in three more symphonies, two operas, and numerous other works. During this period, the power struggle between the "progressive" and "conservative" aesthetic positions was coming to a head, with the conservatives ultimately winning. In 1936 the axe fell on Shostakovich. His opera, *Lady Macbeth of Mtsensk*, was denounced on the front page of *Pravda*. He publicly issued an abject apology (which had been written for him by a party functionary). In it he expressed his profound regret that he had allowed himself to be led astray by decadent Western bourgeois elitist formalist (etc.) influences, but pledged to do better in the future. At this time, he had good reason to fear for his life: many Soviet artists in similar positions were disappearing or being murdered. His *Fifth Symphony* of 1937 brought his return to favour. It uses a formal device that Shostakovich was to favour in many works: gloom and conflict in the early movements give way in the end to a triumphant conclusion. This managed to satisfy the Soviet aesthetic watchdogs in that it could easily be allegorized as representing the sufferings of the people in the bad old days before communism, the struggles and conflicts of the revolution, and finally the great happiness enjoyed by all in Joseph Stalin's blissful Utopia. (Composers of instrumental music had definite advantages in this period over writers and visual artists. Words and images carry immediately apparent denotations; a symphony is far more nebulously connected with concrete subject matter.)

In 1948 Shostakovich's work came under attack once more. Again his works were withdrawn from performance; again abject apologies were issued over his signature. He was fired from his teaching position at the Leningrad Conservatory for "professional incompetence." This time, there was no quick return to favour, and his career languished for a decade during which he led a sort of double career: composing music for public consumption—film scores and an oratorio glorifying reforestation projects—while at the same time composing powerful and personal works "for his drawer", to be played only after the political climate had changed.

It was during this second period of disgrace that Shostakovich began taking an interest in Jewish folk music and poetry. He felt a strong identification between the general conditions of life under Stalin's terror and the sense of insecurity experienced by the Jews for centuries. "Jews became a symbol for me. All of man's defencelessness was concentrated in them."[7] He also admired certain characteristics of their folk music:

> Jewish folk music has made a most powerful impression on me … It's multifaceted, it can appear to be happy while it is tragic. It's almost always laughter through tears. This quality of Jewish folk music is close to my ideas of what music should be. There should always be two layers in music. Jews were tormented for so long that they learned to hide their despair. They express despair in dance music.[8]

Jewish folk music is featured in several of the works Shostakovich composed "for his drawer" in this period.

It is evident that the periods of attack on Shostakovich correspond with Stalin's major purges of "enemies of the people". This is, of course, no coincidence. As noted earlier, Soviet artistic policy was influenced to an almost incredible extent by political considerations. The "thaw" of the early 1960s, in which artists enjoyed a brief period of relative artistic freedom, occurred for similar reasons.

In 1956, Nikita Khrushchev, the premier of the Soviet Union, denounced the legacy of Stalin in a secret speech to the Party Congress. Over the next four or five years, Khrushchev worked for the elimination of Stalinist policy. By 1961, Stalinist forces were struggling to depose Khrushchev, who in a preemptive move, went public with his denunciation of Stalin. In October, Stalin's body was removed from its public display in a mausoleum in Moscow. Supporters of Stalinist artistic policy were removed from office and artists were encouraged to attack the Stalinist legacy. Khrushchev himself intervened personally to secure the publication of Alexander Solzhenitsyn's *One Day in the Life of Ivan Denisovich*, a grimly powerful novel about life in a Siberian labour camp. It is in this brief period of "thaw", that lasted from October 1961 to December 1962, that several previously unheard works by Shostakovich were played for the first time, and during which he composed his *Thirteenth Symphony*, "*Babi Yar.*" By 1964, Khrushchev had been deposed and replaced by Leonid Brezhnev, who put an end to the period of "de-Stalinization".

One of the most remarkable artistic figures to emerge during the 1961 "thaw" was the young poet Yevgeny Yevtushenko. He rapidly rose to fame on the basis of both his poetry, with its vivid language and imagery, and his great gifts as a reciter. (In Russia, one should note, poets reading their work attract a far wider audience than they do typically in the west. It is regarded more like "performance art" than mere reading aloud.) In 1961 he created a sensation when he stood up at a reading in Kiev and recited his latest poem, *Babi Yar*. The poem uses the memory of the Nazi massacre of Jews at Babi Yar in 1941 as the starting point for an attack on anti-Semitism in the present.

Shortly after the poem was published, Yevtushenko got a telephone call from Shostakovich asking permission to set *Babi Yar* to music. The poet confessed himself deeply honoured by the request. "Good," said Shostakovich, "I've already composed it. Would you like to hear it?"

Yevtushenko recalls:

The most thrilling performance was the very first one, when Shostakovich himself sang it for me, sitting at the piano. He played and sang all the parts: the soloist, the chorus, and the orchestra. His eyes were filled with tears. ... The way he had [set the text to music] amazed me. If I had been able to write music, this is exactly the music I would have written for this poem. For he had combined seemingly incompatible things: requiem, satire, and sad lyricism.[9]

Shostakovich decided to use his setting of *Babi Yar* as the first movement of his *Thirteenth Symphony*. For the remaining movements he set four other poems by Yevtushenko, all of them obliquely critical of aspects of Soviet society.

The symphony is darkly scored for a bass soloist, a unison chorus of basses, and large symphony orchestra. The work was finished in August 1963 and the premiere was scheduled for 18 December in Moscow. At this point troubles began. The artistic "thaw" was abruptly coming to an end. On December 1 Khrushchev had seen an exhibition of abstract art and reacted with a blistering attack on modernism in the arts—he called the artists degenerate and perverted pederasts and said, "Gentlemen, we are declaring war on you."[10]

At this point, party bureaucrats began to make difficulties for Shostakovich and Yevtushenko. First of all, the text of the poem *Babi Yar* was declared unacceptable because, among other problems, it did not mention that others besides Jews had been killed at Babi Yar. The published poem had already been set to music, so Yevtushenko, in consultation with Shostakovich, replaced certain objectionable lines with new ones that kept the original poem's metre and phrasing. The poem is considerably weakened by the substitutions.

In the original poem we find these lines:

I feel myself a Jew.
Here I tread across ancient Egypt.
Here I die, nailed to the cross.
Even now I bear the scars of it.

In the revision, these lines were changed to:

Here I stand as if at the fountainhead
That gives me faith in brotherhood.
Here Russians lie, and Ukrainians,
Together in the same ground with Jews.

Later in the poem, the original version has these powerful lines:

> I become a gigantic scream
> Above the thousands buried here.
> I am every old man shot dead here.
> I am every child shot dead here.

They were replaced by:

> I think of Russia's heroic deed
> In blocking the advance of Fascism.
> To the smallest flower, she is dear to me
> In her very being and her fate.

One senses that Yevtushenko was here deliberately writing flat and conventional lines as a message in hidden code to his listeners: "You know that I am capable of far better poetry than these feeble and platitudinous lines; they are just filler, put in under duress." (In recent performances, the original lines have usually been restored.)

Shostakovich ran into other problems in connection with the premiere. The bass originally scheduled to sing the solo part was pressured into refusing; Shostakovich and his allies found another one willing to perform. The day before the performance the authorities announced that the replacement bass could not perform because he was needed to sing at the Bolshoi opera that night. Fortunately, Shostakovich had secretly been coaching a third bass in the part, and he sang at the premiere. At the dress rehearsal, the men's choir announced that they were refusing to sing; Yevtushenko gave a desperate speech shaming them into agreeing to perform. The television and radio equipment was removed from the hall just before the performance so the scheduled broadcast could not take place. In the end, the symphony was given two triumphantly received performances, then the work was banned. A copy of the score was smuggled to the west where several successful performances were given, but the piece went unheard in Russia for a decade.

When an artist uses an historical event as the subject for a work of art, he is not principally concerned with recreating that event in its historical context. Rather, he is concerned with the *present* relevance of the subject. This is nowhere more apparent than in Yevtushenko's and Shostakovich's *Babi Yar*. The massacre at Babi Yar, and the other incidents from Jewish history recalled in the text, are mentioned primarily as a warning against present anti-Semitism. Anti-Semitism has a long and shameful history in Russia and the Ukraine, and it continued to flourish (with only few periods of relaxation) under the communist regime. (Unfortunately, it is still present today.) In the late 1940s and early 50s, for example, at the same time as Shostakovich's second period of disgrace, Stalin went on a ruthless campaign against Jews and Jewish influence (somewhat ironically, considering Karl Marx's Jewish origin).

In the period immediately following Shostakovich's "Babi Yar" Symphony, the Soviet regime once again manifested overtly anti-Semitic policies. Although they stopped at the indiscriminate imprisonment and slaughter characteristic of earlier regimes, a climate of fear was created in which Jews were targeted as social misfits, dissidents were put in prisons and mental institutions, synagogues were closed, Jews suspected of wanting to emigrate lost their jobs. Throughout this period, the banned words and music of Shostakovich's Symphony stood as a silent accusation.

A few points of similarity between Shostakovich's "Babi Yar" Symphony and Schoenberg's *A Survivor from Warsaw* should be noted. In spite of the radical difference of harmonic language between the two pieces, both works share certain concerns. One is the great care taken to ensure that the words are readily audible. Both composers were capable of writing dense and complex textures, but in these two pieces, their concern with maximizing the impact of the text led them to use only a vocal soloist and a unison chorus. In addition, both works were composed very rapidly. Schoenberg completed the *Survivor* after only twelve days of work, Shostakovich sketched his setting of "Babi Yar" almost overnight. Although the emotional immediacy of a work is not necessarily related to its speed of composition, in each of these two works one senses that the subject matter tapped deep roots in the composer's inner being. The rapidity of composition is a reflection of this deep involvement, and it is this quality that gives both these pieces their immediacy. As we listen to these works by Schoenberg and Shostakovich, we feel that their souls are speaking directly to ours.

Poetry

Carrie Bacher

THOUGHTS AS WE WALKED

We walked, holding hands, wondering
what we were supposed to be feeling.
We walked, supposed to be silent,
yet talking about Israel, Poland, and home.
We walked, six thousand of us.
One, for every hundred thousand gone?
We walked, watching the Israeli flags,
bright Blue and White against the
drab grey Polish sky.
We walked, wondering what it meant
to those who watched us from the
sidelines.
We walked wondering. . .
Would we ever be the same?
We walked, talking to fill the
void of wonder. . .
We walked, with hope, with expectations,
with a spring in our step
and in warmth.
We walked together, and yet,
We walked Alone.

They walked, holding hands,
supporting their neighbour.
They walked, silent as death,
in the black of night, the hush of day.
They walked devoid of hope
hearts filled with fear.
They walked, trying to keep up,
seeing others fall as they gave in.

They walked, wondering. . .
Where the road led. . .
They walked, fear overtaking all other emotions
as they approached
Death
at the other side.

They walked, cold, hungry, in terror, in pain,
wondering when it would end. . .
They walked alone, and yet.
They walked Together.

I walked, friends on each side.
Israeli flags up ahead, security all around.
I walked, talking with the people
who I had met just days ago.
Bound to them for Life.
I walked, and as I walked
I recited silently, over and over again
to myself:
Ani Maamin, I do believe,
Am Yisrael Chai! The people of Israel live on!
I walked wondering why so many
had to fall. But I walked sure that Hashem had
a reason, glad I didn't understand,
scared of how I'd feel if I did
understand.
And I walked, Jews all around me,
brothers and sisters all of my own.

And we walked. . .
Our walk, a March of Life
Just as they walked. . .
                Only theirs was a
                        March
                                Of Death.

Ray Shankman

FIRST THEY KILLED THE SHEEP

for sacrifice they killed the sheep
for Aryan purity they killed the lame and infirm
those with hair-lips and double chins
then they killed the Jews and the Gypsies
to propitiate the swastika God
whose petty black moustache
trembled to welcome the odious odour
of charred corpses
ash drifting lyrically in the wind
descending on the land
like snowflake fallout
while outside muted villagers
hell bent on redemption
revelling in their reawakened primitive appetite
revile the victims
heap scorn and curses
upon their neighbours
                          the sweet smell of death
saves them from their sins

first they killed the sheep

FOR THE BOY WITH UPRAISED HANDS

on this day
there is birth death memory
you remember a love
that lasted an eternity
in a moment
of anxious anticipation
a love that vocalized an aria
of passion into some primitive room
you have never inhabited
and you remember
(how can you ever forget)
you were born into a blessing
of survival and comfort when others
were being killed, starved, tortured

and you wonder
if the soul of the dead
(you know the photo of that little boy
with his hands upraised
while the Nazis mocked God
with their derisive laughter)
entered your alive soul
to arm you with the words
to raise you to the Divine
to help you ask for strength
so others will remember

TO MY VIRTUOUS JEWISH WOMAN

To my virtuous Jewish woman
who sews my coat patiently and cries
listening to Leonard Cohen
pigtails framing ancient ghetto suffering

pogroms murdered your Polish grandparents
your Kiev family now the dust of Babi Yar
alone you survive
in the family of your imagination
braids thin with worry splitends
the story of your life and your mother's death
swaddled in plastic at the hospital morgue
mirrored in the soul of your face
                        reflects my soul

O my virtuous Jewish woman
you who hold my hand eternally
you who watch the night with me
the full moon lights the way
listen to the manic laughter of the loon
hear the fish splash

I've heard the loon mates forever
and he has a weird holy cry

Endre Farkas

WITNESSES REPORT

20,000 a day gassed.
Every week a city disappeared.

And when the killing didn't go fast enough
children were thrown into fires,

alive;
like potatoes.

No one smelled anything.
Nothing happened.

HEIRLOOM

for A.M. Klein

I was conceived by lovers bound for Auschwitz,
Belsen, Birkenau, Buchenwald, Mauthausen,
and every other camp that was,
is and ever will be.

I am the seed of every man-child
who was rounded up like livestock,
loaded into cattle-cars
and shipped off to a final solution.

I grew in the womb of every woman
who was shaved, tattooed
and lined up naked
next to gas chambers.

I am a child of children
stripped of their innocence in death camps;
torn from grief-numbed parents who knew
but were helpless and were gassed
and cremated into Pure Jews.

I am their next day
starved on stale bread
and crumbs of that
saved for tomorrow
in case things got worse.

I am their rememberance of home;
how right now,
this would be happening,
that would be talked about,
and Oh the food—
cooked,
served,
given thanks for,
eaten!

I am their luck, stumbled into;
an extra potato peel in the slop
grabbed quickly, gratefully,
without the strength to question.

I am their songs
begun by mad, angelic voices
which would not be silenced:

which grew wings and flew into their hearts,
and let them escape for a minute
the barbed wires, the towers,
the smokestacks and the soap.

I am their endless stories
retold between endless roll-calls,
between endless hard labour,
between endless beatings,
between endless deaths,
and a moment of sleep.

And through the telling
be safe, beautiful,
full of life.

I am their hope
(some called it God)
when none is possible
because they know no better
because they know nothing else *is* possible.
I am their noble lineage,
their proud ancestry.

I am their priceless heirloom
hidden from murderers
where it could not be found.

I am their surviving words.

Memory

Freedom of Expression, Hate Speech and Holocaust Denial

Irwin Cotler

THE HOLOCAUST evokes for me a sense of awe and reverence—indeed, humility—and I address it with a certain degree of hesitation, and not without a certain measure of pain. For I am reminded of what my parents taught me while still a young boy: that there are things in Jewish history that are too terrible to be *believed*, but not too terrible to have *happened*; that Oswiecim, Majdanek, Dachau... these are beyond vocabulary. For the Holocaust, as Professor Yehuda Bauer stated, is "uniquely unique." It was a war against the Jews in which, as Elie Wiesel put it, "not all victims were Jews, but all Jews were victims".

But if the Holocaust is uniquely unique—if it is beyond vocabulary—it is, arguably, beyond law. But if it is beyond the law, it may also escape the law, so that the very profundity of the horror—be it the Holocaust or its denial—becomes the basis for its immunity from law. Conversely, if law is to address it, it must somehow normalize the evil. Yet the very "normalization," while legally exigent, is somehow existentially unreal. And so the paradox: the very transcendental character of the evil defies legal remedy; while the very use of legal remedy—the "banalization" of evil—is the banality also of the law. An evil, then, that is "uniquely unique" requires an imaginative use of law and legal remedy that is unique, if not uniquely unique.

There is yet another paradox: how is one to be imaginative in speaking of freedom of speech, or freedom of speech in relation to hate propaganda (and the specific hate propaganda of the Holocaust denier), when one is reminded of the words of John Stuart Mill, who in an apology at the beginning of his famous essay titled *On Liberty* said:

> Those to whom nothing which I am about to say will be new, may therefore, I hope, excuse me, if on as subject which for now three centuries has been so often discussed, I venture on one discussion more.[1]

Speaking 140 years after John Stuart Mill uttered his apology, I too must beg your indulgence for beginning still another discussion on the issue of freedom of speech. As I said earlier, the subject matter of my speech—Holocaust denial hate propaganda—appears as difficult to comprehend as the burden of banality surrounding five hundred years of discussion of freedom of expression.

Yet there are some compelling considerations today that justify, and invite, "one discussion more." First, there is the very existential character of the discussion. In other words, we are not simply discussing freedom of speech *in abstracto*; rather, we are discussing the balancing—or even the collision—of two core values: the principle of freedom of speech, on the one hand, and the right of minorities to protection against group vilifying speech, on the other. The philosophic and normative inquiry here, I submit, is more profound and more compelling than that addressed by Mill.

Second, there are important legal, indeed constitutional, considerations which did not even arise for Mill, but which today have not only a national but international juridical resonance. More particularly: Is anti-hate legislation—the panoply of civil and criminal remedies developed to combat hate literature—constitutional? How does one address, let alone determine, its constitutionality? Is such anti-hate legislation, given the enormity but ephemeral character of the evil, necessarily overbroad and all-encompassing, or is it rendered void by its vagueness? And, if narrowly tailored so as to meet a constitutional challenge, can it be effective in combatting the evil?

Third, there are important sociological considerations which Mill did not face, or could not even imagine. In a word, there is a veritable explosion today of racist hate speech—a global web of hate—not only of a kind and character that Mill could not envisage, but conveyed by a technology of cybernate that even post-modernists did not foresee.

Fourth, there is a particular socio-legal dynamic that did not, and could not, obtain in Mill's time, or at any time since. I am referring to the explosion of "Holocaust denial"—perhaps the most obscene form of hate propaganda—and the little-known but not insignificant fact that Canada has emerged as one of the world centres for hate-propaganda litigation in general, and Holocaust-denial litigation in particular. This is not because Canada is an international centre for Holocaust deniers, or a centre for the international dissemination of hate propaganda; rather, it is because Canada, while certainly not without its hate propagandists,[2] has developed one of the most comprehensive legal regimes to combat hate propaganda.

Indeed, it is the dialectical, or what I would call dynamic, encounter between the rise in hate speech, on the one hand, and the existence of a comprehensive legal scheme to combat it, on the other, which has produced this Holocaust-denial and hate-propaganda litigation. It is an encounter, and litigation, that would have been alien to Mill; but it is an encounter and an experience that has international, cultural and legal significance.

There is a fifth consideration—a psychological one—that was again unknown to Mill, and is only now becoming known to us. I am referring to the serious individual and societal harm resulting from this scurrilous speech, harm that is only now being appreciated as a veritable assault on our psyches with catastrophic effects for our polity.

Sixth, there are considerations of an international juridical character that were neither existing nor even foreseeable in Mill's time. There exists an international legal regime, anchored in international treaty law, which not only prohibits racist hate speech and excludes it from the ambit of "protected speech," but also obliges state parties to these treaties, like Canada, to enact measures to combat such malicious speech. If countries like Canada had not enacted such measures, they would now be obliged to do so; once enacted, they cannot lightly be set aside.

One can see, therefore, that there are a variety of considerations of an existential, philosophical, legal, sociological, psychological, and international character that simply were not part of Mill's analysis some 140 years ago. Indeed, these considerations alone warrant "one discussion more," and must necessarily be factored into any discussion of free speech and hate propaganda today. This "one discussion more" may also be said to be warranted by its taking place against the backdrop of the most celebrated hate speech litigation in the history of Canadian jurisprudence—and one that embraces all the above considerations. It includes, most notably, the historic trilogy of the *Keegstra,*[3] *Andrews,*[4] and *Taylor*[5] cases, decided together by the Supreme Court of Canada in 1990 and for which *Keegstra* has become both metaphor and message; the *cause célèbre* involving Ernst Zundel,[6] one of the world's foremost Holocaust deniers; still another *cause célèbre,* involving a complaint lodged under the New Brunswick Human Rights Act against Moncton school teacher and hate propagandist Malcolm Ross, currently on appeal to the Supreme Court; and, particularly in the past few years, numerous lower court decisions under the federal and provincial human-rights codes involving hate propaganda, notably the *Heritage Front* case in Ontario,[7] the *Harcus* case in Manitoba,[8] the *Bell* case in Saskatchewan,[9] the *Aryan Nations* case in Alberta,[10] and the *Liberty Net* cases in British Columbia.[11]

In each of the major hate speech cases decided under the *Charter* thus far there have been two central issues before the courts, issues that are likely to be the central concerns of any court in a democratic society called upon to decide a racial incitement case. The first issue is whether incitement to racial and religious hatred can be defined as "protected speech" under the *Charter*'s section 2(b) guarantee of freedom of expression. The second issue, even assuming that racial incitement is *prima facie* protected speech, is whether, and indeed not just whether but how and to what extent, hate propaganda can nonetheless be subject, in the words of the balancing principle stated in section 1 of the *Charter,* to "such reasonable limits prescribed by law as can be demonstrably justified in a free and democratic society."[12]

The Canadian jurisprudential experience is particularly significant as it has generated one of the more instructive and compelling sets of legal precedents and principles respecting this genre of hate speech litigation and the principle of freedom of expression in the world today. Indeed, the importance of these precedents and principles flows from the very spectrum of factors set forth above that make "one discussion more" as pertinent as it is instructive. First, the Canadian multicultural mosaic has been experiencing a dramatic increase in both hate speech and hate crimes targeting vulnerable minorities, mirroring thereby what has become a general, and not just Canadian, phenomenon. Second, and as a corollary, the dynamic and dialectical encounter between the rise in racist hate speech and the existence in Canada of a comprehensive legal regime to combat it not only reflects this situation elsewhere, but emerges as a compelling case-study of both the efficacy and validity of legal remedy.

Third, the encounter, as demonstrated by Canadian jurisprudence, is not only a legal one but a philosophic one; for what is at issue is not only the efficacy or validity of legal remedy, but the balancing under the *Charter* of two fundamental normative principles: on the one hand, freedom of expression as the lifeblood of democracy and of the autonomy of the individual; and, on the other, the right of vulnerable minorities to protection against discriminatory expression and its related humiliation, degradation, and injury. In effect, what is at stake in the invocation of these core principles, at the most profound and painful level, is the litigation of the values of a nation—the competing visions of what constitutes a free and democratic society.

Fourth, the *Charter* emerges in these cases as a double-edged constitutional sword, invoked by both the purveyors and the targets of hate propaganda alike. The "hate-mongers" shield themselves behind the freedom of expression principle. The victims shield themselves behind the right to protection against group-vilifying speech. Fifth, the Supreme Court of Canada, in its hate-propaganda decisions, has articulated a series of principles and perspectives which have placed Canada in the forefront internationally in the development of a distinguishable "hate-speech" jurisprudence for a free and democratic society. Our Supreme Court has done so by pouring content into the *Charter*'s dual guarantee of freedom of expression and non-discrimination, and by using international human rights law as an interpretive source.

Accordingly, this "one discussion more" respecting freedom of expression and hate speech will be organized around three principal topics: a snapshot of the nature and extent of the present hate movement and of hate propaganda in Canada; a review of the Canadian legal regime of hate-propaganda regulation, including a typology of legal remedies to combat hate speech, including in particular a summary of the hate-speech offence in the *Criminal Code*; and, a discussion of the major principles and perspectives articulated by the Supreme Court of Canada in seeking to "balance" competing rights—the freedom to express hate and the right to protection against group-vilifying speech.

The analysis will then conclude with a summary of the basic indices for developing a hate-speech jurisprudence under the *Charter*, or the basic indices underlying a jurisprudence of free speech, non-discrimination and respect for human dignity in a free and democratic society.

I. Nature and Extent of Hate Propaganda in Canada

The Canadian hate movement is a closely-knit group of mainly anti-Semitic and white-supremacist organizations as well as individual purveyors of hate, whose uniting feature is that they all engage in the practice of "generally irrational and malicious abuse of certain identifiable minority groups."[13] The abuse usually takes one of two forms: it can be violent or destructive crime inflicted directly upon members of these minority groups or against their personal or communal property; or the abuse can take the form of hate propaganda—the public promotion of hatred or contempt against vulnerable minorities with Holocaust denial as an organizing motif. The latter, *inter alia*, "propagates the myth that a certain group poses some kind of menace or threat, and in so doing contains an express or implied invitation to mobilize against the group in question."[14] The methods and media through which hate-mongers have endeavoured to spread their message are numerous, and include concerts, rallies, training camps, political campaigns, academic movements, films, radio and television programming, advertisements, posters, audio tapes, telephone hate lines, speeches, teaching, newspaper articles, letters to the editor, as well as the standard methods of promoting hate: pamphlets, books, mailings and the like. Hate propaganda has also begun to appear in significant quantities on computer bulletin boards and on the Internet.[15]

In recent years, the number of hate groups and prominent individual hate-mongers in Canada has multiplied. In addition to the Ku Klux Klan, which has itself experienced a resurgence in some provinces since the late 1980s,[16] there is now a veritable web of hate movements—the Western Guard, the Northern Hammerskins, the Nationalist Party of Canada, Citizens for Foreign Aid Reform, the Church of the Creator, and the currently dominant Heritage Front, to name only the best-known groups. As well, American hate groups such as the Aryan Nations, White Aryan Resistance and others have tried with varying success to get their message heard in Canada, and have established a network of links with their Canadian counterparts.[17] Meanwhile, Jim Keegstra, Ernst Zundel and Malcolm Ross, among others, are not only the case names of the historic *Charter* hate-speech jurisprudence, but passwords into the popular culture of hate propaganda.

It is often assumed that the individuals who make up the hate movement inhabit the so-called "fringes" of an otherwise moderate and rational society. Yet not all hate-mongers are social outcasts, nor does the fact of their extremism appear to diminish their capacity to grow as a movement and to publicize their ideas. Two of Canada's most notorious promoters of hatred towards minorities—Jim Keegstra and Malcolm Ross—were school teachers, and Keegstra was also at one time the mayor of Eckville, Alberta, the town in which he taught. Ernst Zundel, while characterized as somewhat of a social misfit, nevertheless continues, through his Samisdat Publishing company, to make Canada one of the most important sources of anti-Semitic and Holocaust-denial literature in the world, printing hate propaganda in fifteen languages to service the hate movements in forty countries across the globe.[18] Indeed, in the past five years the size and degree of activity of the hate movement in Canada have altered significantly, producing four intimately inter-related trends.

First, there has been a dramatic increase in the number, organization and membership of the hate groups. Although membership figures are difficult to document due to the transient quality of many of the groups, it is estimated that, whereas there were only approximately two hundred serious leaders of the various anti-Semitic and white-supremacist groups during the 1980s, there are today probably at least two thousand committed members, with an additional two thousand casual followers in local cells across the country.[19] This increase is due in large part to a policy of active recruitment recently put into practice by some groups, notably the Heritage Front and the Church of the Creator, with one of the favoured methods being recruitment among the young through the dissemination of hate propaganda at high schools and on university campuses.[20] Admittedly, some of the dominant hate groups such as the Heritage Front and the Ku Klux Klan have experienced financial and organizational setbacks in the past two years due to such factors as fines, judicial cease-and-desist orders, the imprisonment of leaders for contempt of court, and the exposure and defection of major players such as Grant Bristow and Elisse Hategan.[21] This is in itself suggestive of the efficacy of legal remedy. Other groups originating south of the border are rising to take their place, however, while Samisdat Publishing has continued its propagation of hate with renewed vigour since Ernst Zundel's victory at the Supreme Court,[22] reflecting not so much the failure of legal remedy as the invalidity of a particular legal remedy (namely, the "false news" provision of the *Criminal Code*) and the failure to invoke an alternative remedy.

Second, the age and outlook of the hate movement have changed. Whereas in the not-so-distant past most hate groups were composed of fairly inert middle-aged males, today's hate-mongers are often much younger (18-20 years old) and of both sexes.[23] Moreover, the members of today's hate groups are not just racists who enjoy the company of others with like views, but persons harbouring both an angry grievance at "the establishment" and an angry resentment of "the other". One manifestation of this phenomenon is the recent rise in the number of skinheads in Canada and the United States.[24] Some commentators argue that the anger and intolerance of today's youth is further exacerbated by poor economic times, generating a more intensified ill-will and hostility towards immigrants as well as towards society's traditional scapegoats— Jews, Asians, Natives, African-Canadians, and others.[25]

Third, the rise in youth hate has corresponded with an *increase in violence* perpetrated by members of hate groups in the 1990s. A 1993 Canadian Security and Intelligence Service (CSIS) report on hate groups acknowledged "a noticeable shift towards more violence-prone groups" in Canada in this decade,[26] and the League for Human Rights of B'nai Brith Canada has pointed to 1993 as the year in which Canadian racism came "out of the closet and into our streets" in the form of violent crime as well as the active recruitment of new members.[27] A recent study commissioned by the federal Department of Justice and conducted by University of Ottawa criminologist Julian Roberts suggests that the number of hate-motivated crimes perpetrated annually in Canada has risen in this decade to approximately 9000.[28] This view is shared by specialists in the area of hate crimes who point out that the incidence of hate-motivated criminal activity has increased recently, and who suggest that the trend is continuing to worsen.[29] Symptom and symbol of the new violent face of the hate movement is the increased attention and resources devoted by police and various levels of government to combatting hate crime and its underlying causes. Police departments in Ottawa, Toronto and Winnipeg have recently established special hate crime units,[30] while Parliament in June 1995 passed a hate-crimes amendment to the *Criminal Code,* which directs judges to increase the severity of criminal sentences where it is proved that a crime was motivated by hatred of the victim's race, religion, ethnic origin or sexual preference.[31]

Fourth and finally, the 1990s have witnessed a rather dramatic increase in the quantity of reported hate in Canada. The League for Human Rights of B'nai Brith Canada, which has maintained records of anti-Semitic incidents in Canada since 1982, reported in its *1994 Audit of Anti-Semitic Incidents* that it had received the greatest number of complaints of anti-Semitic harassment and vandalism ever. The 290 complaints received in 1994 constitute a 13 percent increase over the 256 received in 1993, and a huge 130 percent increase over the average of 126 incidents reported over the years 1982-1992. In particular, between 1990 and 1994, the average annual number of complaints of anti-Semitic "harassment" (a category which covers complaints regarding hate propaganda) was 170, while the average during the 1980s was only 52. Similarly, the average annual number of complaints of anti-Semitic vandalism was 98 during 1993 and 1994, compared to an average of 43 incidents per year during the preceding years.[32] Although these statistics may not be a reliable indicator of an actual increase in hate-motivated activity in Canada (for instance, they may be evidence of an increased willingness of victims to come forward, or of greater awareness on the part of victims that records of hate-motivated incidents are being kept), they do indicate a greatly increased public awareness of the hate movement and of its broader social implications. Combined with the likelihood that the hate movement is in fact growing in Canada in the 1990s,[33] the rise in reported hate suggests that Canadians—and in particular Canadians who are members of targeted minority groups—today live their lives in the shadow of an expanding culture of hate.

II. The Canadian Legal Regime of Hate Propaganda Regulation—A Typology of Remedies —The Criminalization of Hate Speech

Canada has one of the most comprehensive legal regimes in the world, including a spectrum of remedies, to combat hate propaganda. Both the federal and provincial governments have enacted laws which seek either to punish individual purveyors of hate, or to remedy the discrimination perpetrated through hate propaganda, often by limiting or forbidding its expression by a particular individual or group. The legislation is of several different types. At the federal level, Parliament has criminalized three distinct forms of hate propagation—advocacy of genocide, public incitement of hatred, and wilful promotion of hatred—and has otherwise restricted the ability of citizens to promote hatred, through various provisions in the *Criminal Code,* the *Canadian Human Rights Act,* the *Canada Post Corporation Act,* and the *Customs Tariff Act.* The provinces, although excluded by Parliament's jurisdiction over criminal law from actually punishing as such those who promote hatred against identifiable groups, have also attempted to remedy some of the harms effected by hate-mongers, through various types of human-rights legislation. In the private law area, while Canadian courts appear to have foreclosed a common law of discrimination, Quebec civil law appears to offer a delictual remedy. And international human-rights law has emerged in the post-*Charter* universe as a relevant and persuasive source in the invocation and application of legal remedy.

The enactment, in particular, of Section 319(2) of the *Criminal Code,* and the advent of the *Charter*, have marked a watershed in "hate-speech" jurisprudence. Indeed, Section 319(2) of the *Criminal Code* is the only hate-propaganda offence which has so far been challenged as violating Section 2(b) of the *Charter* which guarantees freedom of expression. The Section reads as follows:

> 319. (2) Every one who, by communicating statements, other than in private conversation, wilfully promotes hatred against any identifiable group is guilty of:
> > (a) an indictable offence and is liable to imprisonment for a term not exceeding two years; or
> > (b) an offence punishable on summary conviction.

The leading cases challenging this Section are *R. v. Keegstra* and *R. v. Andrews and Smith,* decided concurrently by the Supreme Court in 1990, at which time the Court upheld by a narrow 4-3 margin the constitutional validity of the crime of wilfully promoting hatred. The Court also upheld the anti-hate provisions of the *Canadian Human Rights Act* in the *Taylor* case, which had been joined with *Keegstra* and *Andrews* for hearing. What follows is a "snapshot" of the historic *Keegstra* case, whose judgement alone runs over one hundred pages and which transformed the free-speech / hate-propaganda jurisprudence in this country.

James Keegstra was a high school teacher in the small town of Eckville, Alberta, from the early 1970s until his dismissal in 1982. For the better part of a decade, he imposed virulently anti-Semitic views upon his students in the classroom. The character of Keegstra's hate propaganda was succinctly summarized in the majority judgement of Chief Justice Dickson in the Supreme Court:

> Mr. Keegstra's teachings attributed various evil qualities to Jews. He thus described Jews to his pupils as "treacherous," "subversive," "sadistic," "money-loving," "power hungry" and "child killers." He taught his classes that Jewish people seek to destroy Christianity and are responsible for depressions, anarchy, chaos, wars and revolution. According to Mr. Keegstra, Jews "created the Holocaust to gain sympathy" and, in contrast to the open and honest Christians, were said to be deceptive, secretive and inherently

evil. Mr. Keegstra expected his students to reproduce his teachings in class and on exams. If they failed to do so, their marks suffered.[34]

Indeed, the *Keegstra* and *Zundel* cases are both dramatic case studies of Holocaust-denial hate propaganda and Holocaust-denial litigation. They vividly illustrate that, if racist hate propaganda is one of the more insidious manifestations of racism, then Holocaust denial is among the most insidious forms of racist hate propaganda. The cases also demonstrate that Holocaust deniers are not a bunch of social misfits, but part of an increasingly sophisticated and interconnected international movement whose "assault on memory and truth"[35] is the "cutting edge" of anti-Semitism old and new, with all the attending harm and injury that such racist incitement connotes.

But the danger of this international hate movement does not lie only in its denial of the Holocaust, however harmful or injurious such denial may be. Rather, it resides first in the imputation of this "hoax" to the Jews, in the libel that the Jews "fabricated" this hoax so that they could illegally extort reparations from Germany. This constitutes a teaching of contempt and incitement to hatred and violence against the "evil Jew thief." A second danger lies in its whitewashing of the worst crimes and criminals in history. In effect, the Holocaust-denial movement is an international criminal conspiracy to cover up the crime of genocide against the Jewish people, excoriating the crimes of the Jews as it rehabilitates the crimes of the Nazis.

Accordingly, it is not surprising that Austria, France, Germany, Israel and Switzerland have adopted laws to combat this insidious form of hate propaganda, and that the European Parliament itself has called for legislation to prohibit Holocaust denial. For Canada, which has become a world centre of Holocaust denial litigation, and an important supply source for the international hate movement world-wide, the situation might well warrant the consideration of the adoption of a *lex specialis* to prohibit this egregious form of racist propaganda.

III. Hate Speech Jurisprudence: Principles and Perspectives

As set forth above, the "hate speech" jurisprudence of the Supreme Court of Canada, particularly as represented in the historic trilogy of *Keegstra*, *Smith and Andrews*, and *Taylor*, has articulated a series of principles and perspectives which may help to pour content into what American First Amendment scholar Fred Schauer has called the "multiple tests, rules, and principles" reflecting "the [extraordinary] diversity of communication experiences,"[36] which is a matter of particular importance as the rise in racist hate propaganda is now an international and not just domestic phenomenon.

What follows is a distillation from the case-law of some of these interpretive principles and perspectives. It offers a looking glass into the considerations that ought to be factored into any analysis of hate speech, freedom of expression, and non-discrimination, and seeks to strike a balance between competing normative principles.

Principle 1: "Chartering" Rights: The Constitutionalization of Freedom of Expression—The "Lifeblood of Democracy"

Section 1 of the *Charter* sets forth the fundamental premise for balancing competing rights and interests: "The *Canadian Charter of Rights and Freedoms* guarantees the rights and freedoms set out in it subject only to such reasonable limits prescribed by law as can be demonstrably justified in a free and democratic society." Section 2(b) constitutionalizes freedom of expression. It guarantees "everyone ... freedom of thought, belief, opinion and expression, including freedom of the press and other media of communication."

In the words of the Supreme Court, the rights and freedoms guaranteed by the *Charter*, such as freedom of expression, are to be given "a generous and liberal interpretation", as befits constitutionally entrenched rights. The Constitution, said the Court, in its paraphrase of Paul Freund, "should not be read like a last will and testament, lest it become one."[37]

This by no means suggests that the Canadian experience is irrelevant to societies that do not have an entrenched Charter of Rights. As stated by the Supreme Court, "[The notion] that freedom to express oneself openly and fully is of crucial importance in a free and democratic society was recognized by Canadian Courts prior to the enactment of the *Charter*... freedom of expression was seen as an essential value of Canadian Parliamentary democracy."[38] Therefore, freedom of expression was regarded as a "core" right even before the advent of the *Charter*, a perspective that ought to be instructive for societies without a constitutionally entrenched Bill of Rights.

What the Canadian experience demonstrates is that a constitutionally entrenched *Charter* of Rights invites "a more careful and generous study of the values informing the freedom,"[39] and therefore commends itself to those concerned with a more enhanced promotion and protection of human rights generally. But while it regards freedom of expression as "the lifeblood of democracy", it acknowledges that it may be subject to reasonable and demonstrably justified limits; and, as will be seen below, this balancing act involves existential as well as legal questions—rights in collision as well as rights in the balance. On the one hand, there is the "fundamental" right of free speech, a core principle; on the other hand, there is the right to protection against group-vilifying speech—also a core principle. What is at stake, as we have seen, is the litigation of the values of a nation.

Accordingly, one cannot say that those who challenge anti-hate legislation are the only civil libertarians, or the only ones promotive of free speech; or that those who support anti-hate legislation are not really civil libertarians, or are against free speech; rather, there are good civil libertarians and good free speech people on both sides of the issue. Thus, one can adhere to the notion of free speech as the lifeblood of democracy and still support anti-hate legislation.

Principle 2: Freedom of Expression—Fundamental—but Not an Absolute Right
Freedom of expression, then, as Professor Abraham Goldstein has put it, "is not absolute, however much so many persist in talking as if it is."[40] Indeed, in every free and democratic society certain forms and categories of expression are clearly regarded as being outside the ambit of protected speech. Even in the United States, certain categories of speech—obscenity, personal libel, and "fighting words"—are not protected by the First Amendment; such utterances, said the U.S.

Supreme Court in *Chaplinsky*, "are no essential part of any exposition of ideas, and are of such slight social value as a step to the truth that any benefit ... is clearly outweighed by the social interest in order and morality,"[41] while some American scholars argue that *Beauharnais v. Illinois*,[42] which upheld the constitutionality of a group libel ordinance, is still good law.

All free and democratic societies have recognized certain limitations on freedom of expression in the interest of national security, such as prohibitions against treasonable speech; or limitations in the interest of public order and good morals, such as prohibitions against obscenity, pornography, or disturbing the public peace; or limitations in the interest of privacy and reputation, such as prohibitions respecting libel and defamation; or limitations in the interest of consumer protection, such as prohibitions respecting misleading advertising; and the like.

Principle 3: The Scope of Freedom of Expression and the "Purposive" Theory of Interpretation

In the view of the Canadian Supreme Court, the proper approach to determining the ambit of freedom of expression and the "pressing and substantial concerns" that may authorize its limitation is a *purposive* one. This principle of interpretation was set forth by then Chief Justice Dickson in the *Big M. Drug Mart Ltd.* case as follows: "The meaning of a right or a freedom guaranteed by the *Charter* was to be ascertained by an analysis of the purpose of such a guarantee; it was to be understood, in other words, in the light of the interests it was meant to protect."[43]

In the *Keegstra* case, the Court reiterated the three-pronged purposive rationale for freedom of expression that it had earlier articulated in the *Irwin Toy* case as follows:

(1) seeking and attaining truth is an inherently good activity;
(2) participation in social and political decision-making is to be fostered and encouraged; and
(3) diversity in forms of individual self-fulfilment and human flourishing ought to be cultivated in a tolerant and welcoming environment for the sake of both those who convey a meaning and those to whom a meaning is conveyed.[44]

Hate-mongering, however, according to the Court, constitutes an assault on these very values and interests sought to be protected by freedom of expression as follows: first, hate-mongering, and particularly Holocaust denial hate propaganda, is not only incompatible with a "competitive marketplace of ideas which will enhance the search for truth," but it represents the very *antithesis* of the search for truth in a marketplace of ideas.[45] Second, it is antithetical to participation in demo-cratic self-government and constitutes a "destructive assault" on that very government.[46] Third, it is utterly incompatible with a claim to "personal growth and self-realization"; rather, it is analogous to the claim that one is "fulfilled" by expressing oneself "violently."[47] Citing studies showing that victims of group vilification may suffer loss of self-esteem and experience self-abasement,[48] the Court found that incitement to racial hatred constitutes an assault on the potential for "self-realization" of the target group and its members. It is not surprising, then, that the Court anchored its reasons for judgement in the "catastrophic effects of racism."[49]

Principle 4:   Freedom of Expression and the "Contextual" Principle

A fourth principle of interpretation, or "building block,"[50] as Madame Justice Bertha Wilson characterized it, is that of the "contextual" principle. The contextual principle, as with the purposive principle, is relevant both in the interpretation of the ambit of a right and the assessment of the validity of legislation to limit it.

As the Supreme Court put it in *Keegstra*, "it is important not to lose sight of factual circumstances in undertaking an analysis of freedom of expression and hate propaganda, for these shape a court's view of both the right or freedom at stake and the limit proposed by the state; neither can be surveyed in the abstract".[51] As Justice Wilson said in *Edmonton Journal*, referring to what she termed the "contextual approach" to *Charter* interpretation:

A particular right or freedom may have a different value depending on the context. It may be, for example, that freedom of expression has greater value in a political context than it does in the context of disclosure of the details of a matrimonial dispute.[52]

In a recent retrospective on the case, Justice Wilson commented that "there was, for example, no point in assessing the value of freedom of speech for balancing purposes in the context of our political institutions if it had come before the court in the context of advertising aimed at children."[53]

One might equally argue, as will be seen through the prism of the principles below, that it makes all the difference in the world if the freedom of expression principle at issue comes before the court in the context of political speech, or in the context of hate speech aimed at disadvantaged minorities. As Justice Wilson concluded on this point, "a contextual as well as purposive interpretation of the right was required for purposes of Section 1 balancing."[54] In the matter of hate-mongering, then, whether the principle of interpretation adopted is the purposive or the contextual one, both interpretations converge in favour of the right of disadvantaged minorities to be protected against group vilification, while maintaining an "expansive" and "liberal" view of freedom of expression itself as a core right.

Principle 5: Freedom of Expression in a Free and Democratic Society

According to Supreme Court doctrine, the interpretation of freedom of expression must involve not only recourse to the purposive character of freedom of expression (section 2(b)), but "to the values and principles of a free and democratic society". This phrase, as the court put it, "requires more than an incantation ... [but] requires some definition ... an elucidation as to the values and principles that [the phrase] invokes."[55]

Such principles, said the court, are not only the genesis of rights and freedoms under the *Charter* generally, but also underlie freedom of expression (Section 2b) in particular. These values and principles include "respect for the inherent dignity of the human person ... [and] respect for cultural and group identity;"[56] accordingly, anti-hate legislation should be seen not as infringing upon free speech but as promoting and protecting the values and principles of a free and democratic society.

Principle 6: Freedom of Expression in Comparative Perspective

In determining whether incitement to racial hatred is a protected form of expression, resort may be had not only to the values and principles of a free and democratic society such as Canada, but also to the legislative experience of other free and democratic societies. An examination of the legislative experience of other free and democratic societies clearly and consistently supports the position that such racist hate speech is not entitled to constitutional protection.[57]

Indeed, by 1966, the Special Committee on Hate Propaganda (hereinafter the Cohen Committee) had already recorded the existence of legislation in a number of countries which sought to proscribe incitement to group hatred. The countries concerned were demonstrably "free and democratic".

Moreover, the legislative pattern since 1966 in these and other free and democratic societies supports the view that not only is such legislation representative of free and democratic societies, but its very purpose is to ensure that such societies remain free and democratic. Indeed, free and democratic societies in every region of the world have now enacted similar legislation, including countries in Asia, the Middle East, and Latin America, as well as the countries of Scandinavia and Western and Eastern Europe. Such legislation can also be found in the countries of the former Soviet Union.

Principle 7:   Freedom of Expression in the Light of "Other Rights and Freedoms"

The Supreme Court has also determined that the principle of freedom of expression must be interpreted in the light of other rights and freedoms sought to be protected by a democracy like Canada. In the words of the court: "The purpose of the right or freedom in question [freedom of expression] is to be sought by reference to ... the meaning and purpose of the other specific rights and freedoms with which it is associated."[58]

It should be noted that the purpose, if not also the effect, of hate speech is to diminish, if not deny, other rights and freedoms, or the rights and freedoms of others; indeed, such hate-mongering is the very antithesis of the values and principles underlying these rights and freedoms. Accordingly, any reading of freedoms of expression in the light of other rights and freedoms admits of no other interpretation than that such hate speech is outside the range of protected expression.

Principle 8: Freedom of Expression and the Principle of Equality: Hate Propaganda as a Discriminatory Practice

If freedom of expression is to be interpreted in the light of other rights and freedoms, a core, and underlying, associated right is that of equality. The denial of other rights and freedoms, or the rights and freedoms of "the other," makes freedom of expression, or group defamation, not just a speech issue, but an equality issue. In the words of Professor Kathleen Mahoney:

> In this trilogy of cases, the majority of the Supreme Court of Canada articulated perspectives on freedom of expression that are more inclusive than exclusive, more communitarian than individualistic, and more aware of the actual impacts of speech on the disadvantaged members of society than has ever before been articulated in a freedom of expression case. The Court advanced an equality approach using a harm-based rationale to support the regulation of hate propaganda as a principle of inequality.[59]

Principle 9: Freedom of Expression, Group Libel, and the "Harms-Based" Rationale

According to the Supreme Court in *Keegstra*, the concern resulting from racist hate-mongering is not, "simply the product of its offensiveness, but stems from the very real harm which it causes."[60] This judicial finding of the "very real harm" from hate-mongering is not only one of the most recent findings on record by a high court, but may be considered a relevant and persuasive authority for other democratic societies. The following excerpt from the *Keegstra* case, anchored in the analysis and findings of the Cohen Committee, is particularly instructive in this regard:

> Essentially, there are two sorts of injury caused by hate propaganda. First, there is harm done to members of the target group. It is indisputable that the emotional damage caused by words may be of grave psychological and social consequence...[61]
>
> In the context of sexual harassment, for example, this court has found that words can in themselves constitute harassment (*Janzen v. Platy Ent. Ltd.*, [1989] 1 S.C.R. 1252, [1989] 4 W.W.R.

39, 25 C.C.E.L. 1, 10 C.H.R.R. D/6205, 59 D.L.R. (4th) 352, 47 C.R.R. 274, 89 C.L.L.C. 17,011, 58 Man. R. (2d) 1, 95 N.R. 81 (sub nom. *Janzen v. Pharos Restaurant*)).

In a similar manner, words and writings that wilfully promote hatred can constitute a serious attack on persons belonging to a racial or religious group, and in this regard the Cohen Committee noted that these persons are humiliated and degraded (p. 214).

In my opinion, a response of humiliation and degradation from an individual targeted by hate propaganda is to be expected. A person's sense of human dignity and belonging to the community at large is closely linked to the concern and respect accorded the groups to which he or she belongs (see Isaiah Berlin, "Two Concepts of Liberty", in *Four Essays on Liberty* (1969), p. 118, at p. 155). The derision, hostility and abuse encouraged by hate propaganda therefore have a severely negative impact on the individual's sense of self-worth and acceptance...

A second harmful effect of hate propaganda which is of pressing and substantial concern is its influence upon society at large. The Cohen Committee noted that individuals can be persuaded to believe "almost anything" (p. 30) if information or ideas are communicated using the right technique and in the proper circumstances (at p. 8).

In the words of the Cohen Committee:

> ... we are less confident in the 20th century that the critical faculties of individuals will be brought to bear on the speech and writing which is directed at them. In the 18th and 19th centuries, there was a widespread belief that man was a rational creature, and that if his mind was trained and liberated from superstition by education, he would always distinguish truth from falsehood, good from evil. So Milton, who said "let truth and falsehood grapple: who ever knew truth put it the worse in a free and open encounter."

We cannot share this faith today in such a simple form. While holding that over the long run, the human mind is repelled by blatant falsehood and seeks the good, it is too often true, in the short run, that emotion displaces reason and individuals perversely reject the demonstrations of truth put before them and forsake the good they know. The successes of modern advertising, the triumphs of impudent propaganda such as Hitler's, have qualified sharply our belief in the rationality of man. We know that under the strain and pressure in times of irritation and frustration, the individual is swayed and even swept away by hysterical, emotional appeals. We act irresponsibly if we ignore the way in which emotion can drive reason from the field.[62]

The Supreme Court's conclusion on this point, relying as it does on the conclusions of the Cohen Committee itself, is particularly relevant today. In the words of the Court:

The threat to self-dignity of target group members is thus matched by the possibility that prejudiced messages will gain some credence, with the attendant result of discrimination, and perhaps even violence, against minority groups in Canadian society. With these dangers in mind, the Cohen Committee made clear in its conclusions that the presence of hate propaganda existed as a baleful and pernicious element, and hence a serious problem, in Canada [63] (at p. 59).

Again, in the words of the Cohen Committee as quoted by the Supreme Court of Canada:

The amount of hate propaganda presently being disseminated [is] probably not sufficient to justify a description of the problem as one of crisis or near crisis proportion. Nevertheless the problem is a serious one. We believe that, given a certain set of socio-economic circumstances, such as a deepening of the emotional tensions or the setting in of a severe business recession, public susceptibility might well increase significantly. Moreover, the potential psychological and social damage of hate propaganda, both to a desensitized majority and to sensitive minority target groups, is incalculable. As Mr. Justice Jackson of the United States Supreme Court wrote in *Beauharnais v. Illinois*, such "sinister abuses of our freedom of expression... can tear apart a society, brutalize its dominant elements, and persecute even to extermination, its minorities."[64]

Principle 10: Freedom of Expression, Hate Propaganda, and International Law

In the words of the Supreme Court, international law may be regarded as "a relevant and persuasive source"[65] for the interpretation of rights and freedoms under the *Charter*. Moreover, as Chief Justice Dickson wrote in *Keegstra*, "no aspect of international human rights has been given attention greater than that focused upon discrimination ... this high concern regarding discrimination has led to the presence in two international human rights documents of articles forbidding the dissemination of hate propaganda."[66]

It follows that reading the freedom of expression principle in light of international human rights law generally, and under these two international human rights treaties in particular,[67] requires that such racial incitement be excluded from the protective ambit of freedom of expression. Any legislative remedy prohibiting the promotion of hatred or contempt against identifiable groups on grounds of their race, religion, colour, or ethnic origin would be in compliance with Canada's international obligations, and indeed have the effect of implementing these international obligations.

Accordingly, the Supreme Court reasoned in *Keegstra*, after a review of international human rights law and jurisprudence, that "it appears that the protection provided freedom of expression by CERD and ICCPR does not extend to cover communications advocating racial or religious hatred."[68] Of crucial importance was the conclusion of the Court that, in assessing the interpretive importance of international human rights law, the "CERD and ICCPR demonstrate that prohibition of hate-promoting expression is considered to be not only compatible with a signatory nation's guarantee of human rights, but is as well an obligatory aspect of this guarantee."[69]

Principle 11: Freedom of Expression and the Multicultural Principle

Freedom of expression must be read in light of Canada as a multicultural democracy; accordingly, it should be interpreted, to quote S.27 of the Canadian Charter of Rights and Freedoms, "in a manner consistent with the preservation and enhancement of the multicultural heritage of Canadians."

In effect, this interpretive principle admits of no other reading than that such hate-mongering is not only an assault on the members of the target group singled out on grounds of their identifiable race or religion, but it is destructive of a multicultural society as a whole; as such, it falls outside the protection of freedom of speech. Conversely, and again to paraphrase Mr. Justice Cory in *Smith and Andrews*, anti-hate legislation is designed not only "to protect identifiable groups in a multicultural society from publicly made statements which wilfully promote hatred against them," as Justice Cory observed, but are designed to "prevent the destruction of our multicultural society."[70]

Principle 12: Freedom of Expression and the Principle of "Abhorrent Speech"

It is important that one distinguish between political speech—where the government, its institutions, and public officials are the target of offensive speech—and abhorrent, racist speech, intended to promote hatred and contempt of vulnerable and targeted minorities. The hate-mongering at issue in *Keegstra*, and in analogous cases is not the libel of public officials as in the *Sullivan* case;[71] or directed against "the world at large" as in the *Cohen* case;[72] but it is hate-mongering wilfully promoted against disadvantaged minorities with intent to degrade, diminish, vilify. In sum, this is not a case of a government legislating in its own self-interest regarding its political agenda, but an affirmative responsibility of governments to protect the inherent human dignity and equal standing of all its citizens.

Principle 13: Freedom of Expression, and the "Slippery Slope"

Those who reject anti-hate legislation on the grounds that such group libel legislation leads us inevitably down the "slippery slope" to censorship, ignore a different "slippery slope"—"a swift slide into a marketplace of ideas in which bad ideas flourish and good ones die."[73] In fact, it is submitted that the more that hateful speech is tolerated, the more likely it is to occur. As Karl Popper put it, the "paradox of tolerance" is that it breeds more intolerance, so that the tolerance of hateful speech results in more, not less, hate speech, in more, not less harm, and in more, not less hateful actions. For tolerance of hate speech risks legitimizing such speech on the grounds that "it can't be all bad if it is not being prohibited." The slippery slope is there—but it may lead not in the direction of more censorship, which the Canadian experience does not demonstrate, but in the direction of more hate, which it does.

Conclusion

The wilful promotion of hatred may be said to be composed of a number of characteristics whose collection is itself representative, if not determinative, of a genre of expression that is beyond the area of protected speech. These characteristics, taken together, provide a set of indices warranting the exclusion from the ambit of protected speech of such a genre of expression; or if such expression is to be considered *prima facie* protected speech, then such anti-hate legislation as is designed to combat it should be regarded as a reasonable limit prescribed by the law as can be demonstrably justified in a free and democratic society. These indices are:

(a) where the genre of expression involves not only the communication of hatred—"one of the most extreme emotions known to human-kind"[74]—but the wilful promotion of such hatred against an identifiable group, an incipiently malevolent and violent act constituting an assault on the inherent dignity of the human person.

(b) where it involves not only an assault on the inherent dignity and worth of the human person, but on the equal worth of all human beings in society. For the systematic, public promotion of hatred against an identifiable group has the effect of reducing the standing and respect of that group and its members in society as a whole, while resulting in the self-abasement of each.

(c) where such hate-mongering not only does not preserve, let alone enhance, a multicultural society such as Canada, but is destructive of it. In the words of Justice Cory, "what a strange and perverse contradiction it would be if the *Charter* of Rights was to be used and interpreted so as to strike down a law aimed at preserving our multicultural heritage."[75]

(d) where the constitutionalization of the wilful promotion of hatred would not only constitute a standing breach of Canada's international obligations under treaties to which it is a party, but a standing breach of its obligation to implement domestic legislation to prohibit such expression. To paraphrase Justice Cory, "what a strange and perverse contradiction it would be if freedom of expression was to be used and interpreted so as to undermine Canada's conformity with international human rights law."

(e) where such hate-mongering is not only destructive of the values and principles of a free and democratic society, and opposite to the legislative experience of other free and democratic societies, but constitutes a standing assault on the values and interests and the purposive rationale underlying protected speech.

(f) where the hate-mongering not only constitutes an assault on the very values and interests underlying freedom of expression, but is destructive of the entitlement of the *target* group to protection from group defamation.

(g) where the hate-mongering not only lays the basis for discrimination against, and debasement of, members of the target group, but engenders, if not encourages, racial and religious discord, while causing injury to the community as a whole.

(h) where such hate-mongering not only does not partake in the conveyance of ideas or meaning of any kind, but is utterly without any redeeming value whatever.

The wilful promotion of hatred is not only an assault on a free and democratic society, but is an assault on its core principle—free speech. To allow racist hate speech to be protected speech under the *Charter* is to give democracy—and hate speech—a bad name.

Peter Kleinmann's Reflections on Returning to Auschwitz and Flossenbürg

Naomi Kramer

I RECENTLY RETURNED from a trip to the commemorative events of the fiftieth anniversary of the liberation of Flossenbürg concentration camp where, fifty years ago, I was freed from Nazi oppression. Prior to the commemoration I revisited Auschwitz. The journey prompted thoughts about the meaning that this experience has for the world we live in today.

As we approach another epoch in the annals of the *Shoah*, how we view the past and record this event is foremost in the minds of survivors.

That which one cannot speak of is doomed to silence.

It is incumbent on survivors to recount their experiences. We are not only obliged to speak for our fellow Jews who perished, but also to bear witness, ensuring that the past is recorded according to our testimony and not interpreted only through the model of Nazi bureaucracy and the perspectives of the perpetrators and collaborators.

The suffering of Jews and the thousands of Jews who perished in this camp was largely unrecognized at the commemorative "celebration" organized by the Bavarian Government, which took place on 23 April 1995 in Flossenbürg, Germany.

Because there is little physical evidence that can serve as a silent witness, we, the survivors, are compelled to come forward with our testimony. As I walked through the grounds on which fifty years ago I had been selected to die because I was a *Muselmann*, a walking skeleton, I found recently constructed homes where the barracks had once stood. Families now live in former residences of the SS, and conduct their lives unaware of the previous inhabitants. All traces of the Messerschmitt factory where I was used as slave labour have vanished. In this factory thousands of inmates died of starvation and as a result of intolerable working conditions. Labour was a replaceable resource and an indispensable element of the Nazi war economy. The brief three-month life expectancy of a slave was considered a bonus to those who orchestrated the industry of death.

The quarry, in which thousands perished as easily replaceable products of brutal working conditions, is now owned and operated by the Bavarian government. Much of the same equipment and machinery used by the inmates fifty years ago is still maintained. Here the atrocities of the past are known only to those who bring their memories or knowledge with them.

The watchtower used by the SS guards to oversee inmates as they marched from the barracks through the centre of the village to the quarry is today a news kiosk where one can purchase souvenir postcards of Flossenbürg on which unidentified pictures of the former SS guard tower are juxtaposed incongruously with photographs of the town chapel. Flossenbürgers are sold. The inadequacy of language is painfully obvious in the use of the word Flossenbürger. To the survivor this usage is a desecration of the anguish and hardship suffered there

The former *Appelplatz*, where the daily roll call was taken, is now a combination parking lot and children's playground. The laundry and latrines, today a textile factory, were located on the perimeter of this space where men became numbers, faceless presences forced to stand for hours on end, yet refusing to surrender their humanity to their brutal torturers.

The passing of time presents a dilemma to survivors and indeed the world. If we are not left with any of the physical remnants, and such is the case in most of the killing centres, then how do we accurately convey the history? Are we more vulnerable to Holocaust denial? If we restore and preserve the killing centres are we at risk of being accused of fabricating a past? These are questions that occurred to me as I watched a labourer toil with a pneumatic drill under the *Arbeit Macht Frei* sign in Auschwitz. The administration of the State Museum of Auschwitz is installing a plumbing system to accommodate the needs of its 250 employees. The 400,000 internees in this former Auschwitz I / Birkenau /

Buna-Monowitz concentration, killing and forced labour complex did not have such conveniences.

I was liberated by the Ninetieth Infantry of the American army. My life was forever changed and although I was freed from captivity I have always carried with me the tragic outcome of these twelve months. The loss of my family and friends never faded; there are only moments of reprieve. Was liberation possible when survivors' lives were shattered by the annihilation of families and communities, and indelibly marked by months, even years of inhumane treatment? Once again, the limits of language are revealed in the word "liberation."

While in Auschwitz, I met a young historian who found it impossible to consider my testimony credible because it was incompatible with the Nazi records on which he based his interpretation of history. The number 83150, which I had been given upon arrival in Auschwitz, was recorded in the archives as having been assigned to another inmate who was registered as SB (*Sonderbehandlung*), the German code for death by gassing. Because it was not customary for the meticulous record-keeping Nazis to give the same number to two people, or to assign numbers in Auschwitz to those who were being deported to other forced labour camps, I found myself in the bizarre situation of having to defend the fact that the Nazis had indeed branded me 83150 in Auschwitz. This defense was necessary despite the substantiating documentation from the American military I had with me.

Only after much discussion of alternative hypotheses did this young man finally concede that, in Auschwitz, traditional investigative models used in historical research are inadequate because there was no order as we know it, and the unfathomable was possible. He then suggested that since the Nazis realized they were not likely to be victors on the front lines, and concurrently escalated deportations of Hungarian Jews to allow for as many as ten thousand people a day to be killed in the gas chambers of Auschwitz, the procedure for assigning numbers may have changed. This led him to reconsider my testimony and concede that it was possible that I had been numbered in Auschwitz and not, as he originally insisted, in Gross-Rosen, the forced labour camp where I was subsequently

Top: Flossenbürg Camp showing the SS administrative building (left, centre), the barracks which housed the SS troops (right), and the casino and brothel used by the SS (long white building in background).
Bottom: The Flossenbürg crematorium (left) showing the chute which facilitated the transport of bodies.
Courtesy of the Kleinmann Family Foundation.

Peter Kleinmann in Frankfurt airport, 1995.
Photo: Naomi Kramer

deported.

The imaginative leap, taking him outside the usual Nazi methods of number assignment, permitted him to suggest that perhaps this occurred because, in their haste to murder Jews and forward much-needed civilian clothing to labourers in the Buna-Monowitz complex, the Nazis may not have taken the time to remove numbers from the uniforms of their victims before redistributing them to the new arrivals. At this time, in May and June of 1944, transports included up to fourteen thousand people a day. During this mayhem, when the crematoria operated twenty-four hours a day, a Polish Jew, number 83150, was gassed and it is possible that Dezider Wolfe Kleinmann was the recipient of his uniform bearing the number 83150.

This analysis could have a significant impact on the writing of the history of Auschwitz. It will never be known how many Jews were not included in statistics, for, as in my case, they could not have been counted because those doing the counting assumed the same number could not have been used for two people. Interpretation and reality are intricately interwoven and one's biases shape the knowledge that is acquired.

Later during the same trip I visited the former Dachau concentration camp. In the archives there, I discovered the documentation detailing the journey my father took to his death. I last saw my father in Auschwitz. From there he was deported to a labour camp in Warsaw and I to Gross-Rosen. Despite this our numbers were 87232 and 83150, which could only have been the case if they were assigned in the same camp. Ironically it was the fastidious records of the Nazis which confirmed my memory.

The paradox for Holocaust survivors is that, while life is lived in the present, our memories are omnipresent. Even more than this, these memories define us. We cannot and must not forget the past. Those who have not experienced the absolute core of humiliation and degradation cannot fathom us and will never understand.

The array of commemorative events in Flossenbürg had very little relevance for Jewish survivors. Christian clergy marched through the camp with the German flag, adjourning for a service in the Christian chapel. They conducted what was referred to as the celebration of liberation. Later in the afternoon a Christian youth choir gave a concert in the Valley of Death, so named because the ashes from the crematoria were scattered over this area.

While this took place, behind concrete posts that were once wrapped with electrified barbed wire caging the camp, German military police stood on guard, evoking memories of the SS, in the towers and patrolling the camp fifty years ago. Was this image appropriate for the commemoration?

Outside the chapel, in front of a small stone monument, a handful of Jews gathered to say *Kaddish* while the world watched the "commemoration / "celebration" via satellite broadcast. Was this an appropriate ritual marking the liberation of former Jewish inmates in the war against Jews?

The recently constructed synagogue in the camp would have remained closed if the delegates from the group I was with had not insisted that it be unlocked as a symbolic gesture to those Jews whose cries could still be heard, if only we would listen. Was this a fitting and dignified response to honour the memory of those who perished?

This separation of commemoration by Christians and Jews does not inspire hope for a future marked by dialogue and cooperation. No attempt was made to gather survivor testimony, or at the very least, to systematically register the names and addresses of those who attended. Given that this may have been the last opportunity of such magnitude to detail and record the historical events of the Flossenbürg concentration camp, one must question the motivation of the organizers for having neglected to do so. Was this event simply staged for the media and their audiences?

The fiftieth anniversary of the liberation of the camps is a time for reflection and a time for academics, artists, clergy, scholars and survivors to engage in dialogue about the transmission of this legacy. One should not repeat the mistakes of a nation whose members were all too willing to accept the teachings and edicts of authority. From 1933 to 1945 the great majority of German citizens accepted Nazi racial ideology without question. Ordinary people went home at night to their families after spending their days murdering and acting on behalf of a killing machine implementing the atrocities of the *Shoah*.

Our collective memory will be determined in part by the monuments and memorials we erect. Monuments and commemorations can turn the most poignant memories to stone if they are insensitively created and do not evoke the emotional response intended. On the other hand, appropriate monuments and commemorations will arouse within visitors a social conscience, or function as a catalyst inspiring them to action.

The monument and legacy of the *Shoah* is to be found in our future, a future characterized by communication between young people from different countries promoting global understanding in defiance of nationalism, religious fanaticism and ethno-centrism. It is through the transmission of the memory of the survivors that a shared legacy will be provided, one that is characterized by a commitment to freedom and the protection of human rights.

If moral behaviour is taught and not an innate quality of human existence, there is hope for change and for a future that ensures all people may live by their beliefs rather than be forced to conceal them through fear of discrimination and death. Everyone has the capacity to give freedom to all mankind if they care enough and assume this moral responsibility. We must continue to break the conspiracy of silence that characterized the world's reaction to the Jewish plight fifty years ago. We must be vigilant in our teaching of and fight against current atrocities occurring in Bosnia, Rwanda, Sri Lanka, Zaire...

Memory without consequence is futile.

Working for Oskar Schindler

Stefan Lesniak

TODAY WE HEAR from a variety of sources which distort the history of the Second World War and deny the fact of the Holocaust. There is a worldwide resurgence of neo-Nazism, anti-Semitism, genocide and racial cleansing. Furthermore, many schools today do not teach world history to their students. The people who have gone through the Holocaust in Hitler's Europe are getting old and dying off. It is therefore necessary for those of us who still survive, to bear witness and inform the younger generations of the unbelievable madness that took place a long time ago and which should never be allowed to happen again.

Knowing the past is necessary in order to understand the present and help us to decide where we want to go in the future.

The film *Schindler's List* would seem like an unbelievable fairy tale unless understood in the context of World War II. World War II was about a madman named Adolf Hitler and his Nazi Party who came to power in Germany in 1933. Hitler promised the German people that his regime would last a thousand years, and their National Anthem was changed to "*Deutchland, Deutchland uber alles, uber alles in der Welt,*" which translated means "Germany, Germany over everything, over everything in the world." Then through assassination, physical violence, imprisonment and intimidation, the Nazis eliminated all German opposition to their rule. They transformed a democracy into the cruellest dictatorship the world has ever known, and one of the most highly civilized peoples into a race of unbelievable savages.

Hitler set out to conquer and subjugate the whole world. The war he started resulted in the widespread destruction of most of Europe, the death of over forty million people and the torture and murder of six million Jews, whose only crime was to have been born Jewish. So great was his fanaticism that he traced the ancestry of many Germans of the Christian faith and destroyed them as well because they had a great-grandfather or great-grandmother who was Jewish. Hitler annexed Austria and Czechoslovakia, and invaded and conquered Poland, France, Belgium, Holland, Denmark, Norway and Libya. From 22 June 1941 until the end of the war, he was locked in a bitter battle trying to conquer Russia.

Who but a madman during a terrible war would devote so many trains and troops to transport millions of harmless Jewish men, women and children from all over Europe to death camps, instead of devoting these precious resources to the military needs of his hard-pressed armies, especially after they started to lose the war?

Oskar Schindler was a Nazi businessman who, contrary to the policy of the Nazi party, saved the lives of approximately 1,100 Jews by preventing them from going to their deaths in the German concentration camps.

I am sure that those of you who saw *Schindler's List* were very touched by the film. Try then to imagine what I must have felt... This film was a picture of my early life. Each second of Spielberg's film was a day of my life. I relived the fear of death, the horror of having to carry the dead bodies of murdered Jews and the smell of the bodies that the Nazis were burning. Each scene was painful for me and I could not help sobbing throughout the film. Certain scenes were completely unbearable. My thirty-two-year-old son, who accompanied me to the cinema, had never seen his father in such a state. He had heard the story before, but now he saw it before his eyes. He was finally able to understand the emotions I was feeling during the viewing. We, the survivors, lived through the same experiences depicted in the film, but much more than that. Let me tell you about it.

I was born in Krakow, Poland, in 1920. I was very curious and an avid reader and, at age eighteen, I read Adolf Hitler's book, *Mein Kampf* (*My Struggle*), where he expressed his hatred of the Jews and his desire to eliminate them.

The Germans invaded Poland on 1 September 1939 and a few days later entered the city of Krakow. One year later, they herded all the Jews of Krakow and surrounding area into a small district called the Jewish Ghetto, which virtually became a prison. We lived in the Jewish Ghetto in Krakow, as shown in the movie.

At the beginning, living conditions were still bearable, but life in the Ghetto soon began deteriorating daily: the laws imposed on us became more and more restrictive and the number of German soldiers increased. At first, we felt fortunate that our family was still together. As time went on, though, conditions rapidly became unbearable: Whole families were cramped into one room, with little food, frequent starvation, poor sanitation, complete insecurity and violence. Every few weeks, the Nazis randomly rounded up Jews in the streets and transported them to the concentration camps for elimination. In 1942, my mother was caught in such a round-up and we never saw her again. My father, unable to bear the loss, managed to escape from the Ghetto, joined an underground group to avenge my mother and we never saw him again. We heard that he was eventually captured by the Gestapo, tortured for several weeks, then shot and burned.

By the end of 1942, my brother Roman and I were sent to a work camp outside the city and my eight-year-old sister went to live with my aunt. On 13 March 1943, the Nazis liquidated the Krakow Ghetto. They did a selection of all its inhabitants, sending the chosen residents to the Plaszow Work Camp outside the city and then murdering all the remaining Jews. My sister and my aunt perished in this way. By October 1943, my brother and I were also transferred to Plaszow Camp from our original work camp. Plaszow was headed by SS Commandant Amon Goeth, known for his sadism, brutality and bloodthirstiness. Do you remember that scene where he was on his balcony and firing randomly at the people below? Well, that really happened. He did the same thing while riding on his horse. This killing was his morning sport. He also trained his two dogs to attack Jews on command and a number of people were killed in that way.

Life in the camp was a nightmare. We worked twelve hours a day, seven days a week, we slept in narrow, unpadded bunks in long barrack

Lfd. Nr.	H.Art. u.Nat.	H.Nr.	Name und Vorname.	Geburts- datum.	Beruf.
541	Ju.Po.	69398	Senft Wolf.	3. 7.09	Ziegler.
542		9	Goldberger Salomon.	28. 7.20	Autoklempbergos.
543	"	69400	Ehrlich Hirsch.	7. 3.17	Nieter.
544	"	1	Weinstock Joseph	4.10.0	ang. Metallarbeiter.
545	"	2	Weinstock Moniek.	19.11.27	Maschinenschlosser.
546	"	3	Stelzer Alfred.	17. 1.07	Maschinenschlosser.
547	"	4	Sommer Abraham.	22.12.07	Klempnermeister.
548		5	Goldberger Roman.	18. 8.22	Autoklempnerges.
549		6	Knobleh Moszek.	27. 5.20	Zimmerergeselle.
550	"	7	Feeitag Leizon	25. 1.04	Tischlermeister.
551	"	8	Turner Moses.	25. 6.24	ang.Zimmerer.
552	"	9	Eilberg Bernard.	27. 7.11	Baufacharbeiter.
553	"	69410	Seewald Leib.	31. 1.16	Telefonarbeiter.
554	"	1	Sussman Adolf.	12.12.24	Ang. Maurer.
555	"	2	Wildstein Hermann.	21. 8.16	Wasserinst. Ges.
556	"	3	Figowicz Pejsach.	21. 6.13	Tischler.
557	"	4	Wohlfeiler Roman.	13. 2.18	Wassermonteur.
558	"	5	Turner Henryk.	20.10.20	Zimmermann.
559	"	6	Federgrun Moses.	10. 4.12	ang. Mettalbeiter
560	"	7	Puhrman Efroim.	20.12.17	ang. Metallarbeiter.
561	"	8	Haubenstock Jakob.	29. 1.16	ang. Zimmerer.
562	Ju.Ung.	9	Merlstein Alexander.	17. 4.21	Autoschlossergeselle.
563	Ju.Po.	69420	Seidenfeuer Rachmiel.	10. 4.04	Tischlergeselle.
564	"	1	Freitag Hersz.	7. 1.20	Tischlergeselle.
565	"	2	Berger Josek.	15. 7.25	ang. Mettalarb.
566	"	3	Kaus Jakob.	2.12.16	Bauarbeiter.
567	"	4	Lewin Josek.	20.11.24	ang. Tischler.
568	"	5	Nussbaum Henoch.	11. 9.09	ang. Tischler.
569	"	6	Freitag Mendel.	1.10.22	Tischler.
570	"	7	Urbach Salomon.	25.10.25	ang. Tischler.
571	"	8	Freinof Josek.	5. 5.24	Tischlergeselle.
572	"	9	Solinger Lazar.	4. 7.14	Stanzer.
573	"	69430	Scharf Josef.	3.11.16	Bauarbeiter.
574	"	1	Sauerbrunn Dawid.	15. 1.10	Maschinentechniker.
575	"	2	Feinberg Chaim.	5. 1.25	ang. Metallverarb.
576	"	3	Schonherz Siegmund.	20. 6.14	Schlossergeselle.
577	"	4	Degen Leopold	19. 2.25	Automechaniker.
578	"	5	Ickowicz Josef.	8. 5.14	Automenteur.
579	"	6	Seidiger Szymon.	2. 9.91	Stanzer.
580	"	7	Fischgrund Leopold.	26.12.01	Tischlergeselle.
581	"	8	Freihof Fischel.	4.12.02	anf. Tischler.
582	"	9	Monderer Nachum.	10.11.23	Maschinenmech.Ges.
583	"	69440	Minz Iser.	8. 3.18	Malergeselle.
584	"	1	Freimann Anschel.	6.10.23	Malergeselle.
585	"	2	Zukermann Isak.	28. 9.16	Bautechniker.
586	"	3	Goldstein Aron.	10.10.14	ang. Metallarb.
587	"	4	Salzburg Szmul.	30.11.23	Zimmerer.
588	"	5	Eichental Meier.	12. 5.21	Tischlergeselle.
589	"	6	Kern Szyja.	5.11.06	Fahrradmech.Meister.
590	"	7	Grossem an Szymon.	15. 5.01	Schuster.
591	"	8	Grossmann Abraham.	15. 7.20	ang. Elektriker.
592	Ju.Russ.	9	Drisin Chaim.	22. 7.22	ang. Maler.
593	Ju.Po.	69450	Zuckermann Chaim.	26. 3.11	Mechanikergeselle.
594	?	1	Falk Israel.	3. 4.04	Buchalter.
595	"	2	Friedmann Bronislaw.	23.12.22	

Copy of "Schindler's List" (dated 18 April 1945) listing the names of
780 men and 240 women that Oskar Schindler saved. Stefan Lesniak
is number 542 on the list. He appears under his original name,
Salomon Goldberger, before his father obtained a new identity for him—
Stefan (Steve) Lesniak—the name he still uses today.
Courtesy of Stefan Lesniak.

Temporary identification document issued by the Polish Association
of Holocaust Survivors, Krakow district, December 1947.
Courtesy of Stefan Lesniak.

buildings, had little clothing, little food, no sanitation, suffered random beatings and had to endure frequent midnight roll calls outside in the bitter cold of winter. We lived under these conditions for a whole year until our transfer to Gross-Rosen and finally to Schindler's Factory on 20 October 1944.

Again, as was the case in the Ghetto, at Plaszow the Nazis would often round up people and transport them to their deaths in concentration camps. We lived with this uncertainty every day, not knowing when we too would face the "Final Solution." It was also during that period that we first heard about Oskar Schindler.

Rumours in the Ghetto had it that Schindler, the Nazi entrepreneur who had taken possession of a factory in Krakow, was a kind person and treated his employees well. In the beginning, I believe Schindler was an adventurer who simply wanted to make money. He used Jews because, under the circumstances, they represented the cheapest labour. We came to believe that if we were to survive and have good working conditions, we would have to work in Schindler's Enamel Factory. By October 1944, my brother and I learned that Schindler had a list of names of those who would work for him and that our names were on that list. It was the first glimmer of hope that we might survive this Holocaust. I do not know who put our names on Schindler's list and I guess I will never know. But each day of my life, I thank that person. The most extraordinary thing of all was that my brother's name was also added to the list. We both had a chance to survive. We were both very grateful. When you have nothing left but hope, that is enormous. This list was my life. My mother gave me life the first time; Oskar Schindler gave me life a second time.

Oskar Schindler was very tall and handsome. Rumour had it that women were attracted to him and I believe he profited greatly. I heard that he was arrested two or three times for influence peddling and blackmarketeering. When he visited the Plaszow Camp, I guess that he saw the inhuman treatment of the Jews and began to realize that they were actually human beings after all. It is also at that point that he probably began to compile his famous list.

Before proceeding further, it is necessary to understand the progress of the war at this time. After the Germans attacked the Soviet Union in

June 1941, they advanced rapidly to Leningrad in the north, to Moscow in the centre, to Stalingrad in the south and part way to the Ural Mountains in the deep south. In other words, the Germans had captured most of the European part of the Soviet Union. The turning point in the war came at the end of the battle for Stalingrad on 2 February 1943, when the remains of the Sixth German Army under Field Marshal von Paulus surrendered to the Russians. The casualties at Stalingrad were enormous: at least 150,000 German soldiers were killed and almost twice that number were wounded. From then to the end of the war, the German army was continuously driven back toward Germany.

By October 1944, the retreating German armies reached the Polish frontier. On 15 October 1944, we were suddenly transferred in cattle cars from Plaszow to the Gross-Rosen Concentration Camp where we remained uncertain of our fate for five days. Upon arrival there, we were horrified by the tall crematorium chimneys spewing fire and black ash into the sky and the heavy smell of burning human flesh.

The SS guards welcomed us with clubs and whips. They made us undress completely and forced us into a large shower room. We had heard that they often replaced water with poison gas in order to kill large numbers of people at a time. You can well imagine our horror when we went into the shower room and then the incredible relief we felt when water actually came out of the shower heads. That episode was dealt with quite powerfully in the film.

On the fifth day we were transferred from Gross-Rosen camp directly to Schindler's new Ammunition Factory at Brunnlitz. On arrival, Schindler received us personally and informed us that from then on we would be working for him. Conditions were very much improved because he barred the Nazi guards from entering the factory and harassing us. We worked there until 9 May 1945, the day of liberation.

Schindler's Plant was registered as an ammunition factory. We worked there for seven months in 1945, and during those seven months, never did we handle any shells, mortars or any other ammunition. It is said that Schindler bought munitions elsewhere and sold it to the army as though it had been produced by us. We saw Schindler often, but from a distance. Most of us never really talked to him. To us he was *Herr Direktor*, the big boss, and we were his employees. His wife Emilie also worked with him. She was very kind, but had a lot of problems with him.

One day we were informed that the Russians were coming to liberate us. Oskar Schindler was among us at that moment. It was a very moving experience because he had saved our lives and we knew that he would still be obliged to answer for his deeds and be arrested. Just before leaving the factory, all the Jews gave him a ring made from the gold fillings of the inmates. On the ring were inscribed the words from the Talmud: "To save one person from death, is to save a whole nation from extinction." Schindler did even more: He saved the lives of 1,100 people— 800 men and 300 women.

Let me tell you about the day of liberation, and you will understand how we felt. The Russians arrived early on the morning of 8 May 1945. They opened the gates of the factory and told us we were now free. We were suddenly in a state of shock because after so many years of having all decisions made for us, we did not know what to do or where to go. The Czech Partisans arrived soon after and urged us to go to the nearby town of Breznice, enter any home with a white flag and take food and anything else we wanted. The Czechs had obliged all the German residents of the city to put white flags of surrender in their doorways. We left the factory and went to Breznice. During all those years in captivity I dreamed of avenging myself, my family and my people on the Germans. When we finally entered one such house bearing a white flag, we saw a frightened German woman inside clasping her child to her breast. At that moment I realized that I was still a human being with feelings and incapable of atrocities. I simply walked away feeling empty and sad.

For years after the war, I was haunted by terrible nightmares, the illusion of the sweetish smell of burning human flesh in my nostrils, depressed feelings, and I had difficulties in remaking my life.

Reminiscences of the Holocaust

Willie Sterner

I WAS BORN IN WOLBROM, POLAND, in 1919. I was the oldest of seven children. Wolbrom was a small town where the Jewish community, though small and generally quite poor, maintained a thriving religious and social life.

In 1929 my father decided to move to Krakow where he established several businesses, in particular, his own painting contracting company. After I had finished public school, I began to work as a painter in my father's company, work that I enjoyed very much. Since my father wanted me to learn all aspects of the business, I was sent to work in other companies in several cities. For three years I also attended a Technical School for painters, in order to be a certified contractor and, in addition to this, I was enrolled for two years in a pre-military school.

Life in Krakow was good, and there was a vibrant Jewish community, with many synagogues, a Jewish hospital, Jewish schools, theatres, sports clubs, Zionist and socialist organizations, and a Hebrew high school. As a family, we were very happy and all of us were active in the various Jewish organizations in Krakow.

In September 1939, the Second World War began with the German attack on Poland. When Krakow was occupied, our world changed completely. The Germans immediately began to persecute the Jews. They took our freedom, our dignity, our pride. They took our money, businesses, and valuables. We were criminals in the eyes of the Nazis— our crime was that we were Jewish. The Jews were forced to perform humiliating tasks for the Germans: washing toilets for the SS, washing floors, clearing garbage dumps, and so on. We were treated like sub-humans, like animals.

At this time, some friends of mine had decided to go to the city of Lwow in the part of Poland that had been taken over by the Soviets, where, it was hoped, things would be better. I decided to go with them, packed my suitcase, said goodbye to my family. But as I was about to depart I realized I could not bear to leave my family, and, in spite of their protestations, I remained with them.

In December 1939, along with my brothers, Yosel and Abraham, I was sent by the Germans to Puskow-Dembica, a camp where we had to carry trees and lumber. In this camp, the first of several I was to be in over the next few years, we lived in freezing barracks, racked by frostbite, hunger and fatigue. Many people died of the cold and lack of food and the brutality of the guards. My bothers got frostbite and were sent home. Desperate that I would not survive much longer in this camp, I managed to escape with a friend to Krakow. At the sight of me and my friend, my family cried tears of joy.

By 1941, life had become so unbearable in Krakow under German rule that my father decided that we should move back to Wolbrom. Travelling in a large wagon pulled by two horses, we carried with us only those things which we could transport in this manner. After arriving in Wolbrom, my father went to the Jewish Committee and asked for a room for our family. We were told that if I agreed to join the Jewish Police, we would get a room, but I refused. We managed to spend the night in the room of a kind man who worked as a water carrier and, fortunately, the next day we obtained two rooms with a Polish family, by the name of Strzalka. This entire family was very good to us, helping us with food and friendship. One member of this family in particular, Kazia Strzalka, was very helpful to us. All my life I have remembered the kindness and compassion shown by the Strzalka family.

Not long after our arrival in Wolbrom, my father, myself and my brothers, Abraham and Yosel, were hired to paint the house of the new German Commandant of the *Gendarmerie*. We did the job to his satisfaction (we had been threatened with death if the work was not done properly) and received and extra ration of food for our family as a reward.

The end of the summer of 1942, however, brought our greatest tragedy. The order came to deport all the Jews from Wolbrom. During the assembling of the Jews, everyone was helpless and terrified. People were beaten, others were shot on the spot. There was a selection and families were brutally separated. Those who were selected were then crowded into cattle wagons and sent to Treblinka extermination camp. Included in this transport were my mother and my four sisters. They were murdered in Treblinka. By a twist of fate, my father and I and my two brothers were sent to the Krakow ghetto.

Devastated by the loss of my mother and sisters, we now were faced with the horrific living conditions in the Krakow ghetto, where hunger, starvation and humiliation were part of daily life. Along with my father, my brothers and I got a job working for the SS as painters. I was able to obtain permission to go to Wolbrom and bring back clothing left there in our home. Staying with friends in hiding in Wolbrom, I assembled a suitcase full of clothes and was preparing to return to Krakow when I heard the news: there had been an *Aktion* in the ghetto and my father and brothers had been transported to their deaths in Treblinka.

My heart was broken. I was now totally alone. With the death of all my family, the Nazis had destroyed what I held most dear.

Not long after the death of my father and brothers, I was taken along with other Jews to work at a camp at the Krakow airport. The camp was a terrible place, the work back-breaking. After working there for quite some time, I was able to get a job in the city working as a painter. After successfully completing a difficult job for the German boss, involving a new process of painting, I received a special ration of food and cigarettes. This would not be the last time that my knowledge of painting stood me in good stead.

The airport camp was closed down in the fall of 1942 and during the winter I was sent to Plaszow camp, where I worked as a painter in the paint shop with several other painters, including Greenberg, our foreman, whom I had known before the war. While conditions in the camp were bad, they soon got worse with the arrival of the new camp Commandant, Amon Goeth. Daily life at Plaszow camp under Goeth was a living hell. Upon his arrival, Goeth hanged several people to demonstrate his power. For his own sadistic pleasure, Goeth arbitrarily shot people, using them as target practice. Goeth had a vicious dog, who was not much better

Willie Sterner (fourth from right) in pre-military
school in Hermanice, Poland, 1937.

Courtesy of Willie Sterner.

Willie Sterner's family in Krakow, Poland, 1938.
Back row, left to right: Willie, Hinda Resel (mother),
Hersh Leib (father), Yossel Meier (younger brother).
Front row, left to right: Ita, Rachel, Sara, and Genia
(sisters), Abraham (brother).
Courtesy of Willie Sterner.

than Goeth. After a day of killing, Goeth would have the Rosner brothers, two musicians working in the camp, to serenade him in the evening. Daily murders, hunger, brutal beatings, food not fit for animals— these were part of everyday life at Plaszow camp. Some people were so hungry they resorted to eating the flesh of inmates who had died.

One example of Goeth's cruelty stands out in my mind. It so happened that one day a group of about thirty new painters from the Krakow ghetto arrived and were sent to our shop. Since they had just arrived, we did not have work for them. Our foreman, Greenberg, went to see what work could be found for them. In the meantime, Goeth arrived unaware of the situation. On that day our job was to paint a red stripe around fifty poles. Seeing all these new men and not realizing they had just arrived, Goeth asked what the work was for the day, and when the poles were pointed out to him, he asked one man how long it would take to paint a stripe on the pole. When the man could not answer, Goeth took a man from the lineup and ordered him to paint one pole. It was done in about two minutes. When Goeth asked the man what other work he had to do later, he replied that he did not know. Goeth then took out his revolver and shot the man dead on the spot. The man's father was there in the lineup and he fainted, but was supported by the men next to him. Goeth ordered that every second painter was to be shot. It was death for all of us. I asked one of the Rosner brothers to explain the situation to Goeth. When he realized that there were newly arrived painters, Goeth got furious that he had not been informed immediately. Goeth changed his order, however, from shooting to twenty-five lashes for the new painters and, for the rest, five lashes.

In the spring of 1943, we received an order that a painter was required to do artwork and signs. Because of my experience, I was the only real candidate for this job, and my foreman ordered me to go and do this work. It was a factory, *Deutsche Emailwaren Fabrik*, directed by a man named Oskar Schindler. Life in Schindler's factory was very different, the living conditions were better, the guards did not beat anyone up or kill them, and workers were of all ages. In short, Schindler made us feel like human beings again.

Schindler sent for me and asked me to do restoration work on some old paintings and antique furniture. Working slowly and carefully, I was able to do the work to Schindler's satisfaction. During the approximately eighteen months that I was working for him, Schindler gave me many other jobs to do. For example, I applied a special finish to the wood in his den, I painted a map of Europe on the large dining room wall, and I worked in the factory decorating special plates and coffee mugs. Schindler was pleased with the work I did for him.

Schindler used all the oil paintings, the antique furniture, as well as other things he procured, such as furs, jewellery, liquor, to bribe the German authorities. The pots and pans produced in his factory and sold on the black market also made a great deal of money for Schindler and this money was used to obtain further items to bribe the German officials. Money was no object. As a result of his wheeling and dealing, his bribes, his plying the Berlin officials with liquor, Schindler was able to control the Germans to an enormous extent and had them working to his advantage.

On many occasions, Schindler personally helped to save the lives of his workers by intervening when there was to be a selection for the death camps or preventing individual workers from being severely beaten or shot. When a German inspector came to the factory, the Polish workers who were working there would be sent home, leaving only the Jewish workers. This left the impression that the Jews were indispensable and that the work would not be completed without their continued presence. Schindler was a genius, a brilliant man, with spirit. He worked very hard and was determined to save the lives of the Jewish workers. He was a fine man, an angel of mercy. I will never forget him.

In August 1944, because of the advance of the Soviet army, Schindler's factory had to be closed. Schindler decided to send his Jewish workers to Brinnlitz in Czechoslovakia. Unknown to Schindler, I, however, was sent to Plaszow, and then, in crowded cattle cars, to Mauthausen camp in Austria. At Mauthausen, we were put to work in a quarry. The work was horrendous. We had to carry huge stones up 150 steps by hand. The workers were arbitrarily beaten and killed by the guards. After three weeks there I was sent to another camp, Guzen 2, near the Messerschmitt factory, where they made airplanes. Here we loaded cement, built roads, made tunnels for factories for the German air force. In one of these underground factories I had to spray airplanes. With no ventilation, the paint made me sick.

Following this I was able, because of my knowledge as a painter, to get a job painting the barracks. As a result of doing this job to the block commander's satisfaction, I was asked by other commanders to work for them. I was given permission, and, for my work, was fortunate to receive extra food rations.

In April 1945, I finished the painting jobs and was sent to work in the camp "hospital". Here crude operations were performed by a Russian doctor who was a prisoner. He had no medical instruments, no anaesthetics. There was always a lineup for these operations, but there was only time to do a few. The first day I worked in the so-called hospital, it was a terrible experience, but I got used to it, and I was glad I could be of some help.

At this time, an order came to move everyone to Gunzkirchen camp about fifteen kilometers from Mauthausen. We were moved to Mauthausen and from there we walked the rest of the way. Exhausted, many could not keep up and were shot. Hundreds died on the way. It was on this trip that I met Eva, the woman who was to become my wife. We were both looking for members of our family and hearing that she was from Sosnowiec, I asked her if she knew my family or if she had any idea where they might be. She replied that she didn't know and our conversation ended.

In Gunzkirchen camp, we did no work. Although we didn't realize it, the war was almost over. The thousands of Jews here were crowded into barracks. Everyone was hungry, dirty. People had lice. There were bodies everywhere. One day, I worked with the burial commando, carrying the corpses to the mass graves. It was horrific.

On 5 May 1945, the German Commander of our camp surrendered to the American army. The Americans liberated the camp just in time. In another couple of weeks no one would have been alive. Not realizing the consequences of their action, the Americans gave the people candy, chocolates, canned meat and other "rich" food. Unfortunately, many were so hungry that they ate too much and this proved fatal. In spite of medical care, many still died as the result of their hunger and disease. I too got very sick with typhus. I had to force myself to eat. After several weeks, my physical health improved but my morale was low. I knew I was alone in the world, that my family and my previous life had been destroyed. I was moved to a Displaced Persons' camp. Along with thousands of others, I was still plagued by lice. We couldn't get rid of them. One day, American soldiers arrived and sprayed us with DDT powder, and, finally, we were rid of the lice.

About four months after liberation, I was living in another DP camp. A nice blond girl, very good looking, came to the camp to visit friends. She looked at me and said, "Hi, Willie." At first, I didn't recognize her, but then realized it was the girl, Eva, whom I had met at Gunzkirchen camp. She, too, had suffered with typhus, but she was now recovered, and from this moment on we became good friends.

As time passed, things improved, although I was never free of the nightmares and memories of the past. I even had a visitor one day— Oskar Schindler. We were both happy to see each other. But Schindler was changed. He was not the Schindler I had known, full of energy; now, he seemed a broken man. He did not smile. He asked if I had found any members of my family or if I had met people from his factory. After an hour, we said goodbye. I hoped that I would see him again soon, but this did not happen. I was unable to find him.

On 16 July 1946, Eva and I were married in Salzburg, Austria. Two years later, in October 1948, we arrived in Halifax and from there we came to live in Montreal. During the next several years, I worked hard at various jobs and in 1951 I started my own painting contracting business. Later, I gave up the painting business and opened a cigar store and a restaurant. Our two sons were born in Montreal and, today, Eva and I have lovely grandchildren. Since my retirement, I divide my time between Montreal and Miami. In both cities, and elsewhere, I give lectures on my experiences during the war, speaking to different organizations as well as to students. It is hard for me to do this, but I feel it is my duty as long as I am able to do it. The young people of the world must be made aware of the past. The past must be remembered if we are to free the world from the hatred that produced the Holocaust.

DACHAU DETACHMENT
7708 WAR CRIMES GROUP
APO 407   U. S. ARMY

13 March 1947

SUBJECT: Austrian Witnesses

To Whom it may Concern:

1. Mr. Sterner, Willy, is in charge of three persons, SMOLARZ, Leon, GRUBER, Markus, and GOLDSTEIN, Bernard. Together with Mr. Sterner these men were witnesses in the Mauthausen Concentration Camp case at the convenience of the United States Government and are being returned to Linz, Austria.

2. Mr. Sterner is permitted to carry a package containing approximately 3,000 pictures of Mauthausen suspects.

3. In addition, all four persons are allowed to carry with them whatever personal articles they may possess.

WERNER CONN, 2nd Lt.
2nd Lt.   AUS
Mauthausen Sub-Section

Telephone Munich Mil. 2741, Ext. 391

Letter, 13 March 1947, pertaining to Willie Sterner's appearance as a witness at the Dachau trials after the war. Sterner, in charge of a group of three other former inmates of the Mauthausen Camp, testified against the Nazis.
Courtesy of Willie Sterner.

Willie and Eva Sterner (on the right) aboard a train in
Austria, 1948, as they begin their voyage to Canada.
Courtesy of Willie Sterner.

The Anguish of "Liberation"

Avrum Feigenbaum

I WAS BORN IN 1919 and grew up in Lodz, Poland. From the age of eleven I was an activist in Jewish cultural and political life in Poland in an organization called the Jewish Labour *Bund*. My upbringing, both inside and outside the home, was politically and culturally *Bundist*.

I was in Lodz when, in 1939, the Germans occupied Poland. In May 1940, along with my sister and brothers and my parents, I was sent to live in the Jewish ghetto in Lodz. All the Jewish groups in Poland which had been active earlier continued to exist during the war. While in Lodz ghetto, I too remained a member of the *Bund*.

I worked in a factory as a cabinet maker in the ghetto. The ghetto was completely cut off from the world around us. The most important thing the *Bund* did was to bring news from the outside world by means of illegal radios that were operated in the ghetto. I was active in my organization, but essentially the same activities were going on in all the other organizations, especially youth groups like my own.

I was in the Lodz ghetto until September 1944. At that time, the ghetto was finally liquidated and the Jews were sent to Auschwitz. We had heard about gas chambers and crematoria before we got to Auschwitz, but it was upon our arrival there that we were confronted with their reality. I was in Auschwitz for five weeks. Some Jews were sent to work in various other camps. I was transported to a camp called Gorlitz, a part of Gross-Rosen camp. There I worked in a factory producing armoured vehicles for the Germans. On 9 May 1945, the day after the war officially ended in Europe, we walked through the gates of the camp.

By June 1945 I was back in Poland. I soon became active again in Jewish cultural and political life. We tried to rebuild, on a smaller scale,

Jewish life in Poland, by establishing Jewish theatres, choirs, orchestras, sports organizations, schools and co-operatives. But under the communist regime this was not possible. In 1948, all political parties other than the communist party were suppressed, and, not willing to join the United Communist Movement, I had no choice but to leave my homeland. I went to Germany illegally with the help of the Jewish Labour Committee in New York. The same organization also arranged for me and my wife, whom I had married in April 1946 in Lodz, to emigrate and stay for almost one year in Sweden. As well, they also arranged for me a special permit to enter Canada as a political refugee from Poland. We came to Montreal in June 1950 and have lived here ever since.

The foregoing summarizes the main features of my experiences. What I really want to do here is to express some sense of what it is like to be a survivor of the Holocaust, to try to convey the pain that is so much a part of our thoughts.

I remember when I was in Auschwitz. As I noted earlier, we saw the crematoria and were told, "You see those chimneys? That is Jewish smoke coming out. This is what you came here for. You did not come here to live, you came here to die, and you will. If it is not tomorrow, it will be the day after. You are not here to survive, you are here to die." And we believed it when we saw what happened there. Yes, we believed it.

In Auschwitz we asked ourselves questions: Did the outside world know what was happening in Auschwitz? Was it possible that the world did not know that people were being systematically exterminated? Today, in hindsight, we know that the outside world did have knowledge of the widespread organized slaughter of the Jews, and that by the time I arrived in Auschwitz what was taking place there was known in considerable detail.[1]

Auschwitz was really an immense series of camps and I was in the part known as the *Zigeunerlager*, or Gypsy camp. The name derived from the fact that earlier, before they were gassed, the previous inmates of this section had been Gypsies. One of the crematoria was destroyed with the help of four Jewish girls, who, as prisoners working in the nearby German chemical factory IG Farben, which was part of the Auschwitz complex, stole the explosives used to blow up the crematorium. These unarmed prisoners succeeded in destroying at least one crematorium on their own, but the free world, with its armies of millions of soldiers, was unable to destroy anything. We, the prisoners of Auschwitz, wondered at the time: Is it possible that no one cares about us? Are we really forgotten by God and our fellow men?

On 12 May 1943, an event took place in London which attempted to focus attention on the plight of the Jews. Two Jews, Ignacy Schwarzbart and Arthur Zygelboym, were members of the Polish National Council in London. After desperate but futile efforts to get the British government to act to save the Jews, Zygelboym committed suicide. In a farewell letter, Zygelboym wrote: "I cannot be silent. I cannot live while the remnants of the Jewish population of Poland, of whom I am a representative, are perishing... By my death I wish to make my final protest against the passivity with which the world is looking on and permitting the extermination of the Jewish people."

This is how Zygelboym died. He died, giving his life voluntarily, hoping to shake the conscience of the free world. But the conscience of the world was not shaken.

A similar reaction of indifference to information about the murder of the Jews had occurred in February 1943. A German embassy official in Switzerland sent reports to the American embassy, reports which the Americans were not interested in receiving. In response to a final telegram the state department ordered, "Do not use our diplomatic telegraph anymore for personal information." Thus, reports about what was happening to the Jews were seen as being merely "personal information". The Jews were not important, they were not part of the war effort, they were not recognized as a people. (Only the Germans identified the Jews as a people, a people to be annihilated.)

When the nations of the world finally did get together and held a conference on refugees in Bermuda in April 1943, Jews were not officially represented at the conference. There was a Jew, an American congressman named Bloom at the conference, but this was a coincidence. He just happened to be Jewish. He did not represent the Jews as a group. The upshot of this Bermuda Conference was that nothing constructive was done to rescue the Jews. In fact, the reason that a resolution to demand that Hitler permit the Jews to leave Europe was never ratified was not the fear that Hitler would refuse this demand, but that he might actually agree to it. The world was not ready or willing to take the Jews. That was the bottom line.

My main topic here is "liberation." I have waited until the end to discuss this because for many readers my thoughts on this may be difficult to understand. Like the pain we survivors felt at the time as well as after the war, when we discovered that the world was unwilling to attempt to deliver us from the Nazis, this word "liberation" is a word that for us is filled with anguish. It is simply because we were not liberated. We just happened to be there when the allied armies had made their way to the camps. This had nothing to do with Jews as Jews. I was not liberated on 27 January 1945 when Auschwitz was liberated. I was not liberated on 9 May 1945 when I left Gorlitz camp. I was not free. We survivors have no nights in which we feel liberated. However difficult it may be for young people reading this to understand, I must say that, literally, our nights are still spent in the ghettos and in Auschwitz. We play the happy people, it is a role we play. We live happily. I live with my family during the day and in Auschwitz at night, and this is why I cannot use the word liberation.

Others might use it. They shared a victory. They celebrated a liberation. Jews have no victory. We were physically destroyed, including so-called survivors. Most emerged at the end with no one, no friends, family, loved ones, parents, children, brothers, sisters. Jews had to start living again, to build from scratch. We tried. We went to Poland, back to our homes. But it did not work out. We could not forget that in the moment when the tormented Jewish people of Europe were bleeding to death, children, the noblest sons and daughters, were butchered daily. We stretched out our hands for help in those days in the name of humanity, not in the name of Judaism, but in the name of humanity. We felt then and we feel today that we had the right to speak in the name of humanity, with our hope, to reach to the end of that darkness in that long night in May 1945.

The light went on, yes it did, for the victorious armies of the allies. The light of victory did not bring us happiness. We will never have true happiness. I am not a young man. I feel almost at the edge of my grave. If

Postcard from the Lodz Ghetto, Poland, 1940. (Renamed
Litzmannstadt by the Germans).
From left to right: Mordechai Feigenbaum (Avrum's brother),
Minka Feigenbaum (Mordechai's wife), and Avrum Feigenbaum.
Courtesy of Avrum Feigenbaum.

Photograph taken in the Lodz Ghetto by Mendel Grossman
who kept a secret photographic record of ghetto life.
The man on the upper left is Avrum Feigenbaum.

Photograph published in *With a Camera in the Ghetto*
by Mendel Grossman (Ghetto Fighters' House/Hakibbutz
Hameuchad Publishing House, 1970).
Reprinted with permission.

I have not yet felt the happiness of liberation, do not feel it now, I, and others like me, will never feel it.

Not only a people, but a civilization was destroyed by the Germans. Jews were the main victims, physically. But we did have one victory over Hitler. The Germans tried deliberately to dehumanize us. In the end, this plan of Hitler did not work on us—it worked on *his* people, but not on us. I am proud to say we came out from ghettos and camps, not as a liberated people, but as a proud people with dignity. We were not dehumanized. We retained our humanity and today we remind the world that tomorrow it can happen again. If not to the Jews, to others. Other groups might find themselves in a situation where a new Holocaust could happen to them.

Today we often hear people speak of the need for love between the nations of the world. This, of course, is a good thing. But for me, given my experience of the Holocaust, I would settle for something less than love if love is too much to demand of the world. I would settle for learning simply to live together, for simple tolerance. We, all of us, have one world together and this is the world that we have to watch and care for and build every day of our lives. It is possible that some young person reading this today might be a future Prime Minister of Canada or might be a leader in some other capacity. I hope that that person's generation will produce better leaders than my generation did. So we rely on you, on the new generation, to create a better world than the one we had in our time.

Memories

Ann Kazimirski

IT MUST BE REPEATED and remembered that from 1939 to 1945, six million Jews, including one million children, were systematically killed by a German machine of destruction. Poland, my native country, had a large Jewish population of approximately 3,100,000. By the end of the war three million of these Jews had been murdered.

Fifty years later, I cannot forget the scenes of incredible brutality, torture and killing that my eyes witnessed. The same questions repeat themselves over and over again after all these years: Why? Why were so many people killed and why did the world choose to remain silent?

I was born and raised in the town of Vladimir Volynski, where Jews had settled as early as the twelfth century. My father, Joshua, originally had been a teacher of Russian and my mother, Matilda, had been one of his students. They fell in love and married against the wishes of their parents. As time passed my father could no longer earn his living teaching and so my parents became merchants, selling coal and wood. The living conditions in my home town, when I was a young girl, were primitive. There was no running water, no hardwood floors, no indoor plumbing, and no cars. We did not know anything better, however, and life seemed beautiful. My parents were able to provide an excellent education for my brother Benny and me, an education that included Hebrew school, private high school and music lessons.

I was seventeen years old when the Germans invaded Poland. My father and my eighteen-year-old brother Benny were among the first group of Jews to be rounded up and then executed in the town prison. I saw my best friend Sarah being raped by German soldiers. As a result of this brutal attack she died.

The Germans killed my *Zeide* Aaron, my grandfather. He was a very pious, orthodox Jew. He spent day and night studying the Bible. His heart and soul were buried in his religious studies. He was a genius. It is probable that he never went to a regular school, only to a *Cheider*. But he was a role model to his children and grandchildren. He taught us the blessings of nature, work, rest and the Sabbath.

I remember his story about the creation of the world. He said in a sweet voice, "Long, long ago, there was nothing in this world. No trees, no sun, no moon, no stars. Nothing but darkness. But God wanted a beautiful world where people could live and be happy, so He made the world in six days..."

In a period of six years, from 1939 to 1945, my world, and my grandfather's Jewish world was almost completely destroyed. Instead of a "beautiful world where people could live and be happy," it became a world of concentration camps, ghettos, and systematic mass murder. Soon after the arrival of the German soldiers, the Jews of Vladimir Volynski were forced into a ghetto surrounded by barbed wire. Then the systematic killing began with the first of three *Aktionen*, or killing operations. During the first *Aktion*, my husband Henry and my mother and I were hidden in the attic of a military dental clinic. A German dental technician, who was a friend of my husband, had agreed to let us hide there. This man, whose name was Hahn, risked his own life to save us.

The clinic was right across from the ghetto. Early one morning we heard terrible screams, and from a small window in the attic we saw the *Aktion* unfold. There were big trucks scattered around, and men wearing prayer shawls were being beaten with clubs and shoved into the trucks. With arms raised to the sky they were screaming, "*Lama Hazavtonu?*" (Why have You forsaken us?)

Mothers were crying at the top of their lungs, some clutching their babies and trying to hide them under their dresses. But the little children were grabbed by the Nazis and thrown into the trucks. Blood stained the ground and the children's clothing. I covered my ears, I could not listen to the screaming any longer. Even today I still hear it in my dreams.

During the second *Aktion*, we were hidden in a stable and then in an attic by a Polish woman, Maria Wierzbovska. We stayed there for weeks until we were discovered by her husband. He was a bailiff and a anti-Semite, and when he discovered our presence he threatened to report us to the Gestapo. We were finally forced to go to the ghetto.

We were in the ghetto when the third and final *Aktion* broke out on 13 December 1943. This third *Aktion* was to accomplish the goal of making our town, Vladimir Volynski, "*Judenrein*"—cleansed of Jews. German soldiers overran the ghetto and shot Jews at random. Many were killed trying to escape by climbing the barbed wire fence.

Miraculously, Henry and I found a cramped hiding place in the attic of a house, but we were separated from my mother. During the next few days we watched from our hiding place as German and Ukrainian soldiers searched the ghetto for any remaining Jews. To my horror, I recognized my mother in a group of five people being dragged from a hiding place in a nearby house. The five were lined up against a wall and shot. I will never forget the image of the red blood staining the white snow. I saw my beloved mother die—and there was nothing I could do. To even cry out would have endangered the lives of everyone in our hiding place in the attic.

Earlier, my mother had told me that she would die, but that I would survive. I can still remember her voice: "*Chanale*, we are all going to die, but you will be the one to survive. Live! Fight! You will tell them, tell the world what the beasts have done to us. Do not give up, and do not forget!" I will carry this responsibility for the rest of my life.

In all, nineteen thousand Jews, including one thousand children, were killed in Vladimir Volynski. It was truly a miracle that Henry and I survived this third killing operation. While we had managed to survive we still faced an enormously difficult road ahead. In March 1944, after escaping from the destroyed ghetto, we joined a group of Polish partisans. When it became obvious that the group did not want Jews, we ran away and headed on foot for the Russian front. Finally liberated by the Russian army, we were hungry, filthy, covered with lice and sores, and homeless. But our immediate reaction was one of joy. It was an incredible feeling— to be able to go outside without being afraid for our lives, after years of hiding in attics and cellars.

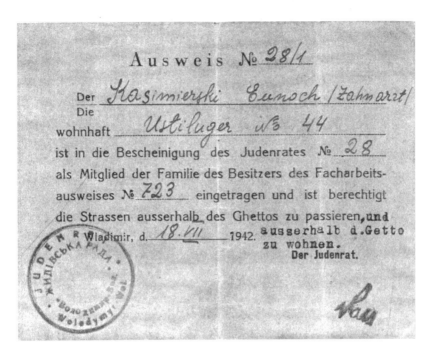

Ausweis № 28/1

Der _Kasimierski Enoch (Zahnarzt)_
Die
wohnhaft _Ustiluger № 44_
ist in die Bescheinigung des Judenrates № _28_
als Mitglied der Familie des Besitzers des Facharbeits-
ausweises № _723_ eingetragen und ist berechtigt
die Strassen ausserhalb des Ghettos zu passieren, und
Wladimir, d. _18.VII_ 1942. ausserhalb d.Getto
zu wohnen.
Der Judenrat.

Ann Kazimirski's identity card allowing her to leave
the ghetto in Vladimir Volynski, Poland.
Courtesy of Ann Kazimurski.

Ann and Henry Kazimirski's Canadian visa,
issued in Munich 28 June 1948,
allowing them to travel to Canada.

During the following three months we began to recover our health, and our first son, Mark, was born in Lwow. Our intention at this time was to get to Berlin. We made a stop in Krakow on our way, and to our great dismay we found ourselves in the middle of another pogrom. It was being conducted by Polish neo-Nazis who were determined to kill the remaining Jews. We managed to reach Berlin, but it was only to discover that we were stepping into an inferno. The Russian bombardment had put the city on fire and epidemics of dysentery and cholera were raging. Our son Mark took sick and we almost lost him.

From Berlin we went to Munich, where we applied for help from the United Nations Relief and Rehabilitation Administration (UNRRA), and then settled in Garmisch, where our second son, Seymour, was born.

But even now, we were not free of the violent hatred of anti-Semites. A young girl, named Pela, we had hired to help us in the house, made an attempt to poison our son Mark. We found out later that she had been active in the Hitler Youth. When we received our visa to come to Canada in the spring of 1948, we could not wait to leave behind us the war-torn and bloody soil of Europe. I will never forget the day we arrived in this country. We were greeted by a large sign saying WELCOME TO CANADA. Overwhelmed, we cried tears of joy.

We settled in Ste. Agathe, north of Montreal, and it was here that our daughter Heidi was born. Like many other survivors, I did not discuss the Holocaust with my children until they were older, and even then, not in any detail. It was still too painful. The wounds were too deep. They had not yet begun to heal.

And even here in Canada, there were reminders of the Holocaust. I met a woman named Danka, who was living in Ste. Agathe. She was a survivor of Auschwitz. I was shocked when I met her. I could not figure out whether I was looking at a man or a woman. Once I got to know her, she was glad to talk to me as one Holocaust survivor to another. In Auschwitz she had been chosen for medical experiments. She was given injections in her uterus over a period of two months. Gradually she began to notice changes in her physical appearance. She became hysterical, screaming like a wild animal. The Nazi doctors gave her pills which made her feel less than a human being. Again and again, she was taken to the hospital for more injections and more tests. She began growing a beard, her breasts disappeared and her voice deepened.

Five years after the war Danka still felt nothing but shame and was profoundly depressed. In 1950, in Ste. Agathe, she killed herself. The inscription on her tomb reads, "A victim of suffering in Auschwitz." Surely, this was the greatest violation of human rights.

I know there were, and are, many victims like Danka who did not come forward with their testimonies. Women were raped, prostituted, tortured, sexually assaulted, and used for medical experiments, but their stories have not been told or documented.

In 1942 and 1943, sterilization experiments were carried out on women at Auschwitz and Ravensbruck, by Professor Carl Clauberg. The aim of his "research" was to determine the feasibility of mass sterilization by a single injection of a chemical into the womb. He reported the results of his experiments to Heinrich Himmler, the head of the SS and the German police. In 1948 Clauberg was arrested and tried by the Soviets. He was sentenced to twenty-five years imprisonment. Clauberg showed no regret for his experiments and even boasted about his "scientific achievements." The records of the medical experiments are available, but there is a debate in the medical community as to whether it is ethical to use the results, considering the circumstances under which the results were obtained.

In 1971, and again in 1982, I was invited by the German government to be a witness at Nazi war crimes trials. At one of these trials, *Gebietskommissar* Westerheide, the German regional commander who was in charge of the massacre of eighteen thousand Jews in my hometown, was tried and found not guilty. As far as I am concerned, this was the final injustice. Like many others, Westerheide maintained that he had not been in charge and that he had only followed orders.

In 1993 I published a book called *Witness to Horror*, an account of my experiences during the Holocaust. It is my legacy to the world, to my children, to my grandchildren, and to future generations. In the Torah we are taught that we are responsible for three generations—our own, that of our children, and that of our grandchildren. The concept is: "*l'dor v'dor*"—generation to generation. I want to pass on the legacy from my

Zeide Aaron and my mother to my children and their children. My story is happening in many, many families of Holocaust survivors.

In recent years there has been an outpouring of Holocaust memories. There is a rush to get everything down in writing before the generation of survivors dies away. There is also a search for knowledge and understanding by the descendants of survivors, a search that is leading the young to rediscover their Jewish heritage. Jews are proudly calling themselves Jews once more.

To the students reading this, I say that when the Second World War broke out, my brother and I were teenagers like you. We too were students. I hope you appreciate your freedom— it must never be taken for granted! Take advantage of the wonderful opportunities you have living in this country, at this time in history.

But you, the next generation, must also be aware of the Holocaust. You cannot make up for the atrocities and the pain that occurred, but you can prevent such a tragedy from happening again. We put our trust in you. Do not fail us. Never forget. Remember... Remember.

Ann Kazimirski and her husband Henry, with their
son Mark, in Garmisch, Germany, 1948. In the centre
is Henry's brother-in-law Nathan Cytryn, who was a
prisoner-of-war in Germany, 1939-1945.
Courtesy of Ann Kazimirski.

Experiences of the Second Generation

Heidi Berger

MY FIRST REACTION to writing about the Holocaust was that the Holocaust was my mother's story, not mine, even though I am the daughter of Holocaust survivors. Then I remembered a recent incident which brought into sharp focus for me what it means, even today here in Canada, to be Jewish.

I had a business meeting in a fine restaurant with a well-known Canadian film producer. The meeting opened with him saying, "Heidi. Heidi Berger. My goodness, you certainly don't look Jewish." My back went up as the conversation continued along these lines for a few more minutes. Why did this man find it necessary to make an issue of my being Jewish, and why was it somehow implied that "not looking Jewish" was a compliment?

As I look back, I realize that "you don't look Jewish" ran as a theme throughout my life. But as the child of Holocaust survivors, I could not escape being Jewish, nor did I want to escape being Jewish.

Children of survivors have different ways of dealing with the horror and the suffering of the Holocaust. This depends to a large extent on how their parents made them aware of their experiences during the war. There are some parents who could not share their memories with their children. They were silent. This resulted in many children of survivors feeling great frustration, guilt, and sadness.

My brothers and I learned at a very young age that our parents had arrived in Canada as penniless refugees after the Second World War. Although they had been humiliated and persecuted, they had survived and had managed to build a new life for themselves and for their children. Looking back at my childhood and upbringing, what stands out in my memories is the joy we had as a family. In spite of all that my parents had suffered and lost, they were always filled with love and compassion for all of us.

My awareness of the war and my family's trials was acquired mainly through the stories told by my father. And in spite of the horror, we understood that only my father, not my mother, was willing to share some of the terrible events of the tragedy with us. I believe that somehow the qualities that emerged from these stories—the desire to survive and the incredible strength—were passed on to us children.

But there were dark moments in our lives. My father had dreadful nightmares and he would often cry out in German and Polish during his dreams. I remember, when I was about six years old, my father coming into my bedroom at night, in a dream-like state, and moving my bed away from the window. He said, "I had a dream that the Germans were shooting through the window. I want to move your bed so you will be safe." This happened several times.

We realized the extent of my father's anxieties through another incident. He had become friends with one of his patients who was a Catholic priest. One day he brought me to the church to meet the priest, and soon after he came home with a Catholic birth certificate in my name. My father believed this would protect me if there was another Holocaust.

My father's stories eased my way into the larger picture of the war. But I sensed even as a young child the great pain behind the words, which often brought him to tears. How could it have happened? Why did God let it happen? My father grieved terribly. I will always remember his tears.

In the case of my mother, things were very different. She did not want to talk about the war. There was a wall there and we knew it. She opened up a bit later on when we were teenagers, but not as much as my father. We never saw her cry, and she never allowed her children to cry; she viewed this as a sign of weakness.

There were two aspects of her character that we knew were related to her experiences during the war. One was that she made us eat everything on our plates. Having known hunger, she considered it a sin

Heidi Berger, Ann Kazimirski's daughter.
Courtesy of Ann Kazimirski.

to waste food. The second was her phobia about keeping doors locked, because she had seen her childhood friend Sarah dragged from her home and raped by German soldiers. She still worries about unlocked doors, and, to this day, even on the coldest day of winter, she will stand outside my home and wait for me to lock the door before she leaves.

My mother's gift to us was different from our father's, but very valuable. She poured love and affection on us, and she passed on by example her strength, her determination, and her instinct for survival. She taught us from a very early age that when you are in uncertain and difficult times, you must fight, and do everything in your power to survive. Nothing must stand in your way—a message given repeatedly during my life.

I was very happy for her when she was working on her book *Witness to Horror*. Knowing how she had refused to speak about the Holocaust, I believed that writing the book would help her deal with the past. I was right, but she was very upset when she could not help crying while giving lectures about the book. She still felt that tears were a sign of weakness. Then one day I overheard her talking to a friend about this. She said, "You know, I told my daughter Heidi about how difficult it is for me to talk about the Holocaust and how I sometimes burst into tears. And Heidi assured me that crying is not a sign of weakness, it is simply a natural emotion." My mother had realized it was okay to cry after all these years.

We were brought up to be different because we were different. Being Jewish in a small, predominantly French town, Ste. Agathe, we were subjected to racial slurs and segregation. Yet, we not only survived but we rose above it all. This gave us a toughness that cannot be easily learned, cannot be bought, and for many people cannot be understood. I recall once my older brother Mark got into a fist fight to protect our brother Seymour, after someone had called Seymour "a dirty Jew".

On another occasion when Mark went to apply for a summer job at an expensive resort hotel, the Laurentide Inn, he found a sign which said, "No Jews Allowed—No Dogs Allowed"—on the same sign. Mark, who did not look Jewish and who was imbued with our mother's teaching that you never accepted defeat, passed himself off as non-Jewish and got the job. He worked for most of the summer, but then he was fired when someone told the management that he was a Jew.

We were also discriminated against by Jewish people born in Canada, who looked down on Jewish immigrants and called them "Greenhorns". Even though my parents became well-established here, they could not escape the stigma of being immigrants. I resented those racial slurs, but while growing up I became aware that my parents' accent made them different.

I often think of how terrible it was for my mother to see her mother killed and her father and brother rounded up and taken to a prison where they were shot and dumped into mass graves. I particularly remember being envious of children who had grandparents. I know that my mother yearned to have her mother and father here. She told us often of the warm and loving extended family she had shared in her *shtetl*, the small village where she grew up, before the Holocaust. Unlike my mother, as children my brothers and I only had each other.

I will never stop feeling angry and sorry for what has been done to my parents' families and all the other innocent Jewish people. If I had not witnessed my parents' suffering, if I had not been subjected to the rigors of our lifestyle, I would not be what I am today—proud to be a Jew, proud to be the daughter of Holocaust survivors.

We all learn from our parents, and the things we learn growing up stay with us always. Given my parents' experiences and the Holocaust, my brothers and I always try to accomplish the most and the best in everything we do. If I have instilled in my children the love and respect for life that my parents instilled in me, I will have done a good job.

Thoughts of a Grandchild

Jason H. Berger

SIGMUND FREUD NOTED that our earliest childhood memories leave an impression and influence us for the rest of our lives. When I was a young boy of five years, I remember my family gathered around the Passover table in my grandmother's house. Her eldest son Mark pleaded with my grandmother to tell us about her experiences of the Holocaust. My whole family listened in awe as my grandmother began to recount her story of her sufferings in the war. In my innocence I could not comprehend the reason why the Jews were punished and slaughtered. What did they do to deserve this? What did my grandmother ever do to deserve this?

My Jewish History teachers at Bialik High School tried to answer these questions to the best of their abilities. Unsatisfied, I finally went to my grandmother's house for answers. I sat down in her office. On the table was the manuscript of her book, half completed. I implored my grandmother to finish the book and leave, not only for me, but for the world, a legacy. My grandmother could not refuse such a request and eventually we agreed on the title *Witness to Horror*.

My grandmother's book, as well as books and testimonies of other survivors, are a direct source of information for future generations as to the reality of the Holocaust. The brutal attempt by the Nazis to annihilate the Jewish nation must not be forgotten. We must always keep asking the question, "Why did it happen?" More importantly, we answer this question by asking, "How can we prevent these atrocities from being forgotten or repeated?"

Anti-Semitism did not die with the Nazis. There are still today Nazi sympathizers who openly promote anti-Semitism, xenophobia, and other forms of hatred. I myself am a witness to this reality. A year ago, on a

Saturday night, I was at the Old Port of Montreal with some of my friends. The flea market was open and we decided to have a look. One of my friends pulled me by the arm to a kiosk. She told me that I would not believe my eyes. I thought that the kiosk she was bringing me to was full of hockey paraphernalia. I was absolutely shocked when I realized that what they were selling was Nazi propaganda. There were iron crosses, swastikas, copies of *Mein Kampf*, Hitler's autobiography, pictures of Hitler himself, and various anti-Semitic materials and literature. I was paralyzed with disbelief. How could this be happening here in Montreal? I thought that this only existed in backward, rural communities, certainly not in a modern metropolis. I heard my grandmother's voice declare to me: "Never again must we permit such carnage and tribulation to exist!" I took it upon myself to confront the proprietors of this kiosk and in a calm and rational way to explain to them that what they were doing was not only wrong, but insulting to me and to the memory of six million Jews, twenty million people of other nations and races, and to the millions of soldiers who died in defeating the Nazis. The elderly couple behind the counter responded to me by saying, "What do you care what happened? You were not killed, it does not affect you."

It does not affect me? I thought to myself. How could the Holocaust not affect me? Over eighty-two members of my family were butchered and this does not affect me? My uncles got into fights at school because they were Jewish and this does not affect me? While the outside world stood by and watched, over six million people were deliberately and systematically murdered because they were of the same religion as me and this is not supposed to affect me? This devastates me.

The couple went on to say that the Holocaust never existed and that it was a conspiracy started by people like my grandmother. I could not reason with these people any longer. I proceeded to announce at the top of my lungs what this couple was doing and that they must be stopped. People all over the flea market began to congregate around me and my friends and started to support us. Needless to say, the security guards arrived and peacefully escorted us out. One security guard turned to me and said in French, "You should learn your history of the Second World War and of the Holocaust." The final insult of the night: this man telling me that I should re-learn my history. I immediately went home and told my grandmother the story. She was in tears. Her own grandson had to experience things that she went through fifty years earlier. In order to try and put a stop to this, we contacted B'nai Brith and informed them of what had happened. Although B'nai Brith has long been vigilant in opposing hate literature, ambiguity in the laws concerning free speech remains a problem in dealing with Nazi material of this kind.

One fact is clear. We have not overcome anti-Semitism or racism. Today, there are still radicals out there who, like the people in the kiosk, deny the Holocaust and promote violence towards various racial, religious and ethnic groups. If you want to see firsthand where these people are publishing their hate propaganda, all you have to do is turn on your computer and surf the Internet. There are many neo-Nazi hate groups who have their own bulletin boards where they display their lies and falsehoods and where they advocate discrimination and violence against minorities. I have seen this with my own eyes. It is time that governments step in, regulate, and censor these bulletin boards and prevent these purveyors of hate from spreading their message.

How much longer must we wait, how many more reminders do we need, before the governments of Canada and Quebec, as well as the world community, act? In the meantime, we as responsible individuals must speak out. As a grandson of Holocaust survivors, I feel it my duty to inform the young and old alike about what has occurred in the past, is occurring at this moment, and, if not stopped, will continue to occur.

I have faith in the individual. One person can make a difference. We do not want to be an unfeeling world that watches, listens, and yet chooses to do nothing and be silent in the face of anti-Semitism and racism. It is up to individuals of my generation and generations to come to make sure our voices are heard in unison denouncing all forms of hate.

Fifty years from now, I want to be the one seated at the Passover table, telling my children and grandchildren stories about pride, triumph, victory, and love, and never a single story about experiencing and witnessing the horrors that my grandparents had to endure.

Notes

HISTORY

The Contribution of Late 19th Century German Anti-Semitism to the Holocast
[Josef Schmidt]

1. Stuckart-Globke. *Kommentar zur deutschen Rassengesetzgebung*. Bd. 1 (1936) C I, Vorbemerkungen, 15.
2. Alexander Mitscherlich and Margaret Mitscherlich, *Die Unfähigkeit zu Trauern*, (München: Piper, 1967).
3. The most comprehensive historical studies of that period are Helmut Berding, *Moderner Antisemitismus in Deutschland* (Frankfurt a. Main: Suhrkamp, 1988); Shulamit Volkos, *Jüdisches Leben und Antisemitismus im 19. und 20. Jahrhundert: 10 Essays* (München: Beck, 1990); and Uriel Tal, *Christians and Jews in Germany: Religion, Politics, and Ideology in the Second Reich, 1870-1914* (Ithaca: Cornell University Press, 1975). Many of my factual references draw on these works without acknowledging them in detail. I do realize that the question to what extent "modern" anti-Semitism added new dimensions to an old ingrained hatred is a controversial issue. But in my premise that modernity did provide a new kind of anti-Semitism, I follow a trustworthy source: Alphons Silbermann, *Der ungeliebte Jude. Zur Soziologie des Antisemitismus* (Zürich: Interfrom, 1981).
4. Daniel Jonah Goldhagen, *Hitler's Willing Executioners. Ordinary Germans and the Holocaust*, (New York: Alfred Knopf, 1996), particularly Part I, "Understanding German Antisemitism: the Eliminationist Mind-Set."
5. This is not the place to engage in the controversy about this study; and many competent critics have already stated major objections to Goldhagen's analysis. A convincing example is "Blaming the Germans. The much lauded revisionist study of the Holocaust goes too far" by Clive James (*The New Yorker*, April 22, 1996), 44-50.
6. I cannot refrain from this polemical remark since Goldhagen presents, to the best of my knowledge, no substantial new original evidence for his claims covering the period in question. Instead, he relies almost exclusively on a German study by Konrad Felden (*Die Übernahme des antisemitischen Stereotyps als soziale Norm durch die bürgerliche Gesellschaft Deutschlands*, Ph.D. diss., Heidelberg 1963); written more than 30 years ago, this excellent and pioneering analysis works with rather broad categories.
7. Again, two notable exceptions addressing the general question of Christian

complicity or omission are: Georg Denzler/Volker Fabricius, *Christen und Nationalsozialisten. Darstellung und Dokumente* (Frankfurt a. Main: Fischer, 1993, 2nd ed.); and Doris Berger, *Twisted Cross: The German Christian Movement in the Third Reich* (Chapel Hill: University of North Carolina Press, 1996).

8. Translated from the easily accessible German text in Walter Boehlich, ed., *Der Berliner Antisemitismusstreit* (Frankfurt a. Main: Insel, 1988), 13.

9. Goldhagen's book has on its cover one such telling illustration of a rally where this slogan is prominently displayed.

10. Adolf Hitler, *Mein Kampf,* quoted from 558. / 562. edition (München: *Zentralverlag der NSDAP*, 1940), 629.

11. The German original actually renders these two terms in Latin (*igni ferroque*) making it very likely that it was written by a cleric.

12. In a fascinating recent study Marc Angenot has traced this feature back to its origins; cf. *Les idéologies du ressentiment* (Montréal: XYZ, 1996), particularly 17ff.

13. Marc Angenot, *"Un Juif Trahira" Le thème de l'espionnage militaire dans la propagande antisémetique 1886-1894.* (Montréal: Ciadest, 1994), particularly III, pp. 31ff., "*L'antisémitisme des catholiques.*"

14. See John Hellman, *The Knight-Monks of Vichy France Uriage, 1940-45* (Montreal & Kingston et al.: McGill-Queen's Press, 1993); the introduction in particular gives a concise account of this process.

The Initial Reactions of German Jews to Adolf Hitler's Accession to Power
[Klaus J. Herrmann]

1. *Rabbiner* Dr. Elie Munk in his *Judentum und Umwelt*, a collection of sermons that was published in 1933 by the Hermon Publishing House of Frankfurt am Main.

2. Information received in 1956 from the late *Landesrabbiner* Dr. Emil Lichtigfeld of Hessen.

3. During the 1866 Austro-Prussian war, Lieutenant von Hindenburg served with the Royal Prussian army in what was then the Austrian kingdom of Bohemia. Adolf Hitler was born in Braunau on the River Inn in Austria proper, but von Hindenburg recalled a town in Bohemia by the name of Braunau as well. Hence his rather derogatory appellation for a man who had not even attained a non-commissioned officer's rank, much less that of a lieutenant. Von Hindenburg's milieu was dominated by a proverb: "*Der Mensch beginnt mit dem Leutnannt*", that is, the human being begins with the grade of lieutenant.

4. Cited in Klaus J. Herrmann, *Das Dritte Reich und die deutsch-jüdischen Organisationen, 1933-34* (Munich: Carl Heymanns Verlag, 1969), 1. (Hereafter cited as Herrmann, *Das Dritte Reich.*)

5. That the Jews were viewed not merely as part of a religion, but, in fact, as a racially defined *Volk*, pre-dated Adolf Hitler's hatred of the Jews. While baptism into one of the Christian religions substantially satisfied all of the legal requirements of German states insofar as Jews' entry into the officers corps, the judiciary, the professorate and the higher civil service was concerned, baptism failed to pacify the "anti-Semites" and "Germano-folkists". By 1879 at the very latest, perceptions of Jews as a religious community had extensively given way to viewing all people of Jewish descent as being less than "German".

6. Erich Matthias and Rudolf Morsey, *Das Ende der Parteien 1933* (Duesseldorf: Droste Verlag, 1960), 790.

7. Fritz Tobias, Ministerial-Counsellor in Lower Saxony's Office for the Protection of the Constitution, researched the *Reichstag* arson and published his findings in *Der Reichstagsbrand* in 1962. His research conclusively proved the fire was exclusively set by Marinus van der Lubbe and therefore neither by the Nazis nor the Communists. Fritz Tobias, *Der Reichstagsbrand: Legende und Wirklichkeit* (Rastatte: 1962).

8. Herrmann, *Das Dritte Reich*, 2. These statistics were published by Ministerial-Counsellor Leonardo Conti, M.D. Born of Swiss-Italian parents in Lugano in 1900, he formed the "Anti-Semitic Fighting Union of Folkist Student Leaders" as early as 1918 and subsequently built and led the Nazi League of Physicians, served as the "First Physician of the Storm Troopers" during the 1920s. His statistics were re-published in *Der Schild*, the organ of the *Reichsbund jüdischer Frontsoldaten*, in its issue of November 1933.

9. From a copy of a *Reichsverband* document, dated August 1933, given to the author by Hans Faust, who had been a member of this organization.

10. Cited in Herrmann, *Das Dritte Reich*, 9-11.

11. Italy's Jewish Fascists were led by Ettore Ovazza of Turino, who published *La Nostra Bandiera* (*Our Flag*). Its last issue appeared shortly prior to the proclamation of these "Racial" laws. For a detailed description of this phenomenon see Alexander Stille, *Benevolence and Betrayal* (New York: Summit Books/Simon & Schuster, 1991).

12. Herrmann, *Das Dritte Reich*, 155-6.

13. Ibid., 24, 50-1.

14. Ibid., 81.

15. Ibid., 153.

16. This "*Austritts-Orthodoxie*" or Secessionist-Orthodoxy was initiated by Rabbi Dr. Samson Raphael Hirsch, and on 28 July 1876 a law was passed in the *Reichstag*, subject to which the Secessionist-Orthodox Jews were granted authority to establish their own congregation under public law. These congregations, most notably the Israelitische Religions-Gesellschaft of Frankfurt am Main, the Adass Jisroel of Berlin and others in Mayence, Wiesbaden, *inter alia*, functioned aside and apart from the regular Jewish *Gemeinden*. Notwithstanding, other Orthodox protagonists, led by Rabbi

Seligmann Baer Bamberger of Wuerzburg strictly opposed Hirsch's separatist ideology.

17. There were some few German Jews who resisted the Nazi regime, for instance by way of distributing/printing anti-Nazi pamphlets, and in one instance by detonating a bomb at an anti-Soviet exhibition in Berlin in 1942. These actions, leading to arrest, torture and, in the instance of the «Baum Group,» death sentences, were undertaken within the ambit of Social-Democratic or Communist political leadership. Rabbi Leo Baeck is supposed to have been in contact with the Resistance of the Goerdeler circle, leading to the July 1944 unsuccessful attempt by a group of highly placed German officers and civilians to assassinate Hitler. John F. Oppenheimer, *Lexikon des Judentums* (Guetersloh: Bertelsmann, 1967), 868-9.

Reporting Nazi Murder:
The Einsatzgruppen Reports
[Ronald Headland]

A somewhat different version of this paper was presented at a conference entitled "Building History: Art, Memory, and Myth," held in Munich in November 1997. Papers from this conference will appear in a forthcoming publication of McGill-Queen's University Press.

1. See Hans-Heinrich Wilhelm, *Rassenpolitik und Kriegfuhrung: Sicherheitspolizei und Wehrmacht in Polen und in der Sowjetunion 1939 - 1942* (Passau: Wissenschaftsverlag Richard Rothe, 1991), 196.

2. Report by Karl Jäger, leader of *Einsatzkommando 3*, on the operations of this Kommando as of 1 December 1941. For an analysis of this report see Ronald Headland, *Messages of Murder: A Study of the Reports of the Einsatzgruppen of the Security Police and the Security Service 1941-1943* (Rutherford, New Jersey: Fairleigh Dickinson University Press, 1992), 154-58, 189-90. (Hereafter cited as Headland, *Messages of Murder.*)

3. Nuremberg documents NOKW-2302, PS 447. Nuremberg trial documents are essentially divided into two types: those documents that were used as evidence at the Trial of the Major War Criminals before the International Military Tribunal held in Nuremberg in 1945 and 1946; and those documents that were used in the twelve subsequent trials, also held in Nuremberg before American Military Tribunals from 1946 to 1949. The documents in the first case were published in *Trial of the Major War Criminals before the International Military Tribunal*, 42 volumes, Nuremberg: 1948 - 49 (hereafter cited as *IMT*). Many of the documents from the *IMT* series were also published in English translation in *Nazi Conspiracy and Aggression*, 8 volumes and 2 supplemental volumes, Washington D.C.: United States Government Printing Office,

1946-48. The documents from the subsequent trials were more widely scattered and are less easily referred to. The lettering symbols of the *IMT* documents referred to the Allied agencies that processed these documents for use at the trial, whereas in the case of the latter trials the symbols referred to the German organizations to which the documents pertained. (For example, to mention three of the document series that concern us here, the letters NOKW refer to documents relating to the German armed forces and the letters NO refer to German organizations, particularly the SS. The designation PS refers to the Paris-Storey series, which in turn indicates the city where these documents were prepared for trial and the American officer in charge of this task. Document PS - 447 is found in *IMT*, Vol. 26, 53-8.) For more detailed discussion of the Nuremberg documents, see Jacob Robinson and Henry Sachs, *The Holocaust: The Nuremberg Evidence, Part One: The Documents* (Jerusalem and New York: Yad Vashem and Yivo, 1976); John Mendelsohn, *Trial by Document: The Use of Seized Records in the United States Proceedings at Nuremberg*, unpublished doctoral dissertation, University of Maryland, 1974; Headland, *Messages of Murder*, 160-1, 231-2.

4. Nuremberg document NOKW - 256, in John Mendelsohn, ed., *The Holocaust: Selected Documents*, 18 volumes (New York and London: Garland Publishing, 1982), Vol. 10, 1-5.

5. Helmut Krausnick and Hans-Heinrich Wilhelm, *Die Truppe des Weltanschauungskrieges: Die Einsatzgruppen der Sicherheitspolizei und des SD 1938 - 1942* (Stuttgart: Deutsche Verlags -Anstalt, 1981), 145. (Hereafter cited as Krausnick/Wilhelm, *Die Truppe.*)

6. Nuremberg document L - 180, *IMT*, Vol. 37, 670-717.

7. Headland, *Messages of Murder*, 38.

8. Operational Situation Reports 101 and 106, Nuremberg documents NO - 3137 and NO - 3140, respectively.

9. See Headland, *Messages of Murder*, chapters 10 and 11.

10. Michael Musmanno, *The Eichmann Kommandos* (London: Peter Davies, 1962), 242.

11. Raul Hilberg, *Perpetrators Victims Bystanders: The Jewish Catastrophe 1933 - 1945* (New York: HarperCollins Publishers, 1992), 45.

12. Ibid., 44-5. For Ohlendorf's career, see Lawrence Duncan Stokes, *The Sicherheitsdienst (SD) of the Reichsfuehrer SS and German Public Opinion, September 1939 - June 1941*, unpublished doctoral dissertation, John Hopkins University, 1972, 90-192.

13. Nuremberg documents NO - 5050, NO - 4235.

14. Nuremberg document NO - 4314.

15. Nuremberg document PS - 1997, *IMT*, Vol. 29, 234-7.

16. Headland, *Messages of Murder*, 198.

17. Ibid., 92 - 106.

18. Operational Situation Report 148, Nuremberg document NO - 2824.

19. See Headland, *Messages of Murder*, chapters 7, 14 and 15, for more detailed analysis of these two subjects.

20. Raul Hilberg, *The Destruction of the European Jews*, 3 volumes, revised and definitive edition (New York: Holmes & Meier, 1985), Vol. 3, 1012.

21. It is likely that the use of "legal" justifications and euphemisms was the result of a specific directive from Reinhard Heydrich concerning "language rules" to be followed in the reports. See Headland, *Messages of Murder*, 74. Euphemistic language was also routinely used in connection with the murder of handicapped victims within Germany. See Henry Friedlander, *The Origins of Nazi Genocide: From Euthanasia to the Final Solution* (Chapel Hill and London: The University of North Carolina Press, 1995), 57, 129, 158, 188, 231, 233.

22. Operational Situation Report 194, Nuremberg document NO - 3276.

23. Operational Situation Report 146, Nuremberg document NO - 2835.

24. Headland, *Messages of Murder*, 75, 79.

25. For example, see *Case 9, United States of America v. Otto Ohlendorf et al.* (Trial of the *Einsatzgruppen* leaders at Nuremberg), English Transcript of the proceedings, 544, 545, 3065 and 5731. (Hereafter cited as *Tr.*) The court rejected these claims. See *Tr.* 6759-61.

26. *Tr.* 520, 662-3.

27. See Headland, *Messages of Murder*, Appendix A, 217-21.

28. For example, see Operational Situation Report 132, Nuremberg Document NO - 2830.

29. *Tr.* 633.

30. Christopher Browning, *Ordinary Men: Reserve Police Battalion 101 and the Final Solution in Poland* (New York: HarperCollins, 1992), 55-70, 73-4. This battalion shot at least 38,000 Jews and was responsible for deporting at least 45,200 Jews to Treblinka extermination camp. See pp. 191-2. For statements of men who refused to take part in the shooting of Jews, see Ernst Klee, Willi Dressen and Volker Riess, *Those Were the Days: The Holocaust through the Eyes of the Perpetrators and Bystanders* (London: Hamish Hamilton, 1991), 76-80.

31. The *Einsatzgruppen* were not alone in their initial reluctance to shoot women and children. In Serbia, beginning in October 1941, the German army carried out reprisal executions of Serbian male Jews on the ratio of 100 to 1 for German soldiers killed by Serbian partisans. While there was no hesitation in killing male Jews, the army officials considered it unchivalrous to shoot women and children. See Christopher Browning, *The Path to Genocide: Essays on Launching the Final Solution* (Cambridge: Cambridge University Press, 1992), 135. The reluctance of the *Einsatzgruppen* did not last long. By mid - August 1941 Jewish women and children were being routinely killed in the thousands. See Karl Jäger report, entries for August 1941.

32. Jäger report. See Headland, *Messages of Murder*, 187.

33. Krausnick/Wilhelm, *Die Truppe*, 605-6. A photograph of this document is

found in Avraham Tory, *Surviving the Holocaust: The Kovno Ghetto Diary* (Cambridge, Massachusetts: Harvard University Press, 1990), unpaginated section with photographs between pp. 270-1.

34. Operational Situation Report 21, Nuremberg document NO - 2937.

35. Operational Situation Report 92, Nuremberg document NO - 3143.

36. See Browning, *Ordinary Men*, pp. 176-89, for an examination of anti-Semitic indoctrination of Police Battalion 101.

37. Headland, *Messages of Murder*, 25, 237 note 80.

38. These men were Karl Jäger (*Einsatzkommando* 3), Emil Haussman (*Einsatzkommando* 12), Rudolf Batz (*Einsatzkommando* 2), August Meier (*Einsatzkommando* 5), Heinz Seetzen (*Sonderkommando* 10A), Walter Bierkamp (*Einsatzgruppe* D), and Max Thomas (*Einsatzgruppe* C).

39. These men included Edward Strauch (*Einsatzkommando* 2), Gunther Rausch (*Sonderkommando* 7B), Otto Rasch (*Einsatzgruppe* C), and Eduard Jedamzik (*Sonderkommando* 10B).

40. Headland, *Messages of Murder*, 272 note 76.

Arab Nationalists and Nazi Germany, 1939-1945
[Avraham Sela]

1. Unless otherwise noted, the discussion in this article is based on the following sources: Lukasz Hirszowicz, *The Third Reich and the Arab East*, (London: Routledge & Kegan Paul, 1966) and Francis R. Nicosia, *The Third Reich and the Palestine Question*, (Austin: University of Texas Press, 1985). Two recent books which also deal with this subject are Philip Mattar, *The Mufti of Jerusalem: al-Hajj Amin al-Husayni and the Palestinian National Movement*, (New York: Columbia University Press [rev. ed.], 1992), Chapters 7-8, and Zvi Elpeleg, *The Grand Mufti: Haj Amin al-Hussaini, Founder of the Palestinian National Movement*, translated by David Harvey, edited by Shmuel Himelstein (London: Frank Cass, 1993), 56-73.

2. Bernard Lewis, *Semites and Anti-Semites: An Inquiry into Conflict and Prejudice*, (New York: W.W. Norton, 1986), 147-49.

3. Majid Khadduri, "General Nuri's Flirtation with the Axis Powers," *The Middle East Journal* vol.16 (1962), 330-32; George Kirk, *The Middle East in the War*, intro. Arnold Toynbee, (London: Oxford University Press, under the auspices of the Royal Institute of International Affairs, 1952), 37-38, 64.

4. On this episode, see Majid Khadduri, *Independent Iraq: 1932-1958*, (London: Oxford University Press, 1960), 171; Kirk, *The Middle East in the War*, 63-64, 229-230.

5. Geoffrey Furlonge, *Palestine Is My Country: The Story of Musa Alami*, (London: John Murray, 1969), 127-28; Philip Mattar, "Amin al-Husayni and Iraq's Quest for Independence, 1939-1941," *Arab Studies Quarterly* 6:4 (Fall 1984), 271-72.

6. Kirk, *The Middle East in the War,* 64; Salah al-Din al-Sabbagh, *The Cavaliers of Arabism in Iraq* [in Arabic], (Damascus, 1956), 109; memo by Anthony Eden, May 27, 1941, reproduced in Gabriel Cohen, *Churchill and the Palestine Question* [in Hebrew] (Jerusalem, 1976), 85-86.

7. On the revolt in Iraq, see Hirszowicz, *The Third Reich and the Arab East,* 142-81; Geoffrey Warner, *Iraq and Syria, 1941,* (London: Davis-Pointer, 1974), Chapter IV.

8. The Mufti's aims at this stage were announced in his 12 January 1937 testimony before the Peel Royal Commission; text reproduced in Ernest A. Main, *Palestine at the Crossroads* (London: George Allen & Unwin, 1937), 287-309.

9. Warner, *Iraq and Syria, 1941,* 37.

10. On the Mufti's personal involvement in the conduct of Iraq's policy towards the Axis powers and in the revolt, see: Hirszowicz, *The Third Reich and the Arab East,* 90-95, 117-20; al-Sabbagh, *The Cavaliers of Arabism in Iraq,* 218-20; Khadduri, *Independent Iraq: 1932-1958,* 208; Mattar, "Amin al-Husayni," 273-75; idem, *The Mufti of Jerusalem,* Chapter 7.

11. Lewis, *Semites and Anti-Semites; An Inquiry into Conflict and Prejudice,* 152-53.

12. Yigal Karmon, *The Mufti of Jerusalem, Haj Amin al-Husaini, and Nazi Germany during the Second World War* [in Hebrew], (Unpublished M.A. thesis, Hebrew University of Jerusalem, 1987), 161-63 (based on Eichmann's testimony). For a different version, according to which the Mufti personally visited the gas chambers of Auschwitz, see Lewis, *Semites and Anti-Semites: An Inquiry into Conflict and Prejudice,* 156.

13. Lewis, *Semites and Anti-Semites: An Inquiry into Conflict and Prejudice,* 154.

14. Karmon, *The Mufti of Jerusalem, Haj al-Husaini, and Nazi Germany during the Second World War,* 256-59.

15. Lewis, *Semites and Anti-Semites: An Inquiry into Conflict and Prejudice,* 155-56; Karmon, *The Mufti of Jerusalem, Haj al-Husaini, and Nazi Germany during the Second World War,* 242-53.

The Holocaust and the Arab-Israeli Conflict
[Neil Caplan]

I would like to thank Dr. Laura Zittrain Eisenberg for her challenging and pertinent comments on earlier drafts of this paper.

1. For a careful re-examination of relations between Arab nationalists and Hitler's Germany, see the essay by Avraham Sela in this volume.

2. Walter Laqueur and Barry Rubin, eds., *The Israel-Arab Reader: A Documentary History of the Middle East Conflict,* 4th ed. (New York: Penguin, 1984), doc.19; Yehuda Bauer, *From Diplomacy to Resistance: A History of Jewish Palestine, 1939-1945,* (Philadelphia: Jewish Publication Society, 1970), Chapter.6; Michael J. Cohen, *Palestine: Retreat from the Mandate, 1936-1945,* (London:

Paul Elek, 1978), 130f.

3. Abba Hillel Silver, "Toward American Jewish Unity," in *The Zionist Idea: A Historical Analysis and Reader*, ed. Arthur Hertzberg (New York: Atheneum, 1984), 597.

4. For evidence of this during the 1930s and 1940s, see Neil Caplan, *Futile Diplomacy, vol. II - Arab-Zionist Negotiations and the End of the Mandate*, (London: Frank Cass, 1986), 81, 131, 176f., 264-7, 326 (n.83), 333 (n.44).

5. Robert W. MacDonald, *The League of Arab States: A Study in the Dynamics of Regional Organization*, (Princeton: Princeton University Press, 1965), 317f. Compare Geoffrey Furlonge, *Palestine is My Country: The Story of Musa Alami*, (New York: John Murray, 1969), 130-37.

6. William Eddy, *FDR Meets Ibn Saud*, (New York: American Friends of the Middle East, 1954), quoted in *From Haven to Conquest: Readings in Zionism and the Palestine Problem Until 1948*, ed. Walid Khalidi, (Washington DC: Institute for Palestine Studies, 1971/1987), 510-11.

7. For an interesting discussion of the evolution of Israeli fiction reflecting this phenomenon, see Amnon Rubinstein, *The Zionist Dream Revisited: From Herzl to Gush Emunim and Back*, (New York: Schocken Books, 1984), Chapter 8: "The End of the Sabra Myth."

8. Remarks by Prime Minister Shimon Peres at Holocaust Martyrs' and Heroes' Remembrance Day Opening Ceremony, Yad Vashem, Jerusalem, 15 April 1996.

9. For a recent examination, see David Arnow, "The Holocaust and the Birth of Israel: Reassessing the Causal Relationship," *Journal of Israeli History* 15:3 (Autumnn 1994), 257-81.

10. See Tom Segev, *1949: The First Israelis*, (New York: Free Press, 1986); Benny Morris, *The Birth of the Palestinian Refugee Problem, 1947-1949*, (Cambridge: Cambridge University Press, 1987).

11. Isaac Deutscher, "The Israeli-Arab War, June 1967" (from an interview given to the *New Left Review*, 23 June 1967), in *The Non-Jewish Jew and Other Essays*, (London: Oxford University Press, 1968), 136-37.

12. Laqueur and Rubin, *Israel-Arab Reader*, doc. 27.

13. Paragraph 11 of Resolution No. 194 (III), in *United Nations Resolutions on Palestine and the Arab-Israeli Conflict, Volume I: 1947-1974*, ed. George J. Tomeh (Washington DC: Institute for Palestine Studies, 1975), 15-17. Compare Morris, *Birth of the Palestinian Refugee Problem,* Chapter 4; Abba Eban statement at the UN, 4 May 1949, *Documents on the Foreign Policy of Israel, Volume 4* (May - December 1949), ed. Yemima Rosenthal, (Jerusalem: Israel State Archives, 1986), 14-16 (doc. 5).

14. Tom Segev, *The Seventh Million: The Israelis and the Holocaust* (New York: Hill & Wang, 1993), 180-81.

15. Ibid., 185.

16. In August 1952, Israeli government official Rudolph Kastner was publicly

accused of having been a Nazi collaborator during his service as head of the Rescue Committee in Budapest. Kastner, a Mapai party loyalist, brought suit against his accuser, Malchiel Gruenwald. The trial opened in January 1954, and the judgment acquitting Gruenwald was rendered in June 1955. See Segev, *The Seventh Million*, 255-310.

17. See, e.g., Segev, *The Seventh Million*, 323-66; Hannah Arendt, *Eichmann in Jerusalem: A Report on the Banality of Evil* (New York: Viking, 1965).

18. Amos Elon, *The Israelis: Founders & Sons* (New York: Holt, Rinehart & Winston, 1971), 190-98; Segev, *The Seventh Million*, 446-49.

19. Michael Brecher, *The Foreign Policy System of Israel*, (London: Oxford University Press, 1972), 230. Compare Aaron S. Klieman, *Israel and the World After 40 Years*, (Washington: Pergamon-Brassey's, 1990), 171-73; Statement by Ambassador Gad Yaacobi, Permanent Representative of the State of Israel to the United Nations on the Commemoration of the 50th Anniversary of the End of the Second World War, 18 October 1995.

20. Quoted in Segev, *The Seventh Million*, 327.

21. Jay Gonen, *A Psychohistory of Zionism* (New York: Mason-Charter, 1975); Simon Herman, "In the Shadow of the Holocaust," *Jerusalem Quarterly* 3 (Spring 1977), 89-90.

22. Holocaust survivor Yitzhak David, one of the Entebbe hostages, recalled: "Being kidnapped by terrorists reminded me of when the Nazis kidnapped me as a child. And even though the terrorists generally spoke English, I heard it as German." Quoted in Yochi Dreazen, "Miracle in our time," *Jerusalem Post International Edition*, week ending 6 July 1996, 14.

23. Sheldon Kirschner, "Entebbe remains metaphor for courage, daring," *Canadian Jewish News*, 26 June 1986, 10; Sheldon Kirschner, "Israel and the Holocaust," *Canadian Jewish News*, 6 April 1995, 11; Daniel Bloch, "Entebbe: a unique phenomenon in history," *Canadian Jewish News*, 4 July 1996, 9.

24. Elon, *The Israelis*, 198-99.

25. Ibid., 199, 203.

26. Begin speech, Treaty signing ceremony, Washington DC, 26 March 1979, doc.251 in *Israel's Foreign Relations: Selected Documents 1977-1979*, Volume 5, ed. Meron Medzini (Jerusalem: Ministry of Foreign Affairs, 1981), 720.

27. Elon, *The Israelis*, 203.

28. A.B. Yehoshua, "The Holocaust as Junction," in *Between Right and Right*, (New York: Doubleday, 1981), 1-19; Leon Wieseltier, "Auschwitz and Peace," *New York Times*, 10 March 1978. Compare Roger Rosenblatt, "Israel: How Much Past is Enough?" *Time* magazine, 20 September 1982, 42. For a balanced and thoughtful overview of this dispute in a wider context, see Michael R. Marrus, "The Use and Misuse of the Holocaust," in *Lessons and Legacies: The Meaning of the Holocaust in a Changing World*, ed. Peter Hayes (Evanston: Northwestern University Press, 1991), 106-19.

29. Press conference with Prime Minister Begin, IDF Chief of Staff Eitan, IAF

Commander Ivri and DMI Saguy, 9 June 1981, doc.28 in *Israel's Foreign Relations: Selected Documents 1981-1982*, Volume 7, ed. Meron Medzini (Jerusalem: Ministry of Foreign Affairs, 1988), 76.

30. See, e.g., L. Z. Eisenberg, "Passive Belligerency: Israel and the 1991 Gulf War," *Journal of Strategic Studies* 15:3 (September, 1992), 305.

31. "Israel's tradition of swift retaliation, preemptive strikes and bold offensive attacks made a policy of non-response to an Iraqi missile barrage unthinkable. The post-Holocaust legacy, characterized by the vow that 'never again' would Jews wait passively for the blow to fall and brought into sharp relief by the Iraqi threat to gas Israeli citizens, also indicated that an aggressive response would be forthcoming." Ibid., 310.

32. Kach International, Advertisement, *New York Times*, 2 February 1988.

33. Simon Wiesenthal Center Report, *Egypt: Israel's Peace Partner—A Survey of Antisemitism in the Egyptian Press, 1986-1987* (January 1988); Emad S. Mekay, "Local Hero," *Jerusalem Report*, 14 November 1996, 22-3.

34. Palestine National Covenant, Cairo, July 17, 1968, reproduced in Yehoshafat Harkabi, *The Palestinian Covenant and Its Meaning*, (London: Valentine Mitchell, 1979), 123, following the English translation given in a volume produced by Institute for Palestine Studies in 1971. Another translation of the Palestinian National Charter, published by the PLO Research Center in 1969 (ibid., 117; also reproduced in Laqueur and Rubin, *Israel-Arab Reader*, 369) offers a different version: viz., "fascist in its methods," omitting the word "Nazi". For other examples, see Y. Harkabi, *Arab Attitudes to Israel* (Jerusalem: Keter, 1972), 176-77.

35. Shmuel Katz, cited in Mark Tessler, *A History of the Israeli-Palestinian Conflict*, (Bloomington and Indianapolis: Indiana University Press, 1994), 309.

36. Ze'ev Schiff and Ehud Ya'ari, *Israel's Lebanon War*, (New York: Simon and Schuster, 1984), 39, 220; Sheldon Kirschner, "Israel and the Holocaust," *Canadian Jewish News*, 6 April 1995, 11.

37. The works of two well-known North American Jewish authors capture these feelings: Philip Roth's fictional *Operation Shylock: A Confession* (New York: Simon & Schuster, 1993), and Mordechai Richler's travel-memoir *This Year in Jerusalem* (Toronto / New York: Alfred A. Knopf, 1994).

38. Elon, *The Israelis*, 199.

39. Ibid.

40. Rabin address to the Knesset, 27 June 1993.

41. Aharon Klieman, "New Directions in Israel's Foreign Policy," *Israel Affairs* 1:1 (Autumn 1994), 98-99.

42. E.g., Abba Eban, "Why Hysteria on a Mideast Parley?" *New York Times*, 3 April 1988.

43. Quoted in Sheldon Kirschner, "Israel and the Holocaust," *Canadian Jewish News*, 6 April 1995, 11.

The Genocide of Sephardi Jews:
The Impact on a Community
[Yossi Lévy]

1. Isaac Jack Lévy, *And the World Stood Silent: Sephardic Poetry of the Holocaust*, (Urbana & Chicago: University of Illinois Press, 1989), 25.
2. Ibid., 44.
3. Primo Levi, *Survival in Auschwitz*, (New York: Collier Books, 1947); idem, *The Saved and the Drowned*, (New York: Summit Books, 1986).
4. Levi, *Survival in Auschwitz* (1947 ed.), 7.
5. Ibid., 79.
6. Levi, *The Saved and the Drowned*, 21.
7. Ibid., 199.

Anti-Semitism in Québec and Canadian Popular Culture:
Adrien Arcand and Ernst Zundel
[Stanley Asher]

1. Lita-Rose Betcherman, *The Swastika and the Maple Leaf*, (Toronto: Fitzhenry and Whiteside, 1975), 5-6. (Hereafter, Betcherman.)
2. David Rome, *Clouds in the Thirties: On Anti-Semitism in Canada 1929 - 1939* (Montreal: Canadian Jewish Congress,1977-1981), 13 volumes.
3. Betcherman, 9.
4. Ibid., 27-8.
5. Ibid., 103-4
6. David Martin, "Adrien Arcand, Fascist—An Interview," *The Nation*, 26 February 1938, 241-44.
7. Betcherman, 145.
8. Robert Skidelsly, *Oswald Mosley* (London: Macmillan, 1975), 449-501.
9. Betcherman, 146.
10. Much of the information for Zundel's early career comes from Grayson Levy, "Who the Hell is Ernst Zundel?" *Future Tense* (a Canadian Jewish student publication), Fall 1993.
11. Warren Kinsella, *Web of Hate: Inside Canada's Far Right Network* (Toronto: HarperCollins,1994), 79-80.
12. Ibid., 353-54.
13. *Jewish Chronicle*, London, 12 May 1995.
14. See, e.g., Ernst Zundel, German Canadian Human Rights Activist, "An Open Letter," August 1994, 2 pages, as well as an interview he had with Gil Kezwes, in the 24 February 1996 *Globe and Mail*.
15. One of the most fascinating new developments—websites devoted to hate messages on the Internet—raises new questions about access to information and protection of human rights. This issue was addressed during the April

1996 Kleinmann Symposium by media consultant David Abitbol. For a sampling of recent articles on the fight against racist propaganda without attempting to ban it, see: Paul Lungen, "Computer maven fights hate on the Internet," *CJN*, 2 November 1995, 25; Peter H. Lewis, "Group Urges an Internet Ban on Hate Groups' Messages," *New York Times*, 10 January 1996, A10; David Lazarus, "Jewish Web page a community resource," *CJN*, 8 February 1996, p.7; Andy Riga, "Online against hate," Montreal *Gazette*, 16 March 1996, pp.B1-B2.

Two Composers Respond to the Holocaust:
Arnold Schoenberg's *A Survivor from Warsaw* and
Dmitri Shostakovich's *Babi Yar* Symphony
[Robert Frederick Jones]

1. Quoted in H. H. Stuckenschmidt, *Arnold Schoenberg: His Life, World, and Work*, trans. H. Searle (New York: Schirmer, 1977), 26.

2. See his letter of 4 May 1923 to Wassily Kandinsky in Arnold Schoenberg, *Letters*, selected and edited by Erwin Stein, trans. Eithne Wilkins and Ernst Kaiser (London: Faber, 1965), 89.

3. See letter of 16 October 1933 to Alban Berg, *Letters*, 184.

4. See the chapter on this subject, "Unity and Strength: The Politics of Jewish Survival," in Alexander Ringer, *Arnold Schoenberg: The Composer as Jew* (Oxford: Oxford University Press, 1990), 116-149.

5. *Letters*, 164-65 [translation revised].

6. Deuteronomy 6:4-5.

7. Solomon Volkov, *Testimony: The Memoirs of Dmitri Shostakovich as Related to and Edited by Solomon Volkov* (New York: Harper, 1979), 156-67. Readers are warned of the very questionable authenticity of this source. According to Volkov's introduction, his book had Shostakovich's total approval. He smuggled it to the west for publication (after Shostakovich's death). Scholarly opinion of the value of these "memoirs" ranges from qualified acceptance to total rejection. In assessing the reliability of any particular passage it is best to compare it with the recollections of others who knew Shostakovich. In the case of the present quotations about Jewish music, they are close enough in sentiment to those recalled by Rafiil Matveivich Khozak in an interview with Elizabeth White for me to regard them as basically reliable. Elizabeth White, *Shostakovich: A Life Remembered* (Princeton, NJ: Princeton University Press, 1994), 235.

8. Ibid.

9. "Speak, Memory" [interview with Yevgeny Yevtushenko in booklet accompanying Teldec compact disc 4509-90848-2], 6.

10. Ian MacDonald, *The New Shostakovich* (London: Fourth Estate, 1990), 229.

Freedom of Expression, Hate Speech
and Holocaust Denial
[Irwin Cotler]

This paper is a modified version of a chapter that appeared in Irwin Cotler, ed., *Nuremberg Forty Years Later: The Struggle Against Injustice in Our Time* (Montreal and Kingston: McGill-Queen's University Press, 1995).

1. John Stuart Mill, *On Liberty. Representative Government. The Subjection of Women.* (London: Oxford University Press, 1969), 21.
2. See the paper by Stanley Asher in this volume.
3. *R. v. Keegstra*, [1990] 3 S.C.R. 697.
4. *R. v. Andrews and Smith,* [1990] 3 S.C.R. 870.
5. *Canada (Human Rights Commission)* v. *Taylor,* [1990] 3 S.C.R. 892
6. *Zundel v. R.*, [1992] 2 S.C.R. 731.
7. *Canada (Human Rights Commission)* v. *Heritage Front,* [1994] 1 F.C. 203 (T.D.); *Canada (Human Rights Commission)* v. *Heritage Front* (1994), 78 F.T.R. 241 (Fed. T.D.).
8. League for Human Rights B'nai Brith Canada. (Midwest Region) v. Man. Knights of the Ku Klux Klan (1993), 18 C.H.R.R. D/406 (Can. Human Rights Trib.).
9. *Saskatchewan (Human Rights Commission)* v. *Bell* (1994), 114 D.L.R. (4th) 370 (Sask. C.A.).
10. *Kane v. Church of Jesus Christ Christian-Aryan Nations (No. 3)* (1992), 18 C.H.R.R. D/268 (Alta. Bd. of Inq.).
11. *Khaki v. Canadian Liberty Net* (1993), 22 C.H.R.R. D/347 (Can. Human Rights Trib.); *Canada (Human Rights Commission)* v. *Canadian Liberty Net,* [1992] 3 F.C. 155 (T.D.); *Canada (Human Rights Commission)* v. *Canadian Liberty Net,* [1992] 3 F.C. 504.
12. Section 1 of the *Charter* states:
    1. The *Canadian Charter of Rights and Freedoms* guarantees the rights and freedoms set out in it subject only to such reasonable limits prescribed by law as can be demonstrably justified in a free and democratic society.
13. *Report of the Special Committee on Hate Propaganda in Canada* (Ottawa: Queen's Printer, 1965), 11 [hereinafter *Cohen Committee Report*].
14. T. Cohen, *Peace Relations and the Law* (Toronto: Canadian Jewish Congress, 1988), 104.
15. D. Johnston, D. Johnston, and S. Handa, *Understanding the Information Highway* (Toronto: Stoddard Publishing, 1995), 49-50.
16. See Stephen Scheinberg, "Canada: Right Wing Extremism in the Peaceable Kingdom," in B'nai Brith Canada, *The Extreme Right: International Peace and*

Security at Risk (Draft Report) (Toronto: B'nai Brith Canada, 1994), 49-52; Warren Kinsella, *Web of Hate: Inside Canada's Far Right Network* (Toronto: HarperCollins, 1994), 31-49, 283-310.

17. League for Human Rights of B'nai Brith Canada, *1994 Audit of Anti-Semitic Incidents* (Toronto: B'nai Brith, 1995), 12-13 [hereinafter *1994 Audit*].

18. Ibid., 20.

19. These are the figures offered by Warren Kinsella, cited in M. McDonald, "The Enemy Within," *Maclean's,* 8 May 1995, 34.

20. *1994 Audit,* 14, 16.

21. Project for the Study of Anti-Semitism, *Anti-Semitism Worldwide 1994* (Tel Aviv: Tel Aviv University, 1995) 184-185.

22. *1994 Audit,* 20-22.

23. P. Raymont, quoted in McDonald, "The Enemy Within," 38.

24. Scheinberg, "Canada: Right Wing Extremism," 55-58.

25. W. Kinsella, cited in McDonald, "The Enemy Within," 34. See, however, Scheinberg, "Canada: Right Wing Extremism," 57, where he disputes "facile economic explanations" for the rise in youth hate.

26. Cited in McDonald, "The Enemy Within," 17.

27. *1993 Audit of Anti-Semitic Incidents* (Toronto: B'nai Brith Canada, 1994).

28. Cited in R. Corelli, "A Tolerant Nation's Hidden Shame", *Macleans,* 14 August 1995, 40.

29. E.g., D. Dunlop, head of the Ottawa-Carleton Regional Police hate crimes unit, quoted in R. Corelli, *ibid.*

30. The Institute of Jewish Affairs and the American Jewish Committee, *Anti-Semitism: World Report 1995*, (London: Institute of Jewish Affairs, 1995), 21.

31. *Criminal Code*, R.S.C. 1985, c.C-46, as amended by S.C. 1995, C.22.

32. *1994 Audit,* 6-7.

33. According to Kinsella, *Web of Hate*, although Scheinberg ("Canada: Right Wing Extremism") disputes the claim that the hate movement is growing other than in the public eye.

34. *Keegstra,* 714.

35. D. Lipstadt, *Denying the Holocaust: The Growing Assault on Truth and Memory* (New York: Free Pr., 1993).

36. F. Schauer, Book Review, 56 *University of Chicago Law Review.* 397, 410 (1989).

37. *Hunter v. Southam* [1984] 2 SCR 145, 155.

38. *Keegstra,* 726.

39. Ibid.

40. Abraham Goldstein, "Group Libel and Criminal Law: Walking on the Slippery Slope". Paper presented at the *International Legal Colloquium on Racial and Religious Hatred and Group Libel*, Tel Aviv University, 1991, 3.

41. *Chaplinsky v. New Hampshire*, 315 U.S. 568, 571-72 (1942).

42. *Beauharnais v. Illinois* 343 U.S. 250 (1952).

43. *R. v. Big M. Drug Mart Ltd.*, [1985] 1 SCR 295.
44. *Keegstra*, 728.
45. *R. v. Zundel* (1987), 580 R (2d) 129 155-56, and quoted with approval on this point in *R. v. Andrews and Smith* (1988) 28 O.A.C. 161, to the effect that "the wilful promotion of hatred is *entirely antithetical* to our very system of freedom" (emphasis added).
46. *R. v. Andrews and Smith*, Ibid., per Grange J.A. 181-4.
47. See *Irwin Toy Ltd v. A.-G. of Quebec* [1989] 1 SCR 927, 970.
48. See empirical data respecting the harm to target groups as summarized in *Report of Special Committee on Hate Propaganda in Canada* [otherwise known as the Cohen Committee] (1966), 211-215; findings of the Ontario Court of Appeal in *R. v. Andrews and Smith, supra* note 2, per Cory, J., 171; and empirical data cited in M. Matsuda, "Public Response to Victim's Search: Considering the Victim's Story," 87 *Michigan Law Review* 2320 (1989).
49. *Keegstra,* 725.
50. See Justice B. Wilson, "Building the Charter Edifice: The First Ten Years," conference paper, Tenth Anniversary of the Charter (Ottawa, April 1992), 6.
51. *Keegstra,* 737.
52. *Edmonton Journal v. Alta.* (AG), [1989] 2 SCR 1326 1355-6.
53. *See* Note 48.
54. Ibid.
55. *Keegstra,* 736.
56. *R. v. Oakes* (1986) 24 C.C.C. (3d) 321 (S.C.C.) 346.
57. See, for example, the *Study on the Implementation of Article 4 of the International Convention on the Elimination of All Forms of Racial Discrimination* (a report on the United Nations Committee on the Elimination of Racial Discrimination, submitted in May 1983) A/CONF. 119/10 18 May 1983.
58. *R. W.D.S.U. v. Dolphin Delivery Ltd.*, [1986] 2 SCR 573, per McIntyre, J. 583.
59. K. Mahoney, "*R. v. Keegstra*: A Rationale for Regulating Pornography?" 37 *McGill Law Journal* 242.
60. *Keegstra,* 746.
61. Ibid. 746.
62. Ibid., 747.
63. Ibid., 748.
64. Ibid.
65. *Reference re Public Service Employees Act* (Alta) (Dickson CJC dissenting, but not on this point) (1987) 1 SCR 313 per Dickson CJ 349. See also *R. v. Videoflicks*, (1984) 14 DLR (4th) 10 (Ont. CA) 35-6.
66. *Keegstra,* 750.
67. *International Convention on the Elimination of All Forms of Racial Discrimination.* See especially Article 4 (a) of the convention; and *International Covenant on Civil and Political Rights.* See especially Article 20(2) of the convention.

68. *Keegstra,* 752.

69. Ibid., 753.

70. *R. v. Andrews and Smith* (1988) 43 C.C.C. (3d) 193 (Ont. C.A.O. 211).

71. *New York Times v. Sullivan*, 376 U.S. 254 (1964).

72. *Cohen v. California*, 403 U.S. 15 (1971).

73. This principle and perspective find expression in A. Goldstein, see Note 38.

74. *R. v. Andrews and Smith* (1988) 20 O.A.C. 161 (Ont. C.A.), per Cory, J. 178.

75. Ibid., 176.

Peter Kleinmann's Reflections on Returning to Auschwitz and Flossenbürg

[Naomi Kramer]

This paper is a modified excerpt from *The Fallacy of Race and the Shoah*, co-authored by Naomi Kramer and Ronald Headland, published by University of Ottawa Press, 1998.

The Anguish of "Liberation"

[Avrum Feigenbaum]

For studies of what was known, see Walter Laqueur, *The Terrible Secret: Suppression of the Truth About Hitler's "Final Solution"* (London: Penguin Books, 1982); and David S. Wyman, *The Abandonment of the Jews: America and the Holocaust 1941-1945* (New York: Pantheon, 1984). It is from the latter book that the historical material in this lecture is derived.

Notes on the Contributors

Stanley Asher teaches English and film courses at John Abbott College. He is well known in Montreal for his radio broadcasts on CKUT-FM, his recent film (with Dov Okouneff), *Montreal Jewish Memories*, his photographs, and guided walking tours.

Carrie Bacher recently graduated in Fine Arts at York University. Her poetry was inspired by her participation in the 1994 "March of the Living."

Heidi Berger is the daughter of Holocaust survivor Ann Kazimirski. A graduate of McGill University, Heidi has also studied at the Université de Montréal where she obtained a degree in Psychology, and Concordia University, where she obtained a degree in radio and television production. She operates her own documentary and film production company, *The Berger Group*, and lectures at Concordia University in film development.

Jason H. Berger, grandson of Ann Kazimirski, graduated in Political Science at McGill University (spring 1999). Jason is very active in the Montreal Jewish community and in local politics. He plans to continue his studies in law.

Neil Caplan is a graduate of the London School of Economics and Political Science (England) and has taught humanities courses on the Middle East and on the Holocaust at Vanier College since 1973. He has published widely on the historical evolution of the Arab-Israeli conflict. Included among his publications are *The Lausanne Conference, 1949: A Case Study in Middle East Peacemaking* (1993), and his four volume documentary history, *Futile Diplomacy* (1983, 1986, 1997). Most recently he has co-authored with Laura Zittrain Eisenberg *Negotiating Arab-Israeli Peace: Patterns, Problems, Possibilities* (1998).

Irwin Cotler is a Professor of Law at McGill University who has won an international reputation for his energetic and diligent defence of human rights in South Africa, Latin America and the former Soviet Union. Many of his extracurricular activities testify to his strong commitment to developing legal remedies against racism and discrimination in Canada and abroad. Prof. Cotler acted as counsel before the Supreme Court in the major "hate speech" cases, including the Keegstra, Smith and Andrews, Tayler, and Ross cases.

Endre Farkas was born in Hungary in 1948. He and his parents escaped to the West after experiencing mob violence during the Hungarian uprising of 1956. An English teacher at John Abbott College, Farkas has been writing and performing poetry for over twenty years. He has published seven volumes of poetry, the most recent of which is *Surviving Words*, which has been adapted as a play titled *Surviving Wor(l)ds*.

Avrum Feigenbaum is a Holocaust survivor from Lodz, Poland, who, along with three brothers and a sister, was rounded up when the Nazis forced the Jewish population of Lodz into a ghetto. Liberated from Gross-Rosen camp in April 1945, Mr. Feigenbaum came to Canada in 1950, where he worked as a cabinetmaker and carpenter. In recent years he has lectured extensively on the subject of the Holocaust.

Ronald Headland is a graduate of the Faculty of Music at McGill University and the Montreal Museum School of Fine Arts and Design. Since 1977 he has taught in the Music Department at Vanier College. Also a visual artist, he has exhibited his work throughout Canada and abroad. In 1992 he published a book on the Holocaust, *Messages of Murder: A Study of the Reports of the Einsatzgruppen of the Security Police and the Security Service, 1941-1943*. He recently co-authored (with Naomi Kramer) a book, *The Fallacy of Race and the Shoah* (1998).

Klaus J. Herrmann was born in Cammin, Germany, and in 1940 moved to Shanghai, where he lived until emigrating to the United States in 1947. After serving in the American army he taught at the European Division of the University of Maryland and at American University in Washington. He was a member of the Department of Political Science at Concordia University. In addition to serving as Vice-President of the American Council for Judaism, he published a book, *The Third Reich and the German Jewish Organizations*, as well as other publications relating to this subject and Reform Judaism. Klaus Herrmann died in January 1998.

Robert Frederick Jones is a graduate of New England Conservatory and Brandeis University and teaches in the Music Department at Vanier College. He is the composer of more than fifty musical compositions and his works have been performed in Canada, the United States, South America and Europe. In 1992 his *Mass* was performed in England in Westminster Abbey and Salisbury Cathedral. His *Symphony for Chamber Orchestra* was recently played at the Music Gallery, Toronto. He is also Music Director of the Chorale Nouvelle de Montréal.

Ann Kazimirski is a Holocaust survivor who came to Canada in 1949, where she returned to university at the age of fifty-two and obtained a degree in Early Childhood Education. Both as a speaker and as author of the book *Witness to Horror*, published in 1993, she has dedicated herself to furthering public awareness of the Holocaust. She continues to lecture extensively on the subject, and recently she has focused special attention on the suffering of women and children during the Holocaust. In 1997 Ann Kazimirski participated as a survivor in the March of the Living in Poland and Israel.

Peter Kleinmann was born in the Carpathian Mountain region in 1925. He and his family were confined in the ghetto in Munkácz in 1944 and were then deported to Auschwitz. From there he was transferred to the labour camp at Gross-Rosen and was later sent on a death march to Flossenbürg camp where he was liberated. Since his arrival in Canada in 1949 he has rebuilt his life, and following his retirement from a successful business career, he has devoted himself to sponsoring international conferences and speaking about the Holocaust to young audiences in Canada, the United States and in Europe.

Naomi Kramer is Director of Education and Programmes at the Montreal Holocaust Memorial Centre. She has curated numerous permanent and travelling exhibits on the Holocaust. In addition to organizing several international Holocaust conferences in Europe and in Canada, she has recently directed an educational video called *Visualizing Memory....a last detail*, produced by the Kleinmann Family Foundation. Naomi Kramer has also recently co-authored (with Ronald Headland) a book, *The Fallacy of Race and the Shoah* (1998).

Stefan Lesniak was born in Krakow, Poland, in 1920. Along with his family he was confined in the Jewish ghetto in Krakow. After being sent in October 1943 to Plaszow camp and a year later to Gross-Rosen camp, he was transferred to the ammunition factory in Brunnlitz run by Oskar Schindler. It was here that he was liberated in May 1945.

Yossi Lévy was born in Casablanca and emigrated to Canada in 1965.

An anthropologist by training, he is a member of the Département de Sexologie at the Université du Québec à Montréal (UQAM). His wide range of publications and research interests extend to such subjects as AIDS, the Moroccan Jewish community in Montreal, ethnicity and Sephardi Jews in the Holocaust.

Avraham Sela emigrated to Israel from Iraq at the age of five. Pursuing studies in both the history of the Muslim countries and Arabic language and literature, he has been the recipient of numerous scholarships, fellowships and research grants and has undertaken research on a variety of subjects related to Middle Eastern affairs. He is currently a lecturer in the Department of International Relations and a research fellow of the Truman Institute for the Advancement of Peace, both at the Hebrew University of Jerusalem. His latest book is *The Decline of the Arab-Israeli Conflict: Middle East Politics and the Search for Regional Order.*

Josef Schmidt is a Professor of German Studies at McGill University. In addition to publishing numerous articles, he is the author of several books, including one on German Jesuit theater and Jacob Böhme (1967), an anthology of sixteenth-century German literature (1976, and third revised edition 1998), and a study of Reformation satire (1977). Following his latest book on popular religious fiction, he is presently preparing a monograph on nineteenth-century anti-Semitism in the German Catholic press.

Ray Shankman teaches English and Jewish Studies at Vanier College. Previously, he has taught at Lakehead University, Ben Gurion University (Beersheva), and Twin Valleys Educational Community (Wardsville). His first book of poems, *For Love of the Wind*, was published in 1991. His poetry has appeared in anthologies and magazines, including *Aurora* (1978), *The Spice Box* (1981), *Essential Words* (1986), *A Point on a Sheet of Green Paper* (1992), *Prairie Fire* and in *Quebec Suite: Poems For and About Quebec*. Most recently his poems have appeared in *Tel Aviv Review.*

Willie Sterner was born in 1919 in Wolbrom and grew up in Krakow, Poland. The eldest of seven children, he was the only member of his family to survive the Holocaust. Among the camps where he was interned were Plaszow and Mauthausen. He was liberated from Gunzkirchen camp in Austria in May 1945. Mr. Sterner came to Canada in 1948, where he started a family and built his life anew as a painter-contractor. He continues to give lectures on the Holocaust here in Canada and the United States.